'84
The Last of the
Great Tigers

'84
The Last of the Great Tigers
Untold Stories from an Amazing Season

ELI ZARET
Foreword by Elmore Leonard
Introduction by Ernie Harwell

Crofton Creek Press
South Boardman, Michigan

First Edition
10 9 8 7 6 5 4 3 2

Published by Crofton Creek Press
2303 Gregg Road SW, South Boardman, Michigan 49680
E-mail: croftoncreek@traverse.net

Book and cover design by Image Graphics and Design
Ann Arbor, Michigan   E-mail: igd@ic.net

Editor: Stan Stein
Copyeditor: Kate Petrella

Printed by Malloy, Inc.

To Patty:

for inspiring me to write

To Pete and Phil:

for sharing your love of baseball

Contents

Acknowledgments

C'mon. We all know that somebody had to write this book. The story of the '84 Tigers was too special to Michigan, and too remarkable to the sports world as a whole, not to be revisited. So, when 2003 arrived and just one year remained before the '84 Tigers' 20th anniversary, I figured that perhaps I was the guy meant to do it.

I had my recollections and a box full of old videos, but I needed more. So I went to the Bloomfield Township Public Library and found a copy of *Inside Pitch*, a diary of the '84 season by former Tigers pitching coach Roger Craig, a book he co-wrote with the late sportswriter Vern Plagenhoff. We all miss Vern, who left us in his mid-40s, but I still must thank him. Reading *Inside Pitch* helped me remember what it felt like back then, and Craig's wisdom filtered into my recollections.

Also at the library, I read a lot of *Detroit Free Press* microfilm from March '84 through the World Series. Bill McGraw was the Freep's beat writer that year, and Bill did a fine job in covering the team. Thanks to Bill and the *Free Press*, I had thousands of facts to choose from. The headlines that you see throughout the book are actual ones that appeared above the *Free Press* game stories that year.

I then began the process of finding all the players who had disappeared from my woefully un-updated Rolodex. By now, the '84 Tigers were spread all over the country, and Jerry Lewis, the creator and director of the Tigers Fantasy Camp, was immensely helpful in tracking down the players I couldn't locate myself. Jerry is more intimately associated with the men who made Tigers history than anyone else, and his assistance was invaluable.

Detroit News sports writer Lynn Henning was the first person I quizzed about whether a book commemorating the 20th anniversary of the '84 Tigers might resonate with Tigers fans. Lynn's encouraging response and his suggestions for forming a team to put the project together were important kick-starts.

Lynn led me to Stan Stein, my eventual editor on the project. Stan is a veteran public relations counselor and his skills have been instrumental in the marketing of the book.

Through Stan, we went to Bill Haney. Bill has been involved with hundreds of books in a variety of capacities, and his willingness to mentor the project enabled us to allay the gnawing fear that we'd make some critical mistake that would torpedo our efforts. Bill also arranged to have Elmore Leonard read the manuscript. I was thrilled that one of America's greatest novelists would take the time to pore over a baseball story. But he did, and when he told me he actually liked it very much, I took a deep breath and asked if he would agree to write a foreword. He said he would be happy to do so, and it doesn't get much better than that.

Thirty years ago, when I broke into the business, Ernie Harwell told me to come to him whenever I needed. I have taken Ernie up on his generous offer many times, and when I became desperate for a source of box scores, he had the answer. Ernie turned us on to David Smith and his fabulous Web site—retrosheet.org—that provided all the box scores we needed to help us bring the great games of 1984 back to life. I dropped off a manuscript to Ernie one day and by the next day he had read the book and written the introduction. Ernie is over 80 and I don't think he's missed a step.

Through Haney and Stein, I found another old Ann Arborite like myself, Doug Truax. Doug's publishing company, Crofton Creek Press, coordinated the text and design and took charge of publishing the book and making it available to Tigers fans throughout the country.

I've known Ken Calcut since we played softball together in Ann Arbor in the early '70s. His wife, Jacinta, is a brilliant graphic artist and their company, Image Graphics and Design, went far beyond what any of us had anticipated in painstakingly designing and laying out the entire book and cover.

Gathering those pictures was another process altogether. *Free Press* Editor Dave Robinson went deep into his newspaper's archives to help gather many of the photos in the book. I'm also thankful to the photo department at the *Detroit News*, which provided some key photos to fill in the gaps.

Bill Eisner, who has spent decades at the ballpark recording a photo history of the Tigers, also found many of the photos for the book, including some of me with the players in '84. Bill spent many hours digging through drawers and boxes looking for photos from '84. He owed me nothing, yet gave his time and resources generously. Dan Ewald Jr. also came up with some great shots and I'm grateful for his contribution.

Alan Sussman was the only person outside the core team to get an early manuscript. I knew that he would be willing to give an utterly honest opinion on all the material. Sure enough, Alan convinced me to make some critical changes regarding the tone of the book. We all know what we want to hear, but it's the other stuff that we really need to hear. Thanks, Alan.

Finally, at the risk of sounding trite, I must thank the 20 or so Tigers who were interviewed for this book and dug deep into their memories to provide you with their recollections. After all, this book is about them, and I am grateful that they allowed me to become the messenger who enables you, the great Tigers fans, to relive the time of their lives.

Foreword

By Elmore Leonard

This one has to be the best book about a baseball team that I've ever read.

Maybe it's because Eli Zaret's account of the sensational '84 season got me excited all over again. But there is much more than stats and reading about the Tigers' stunning record—taking 35 of their first 40 games, hanging on to first place in their division all season, and then whomping the Padres in a five-game World Series.

What makes the book so readable is that it's loaded with behind-the-scenes stories and incidents that bring it to life. We learn how a tough management put this team together. We learn what players felt and said about personal situations, and how Sparky Anderson, with inimitable quotes, managed and motivated them to be winners.

I've been a fan of the Tigers since they beat the Cubs in the 1935 World Series. I saw player-manager Mickey Cochrane and the "Mechanical Man" Charlie Gehringer, the great DiMaggio during his 56-game hitting streak, and was there when Ted Williams homered in the 1941 All-Star Game. But my all-time favorite highlight was Kirk Gibson taking that Goose Gossage fastball into the upper deck to clinch the '84 World Series. I saw it from the centerfield bleachers and screamed my head off along with 51,901 Tigers fans.

Introduction

By Ernie Harwell

For more than 30 years—most of them in Detroit—Eli Zaret has been on top of every sports happening, as up-to-date as the next swing of the bat.

Life was different for Eli in 1984. He had started his career in the mid-'70s, but was still regarded as a skinny sports reporter for an FM rock station, trying to find a niche in the muscle-and-sweat culture that chewed on longhaired rebels who dared to approach their scene with a discernable edge. At that time, WDIV-TV, for whom he was a weekend sports anchor, assigned him to the Tigers pre-game show.

As you might expect, it was the highlight of his young career. Eli followed the '84 Tigers through their record-setting season. He became almost a part of the team.

Now all of us benefit from Eli's '84 experience. He has chronicled it in *'84—The Last of the Great Tigers*. Zaret gives insight to this remarkable season, taking us down to the playing field and into the clubhouse. He examines the psyche of a fascinating cast of characters.

There is Jim Campbell, clinging to his old-fashioned methods and presenting a challenge to Eli's generation of players and fans. And Sparky Anderson, the my-way-or-the-highway manager. Plus the players, with their diverse personalities.

A highlight of this readable effort is Eli's inclusion of the Tigers' players own views throughout the season. The principals in this soap opera with muscles state their opinions about their own teammates and their manager. It is a remarkable look behind the scenes.

The '84 Tigers were a magnificent one-season team. After a 35-5 start, they won their division with ease. They then swept Kansas City in the playoffs and climaxed their year by beating San Diego in a five-game World Series. The team became the darling of Michigan and its race to glory was a top ongoing story across the nation.

Eli Zaret was there through it all. His compelling retrospective brings to life the thrills we experienced that magical season. It is a wonderful, well-told story.

Chapter 1

The Year the Boys Blessed Detroit

In the summer of 1984, I was privileged to host the Tigers pre-game show on Channel 4, WDIV, in Detroit. It remains the thrill and highlight of my career. After each pre-game episode ended, I would turn to the chroma key screen and "toss it," as they say in television, to Al Kaline and George Kell. George would then say, "Thanks, Eli, and hello again everyone."

To this day, people still imitate George saying those words, and each time I hear them, I marvel at the impact the World Champion Detroit Tigers had on the people of Michigan in 1984. When Kell retired in the late 1990s, the *Detroit Free Press* devoted the entire front page of its sports section to George and his legacy. They also listed about 15 or 20 of his classic phrases. The first one on the list was, "Thanks, Eli..."

As the years rolled by, I began to understand how lucky I was to have been in the catbird seat for the '84 Tigers' race to glory. To have known them and traveled with them, to have been a key participant in presenting their story to their fans, and to have witnessed their growth from promising, unproven pups to celebrated champions have become all the more special over time.

In the latter part of the 20th century, Detroit experienced more major sports championships than any metropolitan area. The Red Wings won three Stanley Cups from '97 to '02; the Pistons won back-to-back NBA Championships in '89 and '90; the University of Michigan and Michigan State University each won an NCAA Basketball Championship; and Michigan shared a national football title.

But none of those great title runs had the impact of the Tigers' 1984 championship. For seven months that year—from the record-shattering 35-5 start to Kirk Gibson's majestic swat off Goose Gossage—the '84 Tigers dominated the sports scene locally and nationally. A record 2.7 million people streamed into Tiger Stadium that year, 25 percent more than had ever witnessed any season at Detroit's historic baseball corner, Michigan and Trumbull. The '68 Tigers had barely broken the 2 million attendance mark, which to that point had been the highest in club history.

Tigers television ratings soared to levels beyond any that had happened before or have happened since. On Friday, June 8, 1984, when the Tigers played at night in Baltimore, the telecast on Channel 4 in Detroit recorded a 62 audience share. That means with dozens of viewing choices, more than 6 out of every 10 televisions turned on in Detroit were showing a regular-season Tigers baseball game. We'll get into a deeper explanation of the numbers later, but from April through October 1984, the Tigers attracted nearly 100 million pairs of TV-viewing eyeballs!

Led by a charismatic and wildly quotable manager who nurtured a core of star players who had been learning, improving and gaining experience over the previous decade, the '84 Tigers became a fan and media phenomenon that arguably stands alone in Michigan sports history.

If you have already been stimulated to pick up this book, I promise you will be amazed by what you had forgotten. Certainly you remember some of what created 35-5, as well as some of the post-season rampage that destroyed the Royals and Padres, but you'll also retrieve many other elements that have fallen through the cracks in your memory since 1984. And some of what you'll read has never been reported.

The "Wave" and its myriad variations debuted and caught fire in '84, raging back and forth through packed stands. There was also the bleacher creatures' rowdiness that distracted the players and drove management crazy. The bleacherites swore in unison and at each other, and harassed the security people who tried to interfere with the continual swatting of beach balls that often wound up on the field, interrupting the game. An extended battle took place over what song would accompany the grounds crew on its fifth-inning infield sweep. Dancing broom man Herbie Redmond became a cult hero, and, rather than capitalize on his popularity, the late Tigers President Jim Campbell fought to quell all the exuberance.

Jack Morris, the ace of the staff, threw a no-hitter and won 10 games before May segued to June. By then, Morris had aroused talk of surpassing Denny McLain's 31 wins in 1968. Then he fell into a lengthy mid-season slump. For a six-week period from July to early September, Jack was in a state of profound confusion, anger and alienation. He pitched miserably, talked barely at all to his teammates and spoke not a syllable to the press. He didn't even win 20 games in '84, but re-emerged as a postseason star.

Meanwhile, the press feasted and fought over the story of this team. In fact, two of them, Jerry Green of *The Detroit News* and Al Ackerman of WDIV-TV, nearly came to blows in the locker room one night late in the season, arguing over Channel 4's decision to trademark Al's pet slogan, "Bless You Boys."

The Tigers rode first place the entire season, winning wire to wire, but couldn't shake pesky Toronto until the final weeks. You may be surprised to recall how at times fans and media became fearful that the occasionally slumping Tigers would find a way to blow baseball's greatest-ever start. Sparky Anderson also shared that same underlying paranoia—what if they did blow it?

How incredibly damning and humiliating would that be?

I shared all of those doubts while sitting in the press box at Kauffman Stadium in Kansas City at 8:30 p.m. on October 2, 1984. Game One of the American League Championship Series was just beginning and I was unable to shake the thought that the dream might be ending soon. After all, these were the young Tigers, up against George Brett, Frank White, Dan Quisenberry and the hardened veterans of Kansas City, a team that had won six American League West titles and an AL pennant in the last nine years. Except for Willie Hernandez, no Tigers player had any postseason experience, and the Royals might soon be bursting the bubble and ruining it for all of us.

Having known most of these Tigers since they were rookies, and some even before that, I had a gnawing feeling that they would wilt under the glare. But moments later, Lou Whitaker led off the game with a single off Bud Black. Alan Trammell quickly lifted me off my seat when he tripled over left fielder Darryl Motley's head, scoring Whitaker.

Soon thereafter, Lance Parrish hit a sacrifice fly and they were up, 2-0. I sat there with my heart pumping, shaking my head in disbelief at the Tigers' readiness to emphatically finish what they had started six months earlier. No, these weren't wide-eyed upstarts about to get spanked by the big boys. Hardly. Although the core of the Tigers was composed of players in their mid-20s, with just four or five major-league campaigns behind them, they were also focused, toughened professionals who were totally prepared and determined to dominate any opponent put before them.

The Tigers went on to win that first playoff game, 8-1, behind a rejuvenated Morris, and took seven of eight in the postseason to finish the year in the same spectacular fashion they had started. They became just the third team to lead wire to wire and go on to win the World Series. And their company was the elite of the elite: the '27 Yankees of Babe Ruth and the '55 Dodgers, teams whose fast-start records had fallen in the Tigers' wake.

As great as the '84 Tigers were, as creatively and scientifically as they were constructed, and as brilliantly as they were led, they won only a single championship. The Blue Jays did to the Tigers in '85 what the Tigers had done to them in '84, just as the Tigers had done to the Orioles what the Orioles did to them in '83.

From 1981 to 1986, six different teams won the AL East, and of the six only the '85 Jays failed to go on to win the AL pennant.

1981	Yankees	1984	Tigers
1982	Brewers	1985	Blue Jays
1983	Orioles	1986	Red Sox

The division was loaded and clearly baseball's best. With their 84-76 record in '84, the AL West Champion Royals would have only finished sixth in the AL East!

I remember standing with Sparky Anderson by the Tigers' dugout around mid-September of '85. The Blue Jays were about to mathematically eliminate the Tigers, and Sparky and I were shooting the breeze waiting for our live shot on the 6 o'clock news.

He said, quite matter-of-factly, "Can't you just feel that little nip in the air? You can always tell when the fall is coming." Sparky was a California guy and loved the slice of fall weather he experienced by touring the country as a baseball manager. I said, "Too bad, huh? I never imagined that it wouldn't happen this year also. You guys out of the race? What a shame."

Strangely, he wasn't ruing the Tigers' disappointing follow-up to '84. He didn't appear crushed in the slightest. Sparky knew that there were reasons, and that most of them were beyond his control. He had come to accept baseball for what it is: a promise of nothing. You get 162 games and you win it or you don't—nothing more, nothing less. They would finish 84-77 in '85. Hell, in '78, '79, '80 and '82 they had also won between 83 and 86 games. I said, "Aren't you disappointed?" All I remember him saying was, "What a great season Toronto had. That's a deserving ballclub, just like we were last year."

In 2003, several of the heroes of that '84 team were brought back to manage and coach the Detroit franchise out of a long period of darkness. Will the lessons derived from their great white-haired teacher and the experiences of pennant fights be implanted within the players of the 21st century? In sports, where rapid change often defies rational explanation, might a transference take place, whereby a team of meager talent with a depleted payroll could rise from the ashes and soar again? Are the seeds of a title being sown just as they were in 1974 when Bill Lajoie drafted Lance Parrish as the first building block of the team that would win it all 10 years later?

That may be far in the offing. Baseball has changed markedly since 1984, and the Tom Monaghan and Mike Ilitch regimes struggled to compete. For now, the '84 Tigers was the last great Tigers team. This was also the last Tigers era in which the players remained in the community, continuing to be visible and raising their families to live among the fans who adored the players' athletic exploits.

You could easily argue that the Tigers have not played a significant game since winning their division in 1987. But that reality also serves to make what happened in '84 all the more significant. The '84 Tigers completed a brilliant 10-year construction project that was conceived by General Manager Bill Lajoie and Jim Campbell, then steered through its final stages by a Hall of Fame manager who helped gather the right players and who also understood how to get the most out of them.

For that season, 1984, the Tigers were one of the greatest teams in baseball history. Here's hoping that in the following pages, you will enjoy reliving it all.

Chapter 2

Just a Fantasy

ach baseball season really begins during the previous winter. That's when teams make efforts to improve by trading, signing and releasing players, and that's when the media and fans make their forecasts. The tendency is often to expect last year's winners to repeat, even though it usually doesn't work out that way.

The Tigers finished six games back of Baltimore in '83. The O's won 98 to the Tigers' 92, blew out the White Sox three games to one to win the pennant, and then disposed of the Phillies in five to win the World Series.

Baltimore had vied with the Yankees as the league's best team the five previous years. In '79, the Orioles won 102 games before losing the Series to Willie Stargell and the "We Are Family" Pirates. They won 100 games in '80, but finished second to the Yankees' 103. They missed out in both halves of the weird, strike-marred '81 season, even though their overall 59-46 record was better than the eventual pennant-winning Yankees. And they won 94 games in '82 but lost the division by one game to Milwaukee.

Going into 1984, the experts liked Joe Altobelli's Orioles to repeat. They had future Hall of Famers Eddie Murray and Cal Ripken to go along with a four-man rotation of Scott McGregor, Mike Boddicker, Mike Flanagan and Storm Davis. They had a pair of bullpen stoppers in Tippy Martinez and Sammy Stewart, and there was no reason to expect the Tigers or anyone else to knock them off.

Altobelli had great flexibility with a left-field platoon of Gary Roenicke and John Lowenstein; he had Al Bumbry and John Shelby in center and Jim Dwyer and Dan Ford in right. His designated hitter, Ken Singleton, was a star in his own right. Even Jim Palmer, at age 38, had a chance of recapturing his youth for a swan-song season.

Clearly, their pitching remained superior to any club in the league. They had also added infielder Wayne Gross from Oakland as well as free-agent A's pitcher Tom Underwood. All the Tigers had done in the off-season to counter was to acquire 36-year-old free agent Darrell Evans.

In January '84, a long-time Tigers fan named Jerry Lewis created the first Tiger Fantasy Camp in Lakeland, Florida. Jerry and his partner, '68 Tigers catcher Jim Price, invited me to attend as a camper. I accepted and decided that while I was there, I would produce a five-part series for Channel 4 News. The '68 Tigers were the stars of the camp, 15 seasons after the World Series triumph that had anointed them as Detroit's reigning baseball heroes. Almost all of the '68 team was in attendance to instruct, play and regale the campers with stories of their exploits. Al Kaline, Mickey Lolich, Jim Northrup, Bill Freehan, Willie Horton, Dick McAuliffe and Gates Brown headed the impressive list of '68 heroes who would suit up to play and schmooze. The only notable absentee was Denny McLain, who had a valid excuse as he served out his initial stint in the federal slammer.

The Fantasy Camp was a very cool concept. My lasting image was the very first scene that I saw as I pulled in to the old Holiday Inn Central where the Tigers used to stay. It was a miserable dive of a hotel on an industrial highway in Lakeland, but it was an authentic Tigers home and therefore perfect for the campers.

I arrived about 45 minutes after everyone else because I had to load TV equipment at the Tampa airport. As I drove into the hotel parking lot, I saw about 30 guys wearing Tigers uniforms attempting to play catch on a strip of lawn next to the parking lot. When the campers had gotten to their rooms, each had seen an official Tigers uniform on the bed with his name sewn perfectly on the back. And here they were, either overweight or undermuscled, their hearts soaring, reveling in the illusion that they really were ballplayers.

Fantasy Camp was the perfect name. To this day, I'm continually amazed at how amateur players allow themselves to imagine that if a few things had gone their way, they could have been big-time ballplayers. I saw it for real that day: they were like little boys masquerading as grownups, warming up their arms and dreaming that they would soon show Al Kaline and Mickey Lolich that they really had the goods.

The '68 team bridged the long gap from the 1945 Tigers World Series winners. Baseball was in a pretty sad state in '45, because World War II had sapped the game of its stars. Except for fan favorite Paul "Dizzy" Trout, aging Hal Newhouser and the great Hank Greenberg, the '45 team had no tangible presence or personalities for Tigers fans to relate to. In other words, in the spring of '84, the '68 Tigers stood as the lone, visible purveyors of Tigers tradition and greatness.

Even if the '45 team hadn't represented an era of watered-down baseball, few of its players maintained any presence in the community. The great Greenberg didn't even live in Michigan, and there wasn't much film or video presence to serve as a reminder of the team. On the other hand, many of the '68 Tigers still lived in the Detroit area and were constant reminders of the greatest season in memory.

The film of their thrilling comeback against a terrific Cardinals team seemed omnipresent. It was a slam-dunk that every time the Tigers were in a rain delay, the Curt Gowdy–narrated '68 Series film would pop up in all its living-color splendor. Tigers fans knew the damn thing by heart.

In fairness, it had truly been a terrific Series and that's why its incessant airing was justified: Horton's throw to nail Lou Brock; Manager Mayo Smith's daring move to put Mickey Stanley at shortstop; Bob Gibson's record 17 strikeouts in Game One; a Tigers team that looked dead after four-plus games; Curt Flood's misplay on Jim Northrup's bases-loaded triple; Kaline's career validation in becoming a World Champion; Jose Feliciano's controversial national anthem; Lolich's three wins and his memorable leap into Bill Freehan's arms after the final out.

That magical '68 season had also been the year of the pitcher, and the Series featured Gibson and his record 1.12 ERA, and McLain of the mind-boggling 31 wins. And rightfully so or not, the '68 Tigers were assigned great social significance for mending the racial disharmony of the explosive 1967 riots.

The '68 Tigers brought a lot to the table, and in the months leading up the '84 season, it was hard to envision any Tigers team equaling or supplanting their substantial legend.

At the Fantasy Camp that January, the '68 stars were respectful of the '84 Tigers and their prospects. Freehan accurately questioned the depth of the starting pitching. In January, they hadn't even re-signed Milt Wilcox, and after Jack Morris and Dan Petry, who was there? The '68 club, with Lolich, McLain, Earl Wilson and Joe Sparma, had a better starting staff. John Hiller was still the Tigers' all-time saves leader, and reigning bullpen closer Aurelio Lopez had faded in '83. Kaline questioned the '84 team's pennant-race experience and ability to deal with adversity.

Northrup, although respectful of Chet Lemon as a center fielder, was concerned about Gibson's chances to succeed as an outfielder, and overall he felt that he, Horton, Stanley and Kaline constituted a superior outfield. In theory, they were all correct.

In the winter of '84, a few months before the season began, no one envisioned that the '84 team would not only surpass the 103 wins of the '68 team, but would also rival their reputation as the greatest Tigers team ever.

Chapter 3

Picking the Pieces

The building of the '84 Tigers began in 1973 with an edict from Jim Campbell to his new director of player procurement, Bill Lajoie, to build the talent end of the organization from the bottom up. Lajoie assembled an eight-man scouting staff to scour the country to identify the human pieces needed to assemble an extremely complex puzzle.

Over the ensuing years thousands of decisions were made on young talent, and hundreds of players passed through. Look at the following list of 19 players who played for the Tigers in '83 with hopes of being a part of the '84 team:

Larry Pashnick	Dave Rucker	Enos Cabell
Pat Underwood	Bill Fahey	Lynn Jones
Bob James	Sal Butera	Rick Leach
Julio Gonzalez	Mike Ivie	Glenn Wilson
Jerry Ujdur	Dave Gumpert	Howard Bailey
Wayne Krenchicki	John Martin	
Bob Molinaro	Bill Nahorodny	

None of them survived. For that matter, with the exceptions of Rick Leach, Glenn Wilson and Lynn Jones, few would become even modestly productive anywhere else.

In 1984, 35 players participated in winning the championship, ranging from bit-part performer to superstar:

YEAR ACQ	PLAYER	HOW OBTAINED
1974	Lance Parrish	1st round draft choice
1975	Tom Brookens	1st round draft choice
	Dave Rozema	4th round draft choice
	Lou Whitaker	5th round draft choice
1976	Alan Trammell	2nd round draft choice
	Dan Petry	4th round draft choice
	Jack Morris	5th round draft choice
	Milt Wilcox	Purchased from Cubs 6/10/76
1978	Kirk Gibson	1st round draft choice
	Marty Castillo	5th round draft choice
	Aurelio Lopez	For Bob Sykes in four-man trade with Cards 12/4/78
1979	Howard Johnson	1st round draft choice
1980	Mike Laga	1st round draft choice
	Dwight Lowry	11th round draft choice
	Barbaro Garbey	Non-drafted free agent 6/6/80
	Roger Mason	Non-drafted free agent 9/21/80
1981	Randy O'Neal	1st round draft choice
	Nelson Simmons	2nd round draft choice
	Scott Earl	14th round draft choice
	Chet Lemon	For Steve Kemp in two-man trade with White Sox 11/27/81
	Larry Herndon	For Dan Schatzeder and Mike Chris in two-man trade with Giants 12/9/81
1982	Doug Baker	9th round draft choice
	Juan Berenguer	Non-drafted free agent 4/4/82
1983	Carl Willis	23rd round draft choice
	John Grubb	For Dave Tobik in two-man trade with Rangers 3/24/83
	Glenn Abbott	Purchased from Mariners 4/23/83
	Doug Bair	For Dave Rucker in two-man trade with Cards 6/21/83
	Rusty Kuntz	For Larry Pashnick in two-man trade with Twins 12/5/83
	Darrell Evans	Free agent from San Francisco, signed 12/16/83
1984	Rod Allen	Free agent cut by Mariners, signed 2/14/84
	Willie Hernandez	For John Wockenfuss and Glenn Wilson in four-man trade with Phillies 3/24/84
	Dave Bergman	For John Wockenfuss and Glenn Wilson in four-man trade with Phillies 3/24/84
	Ruppert Jones	Free agent cut by Pirates, signed 4/18/84
	Sid Monge	Purchased from Padres 6/10/84
	Bill Scherrer	For Carl Willis in two-man trade with Reds 8/28/84

Manager:	Sparky Anderson	1979
Coaches:	Gates Brown	1978
	Billy Consolo	1979
	Roger Craig	1980
	Alex Grammas	1980
	Dick Tracewski	1972

The '84 Tigers were predominantly built through the draft. With the exception of the first major free agent the Tigers ever signed, Darrell Evans, every key member was drafted by Bill Lajoie and his staff of scouts, picked up or purchased for virtually nothing, or acquired in exchange for a player they had drafted.

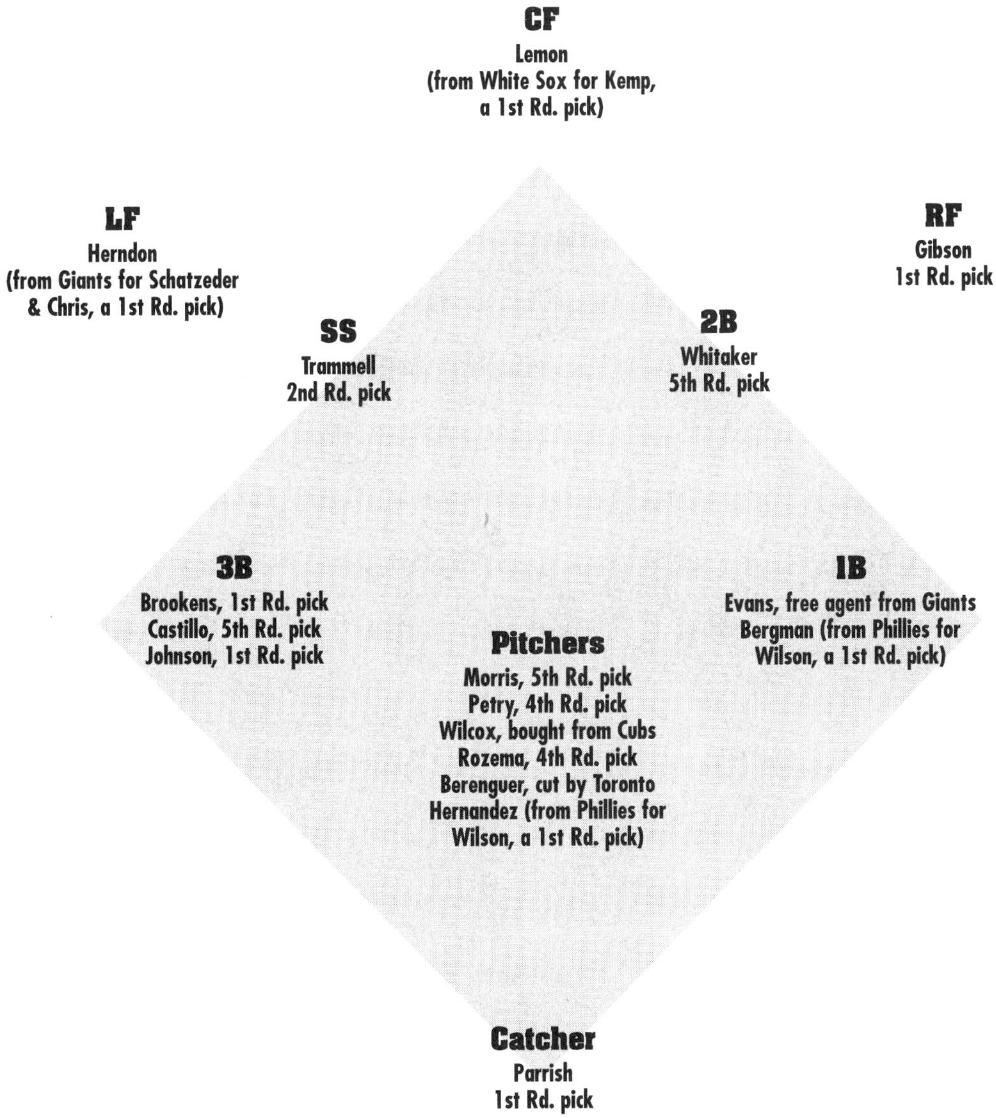

CF
Lemon
(from White Sox for Kemp,
a 1st Rd. pick)

LF
Herndon
(from Giants for Schatzeder
& Chris, a 1st Rd. pick)

RF
Gibson
1st Rd. pick

SS
Trammell
2nd Rd. pick

2B
Whitaker
5th Rd. pick

3B
Brookens, 1st Rd. pick
Castillo, 5th Rd. pick
Johnson, 1st Rd. pick

1B
Evans, free agent from Giants
Bergman (from Phillies for
Wilson, a 1st Rd. pick)

Pitchers
Morris, 5th Rd. pick
Petry, 4th Rd. pick
Wilcox, bought from Cubs
Rozema, 4th Rd. pick
Berenguer, cut by Toronto
Hernandez (from Phillies for
Wilson, a 1st Rd. pick)

Catcher
Parrish
1st Rd. pick

Aside from the big spring trade that brought Willie Hernandez and Dave Bergman to Detroit on March 24, 1984, Lemon, Herndon and Evans were the last three major pieces to be put into place. In the space of several weeks in late '81, Kemp was traded for Lemon, and Herndon was acquired for Dan Schatzeder and Mike Chris. Herndon became an outstanding contributor in '82 and '83, while Schatzeder and Chris went on to do virtually nothing. Lemon played much longer than Kemp, who suffered an eye injury that cut his career short. And although Evans didn't have his best year in '84, he still provided valuable leadership for the still-youngish Tigers.

Spring '84: Tigers up the middle—(l. to r.) Lou Whitaker, Alan Trammell, Chet Lemon, Lance Parrish (and friend).

Evans immediately demonstrated a professional cool and a willingness to counsel all who needed it. But he was far from alone in the leadership category.

Gibson was the most notorious and vocal leader of the '84 champs. Parrish, a more low-key personality, wasn't an "in your face" type of leader like Gibson but had been groomed by Sparky and Roger Craig to be more aggressive and hands-on in leading the pitching staff. Morris' leadership was defined by his defiant determination to win; his inspiration was spread to teammates through his toughness and durability.

For the most part, this was not a boisterous team, and most players were mindful of not being perceived as outspoken. Generally, they were careful to not say the wrong thing. Except for Hernandez, the Latin players rarely spoke at all. But Willie didn't mind letting people know that when he pitched, he was "the boss," and his regal presence and aura of invincibility instilled a sense of well-being in everybody. Veterans like Dave Bergman, Tom Brookens, John Grubb, Lou Whitaker, Larry Herndon, Howard Johnson and Dan Petry preferred to remain in the background and not overtly draw attention to themselves.

Sparky liked this mix of personalities. He respected the style of the quiet guys and appreciated the contributions of the more outgoing players. And although Sparky reigned as the undisputed leader, he recognized the importance of having a self-policing team—a team that embraced his definition of professionalism and had the mettle on the field to emphatically prove it to the world in 1984.

Chapter 4

The Odyssey
of the Obscure

When dissected and analyzed, all baseball rosters reveal the spectrum of success in the game. The core of any championship team will feature at least a handful of players who won awards, amassed vast wealth and left the sport with significant fame. But even legendary teams reveal an underbelly of baseball journeymen and vagabonds who happen to be in the right place at the right time to pull at least a part of the load.

Nearly half of the '84 Tigers were of average or below-average major-league caliber. Even if you followed the team fairly closely that year, you no doubt looked at the list of 35 in the previous chapter and said to yourself, "Oh yeah, I'd forgotten about him," or, "What the hell ever happened to him?" or "Did he really play for that team?"

The phenomenon of the '84 championship team wasn't that there was an inordinate number of bit-part players, because there wasn't. It was a typical team in that regard. What was remarkable that year was that some of them, like Rusty Kuntz, Marty Castillo and Barbaro Garbey, played at a level they never came close to approaching again. Others, like Doug Baker, Sid Monge, Carl Willis, Nelson Simmons and Scotty Earl, arrived for their proverbial baseball "cup of coffee," savored the moment, and then quickly faded from view.

Mike Laga played for the Tigers for parts of five consecutive years, from '82 through '86. A slugger who hit 34 homers at Evansville in '82, Laga struggled through nine major-league seasons, getting a total of barely 400 at bats and hitting .199. But he was called up in September and went 6-11, hitting .545. For what it's worth—very little or nothing at all—Laga had the highest Tigers batting average in '84.

Rod Allen is another. Fans, media and others outside the game don't bother to look into the careers of the non-stars. Who's got time for that? It's tough enough keeping up with the big names. In the spring of 2003, Fox Sports Net in Detroit hired Allen to replace Kirk Gibson as its color analyst.

Allen had been doing similar work for the Arizona Diamondbacks and displayed a deep understanding of the game that he pursued professionally for 15 years. In those 15 years, he got a total of only 50 major-league at bats. He went 8-27 for a .296 batting average in his 10-week stint with the '84 Tigers. Allen was drafted in the sixth round by the White Sox out of high school in Santa Monica in 1977. His major-league affiliations were with Chicago, Seattle, Detroit, Baltimore and Cleveland.

In the minor leagues, Allen was a consistent .300 hitter with modest power. But he was never considered a good fielder—baggage he wouldn't shed until it was too late. Even at the start of '84, Sparky spoke highly of his bat, but said Allen would only hit because he had "problems with the leather." Meanwhile, his leather suitcase got tattered taking him to 17 cities in 3 countries over 15 years in an all-too-typical professional trek:

Year	City	Parent Club
1977	Sarasota	(Chicago)
1978	Appleton	(Chicago)
1979	Knoxville	(Chicago)
1980	Glens Falls	(Chicago)
	Des Moines	(Chicago)
1981	Edmonton	(Chicago)
1982	Salt Lake City	(Seattle)
1983	Seattle	
1984	Detroit	
	Evansville	(Detroit)
1985	Rochester	(Baltimore)
1986	Laredo	(Mexican League)
	Waterbury	(Cleveland)
	Maine	(Cleveland)
1987	Buffalo	(Cleveland)
1988	Colorado Springs	(Cleveland)
	Cleveland	
1989	Hiroshima	(Japan League)
1990	Hiroshima	
1991	Hiroshima	

Calling Allen a vagabond is putting it mildly. The Indians called him up late in '88 and gave him what would be his last 11 big-league at bats before selling him to Hiroshima in the Japan League. He played three years in Japan and made about $1 million there.

Allen, with no bitterness or apologies for spending most of his adult life chasing baseball's wild goose, says, "Japan was wonderful and it got me out of debt. When you play 15 years at minor-league wages, you incur debts and you don't want to leave the game without taking something with you, some security. That's why I didn't quit. I refused to quit."

In the pros, you don't play for the love of the game, as Kevin Costner's character said in *Bull Durham.* You do love playing the game, but the reason you play as an adult is to make a living. And very few succeed at that.

Truth is, most professional sports lives are tragically short, largely unsatisfying and played in relative obscurity. I started covering spring training in Lakeland in 1977, when the seeds of the '84 team were being sown. Of the hundreds of players in Tiger Town in the spring of 1984, 25 went north and the rest were either dispersed to minor-league teams or just released. In fact, '77 rookie Dave Rozema was the only Tiger who went north in '77 and stuck around to ride in the victory parade seven years later. And even he was dumped after the '84 season.

Bruce Taylor was a short-relief specialist with a side-arm delivery that could paralyze right-handed hitters. In '75, he was 8-1 with a 2.22 ERA in Triple A. In the spring of '76, he and a 23-year-old farmhand named Mark Fidrych were impressive enough to become surprise additions to the big-league roster.

But near the end of spring training, Taylor encountered some arm problems. He opened the season in Detroit, then was sent to Evansville to work through it. He had a decent year in Triple A in '76, but now it was '77, his arm felt good and at 24—with four solid years in the minors behind him—Taylor was excited to be on the verge of realizing his big-league dream.

But he had a few rough outings and the walls caved in on him. The Tigers optioned him to Evansville just before the team went north. Briefly discouraged, but still determined, Taylor had another good year at Evansville in '77 as the closer for other young hopefuls like Jack Morris.

Taylor was Evansville's bullpen ace in '77 with a 2.21 ERA, and Morris was ace of the starters with 3.60 ERA. Morris was called up June 25, 1977, to replace injured Mark Fidrych, and went 1-1 in seven starts. Taylor came up a week later and appeared in 19 games and went 1-0. He and Morris were both right on track with bright Tigers futures.

Taylor made the team in '78 but was sent down in April. In '79, when Morris broke through with 17 wins, Taylor made the team again, but was sent back to Evansville in May. Tigers brass had made another of those life-altering decisions, deciding that Dave Tobik, also 27 and a number one draft pick, had the better future. That was the last of Bruce Taylor.

Jack Morris made about $25 million and won 254 games. Taylor finished his career with a 2-2 record and perhaps made a career total of $100,000.

When the Tigers won in '84, I'm sure that wherever Bruce Taylor was, he reflected on what part he might have played if only...if only he hadn't hurt his arm? If only Les Moss, his manager in '79, had still seen Taylor's promise and been more patient?

The shoulders of the baseball highway are littered with thousands of Bruce Taylors, who despite the talent to make it to the majors, wind up with "if only" careers.

There's nothing quite like spring training. The whole scene—the process, the sights and sounds, even just the sun beating down after a cold winter—I love it. On the first day in Florida, I like to pan over and ponder the activity on the many fields where all those hopefuls hit, run and throw in pursuit of their dreams.

Far fewer than 1 percent of them will ever become a Lou Whitaker, Kirk Gibson or Jack Morris. Only about 10 percent will ever get to put on a uniform for even one day in a major-league clubhouse before getting eliminated from the mix. Ninety percent will never get that close before going home to teach school or sell insurance.

Most fans take for granted how talented you have to be and how hard it is just to make it to the majors, no less to actually have a successful career. These odds put into focus what a very special group of Tigers it was that brought Detroit a championship in 1984.

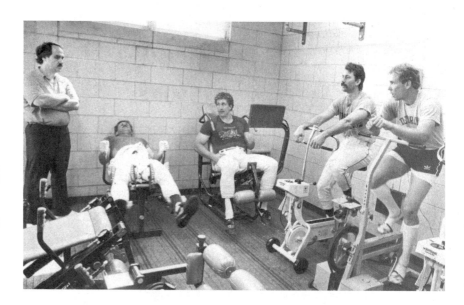

Trainer Pio DiSalvo oversees Petry, Parrish, Brookens and Trammell on the new exercise equipment installed at Joker Marchant Stadium in spring training 1984.

Chapter 5

Bill Lajoie
and the Spirit of '76

*Our athletic director said, "So what do you think about
playing for Ralph Houk?" I go, "Who's Ralph Houk?" He made
fun of me for 10 minutes. Gimme a break. I was disappointed
and confused.*

— Lance Parrish, as a high school senior, on being
informed he'd been drafted by the Tigers

I n November 2002, the Red Sox hired a 28-year-old general manager named Theo
Epstein, making him the youngest to hold that post in baseball history. The Red
Sox also brought in Bill James as a special consultant. James is the self-
proclaimed sabermetrician who revolutionized baseball statistical measuring
devices when he created his breakthrough "Baseball Abstract" in the early
1980s. James had suggested to Epstein that he seek out Lajoie, who by then was
a retired baseball executive turned scout.

Youth, if not stifled by arrogance, looks to its elders for advice, guidance and perspective. Epstein called Lajoie, and in the twilight of his career, Lajoie signed on with
Boston as Epstein's assistant general manager. In 1984, when Epstein was in third
grade, 49-year-old Bill Lajoie was named Executive of the Year for his brilliance in
assembling the '84 World Champion Tigers.

The 1984 season was actually Lajoie's first year as Tigers general manager, having
replaced Jim Campbell, who was bumped up to president and chief executive officer.
Before the '84 season, Lajoie had been promoted from vice president of baseball operations, the last in a series of promotions since he became scouting director in 1973.

Baseball began drafting amateur players in 1965, and in the years since, teams like
the Yankees, Braves, Expos and Twins have done outstanding jobs of building through
their farm systems. Still, James feels that Lajoie's string of successes as Tigers farm
director from '74 to '78 represents the most prolific five-year period in the history of the
baseball draft.

Amateur drafts were held in January and June until 1986, after which the January
draft was eliminated. There was also a supplemental draft that gave clubs a chance to
acquire players that others were willing to set free. Thus, there may be more than one

pick in a particular round in a particular year.

The highlights of that five-year period in Tigers draft history, as well as the four subsequent years, appear in the following list. Names in bold type indicate that the player either played for the '84 Tigers or was traded for a player who played for the '84 Tigers. Following the list of draft picks and the rounds in which they were drafted are the trades Lajoie made using his former draft picks.

Draft Pick/Round

1974 **1st rd. Lance Parrish**; 10th rd. Mark Fidrych; **19th rd. Bob Sykes**

1975 **1st rd. Tom Brookens; 4th rd. Dave Rozema**; 4th rd. Jason Thompson; **5th rd. Lou Whitaker**

1976 **1st rd. Steve Kemp; 1st rd. Dave Tobik;** 1st rd. Pat Underwood; 1st rd. Dave Stegman; **2nd rd. Alan Trammell; 4th rd. Dan Petry; 5th rd. Jack Morris**

1977 **1st rd. Mike Chris**; 7th rd. Rick Peters

1978 **1st rd. Kirk Gibson; 5th rd. Marty Castillo; 16th rd. Dave Rucker**

1979 1st rd. Rick Leach; **1st rd. Howard Johnson**

1980 **1st rd. Glenn Wilson; 1st rd. Mike Laga; 11th rd. Dwight Lowry**

1981 1st rd. Bob Melvin; **1st rd. Randy O'Neal; 2nd rd. Nelson Simmons**

1982 **9th rd. Doug Baker**

Trades

1978	St. Louis	Aurelio Lopez and Jerry Morales for Bob Sykes and Jack Murphy
1981	White Sox	Chet Lemon for Steve Kemp
	Giants	Larry Herndon for Dan Schatzader and Mike Chris
1983	Rangers	John Grubb for Dave Tobik
	St. Louis	Doug Bair for Dave Rucker
1984	Philadelphia	Willie Hernandez and Dave Bergman for John Wockenfuss and Glenn Wilson

Lajoie grew up in Detroit, went to Denby High School and saw many games at Tiger Stadium in the 1940s and '50s. He played at Western Michigan University and in 1955 was an All-American center fielder. Dodgers General Manager Buzzie Bavasi offered him a $30,000 bonus to sign, but Lajoie turned him down. Justifiably dubious about his chances of breaking into a Brooklyn outfield featuring Duke Snider and Carl Furillo, Lajoie took just $4,000 to sign with the struggling Orioles, where he felt he had a much better shot at the majors.

He wound up playing 10 years in the minors, mostly in the Orioles system, and although he hit .300 several times, was never called up to the big leagues. Disappointed, but satisfied that he had given it his best shot, he came back to Detroit and used his WMU teaching degree to teach physical education and coach baseball at Detroit Northern High School.

Bill Lajoie proved to be a drafting genius in rebuilding the Tigers from their '70s swoon.

Still smitten by the pro game, Lajoie became a scout with the Reds, then moved to the Tigers in '68. Bernie Carbo, the very first player he scouted for Cincinnati, made it to the majors. "Bernie was playing for Livonia Franklin High School, right up the street from where I was living at the time," Lajoie recalls in a 1984 *Detroit Free Press* article. "I had to start somewhere, so I started there and got lucky."

By 1970, after working for the Tigers for two years, he moved into the front office and became scouting director in '73. According to Lajoie, "In '73, Jim Campbell said, 'We have to change the way we're doing things.' So he put me in as scouting director and said, 'We will build this team from within.' So I said, 'What do we do for the four or five years until these kids come to the top?' He said, 'I will tell the public what we're doing. We are going to rebuild this franchise.'

"So that was my job, and it worked. You always try and draft the best people but there was a lot of pressure because we were a very bad team. By the same token, we could sell and sign kids on opportunity. I'd tell 'em, 'Come with us and you can play.'"

The Tigers of the early '70s were a case of rapid deterioration. They won the division in '72, bleeding a final hurrah from the heroes of the '68 team. But by '75, when guys like Al Kaline, Jim Northrup, Norm Cash and Dick McAuliffe had left, they were god-awful, losing 102 games. Bill Freehan, Mickey Stanley and Willie Horton were on their last legs, and the Tigers had failed to develop replacements.

Attendance had fallen almost in half, from nearly 1.9 million in '72 to barely a million in '75. Campbell would later say, "Letting that team grow old was the dumbest thing I ever did."

It was time for Bill Lajoie to ride to the rescue.

The first full-blown draft Lajoie was totally responsible for was 1974, when he produced three major-leaguers who had an impact on the '84 champions. With hopes of finding a perennial All-Star catcher, as Freehan had been, Lajoie took Lance Parrish number one to fill that role, and got lucky with long shots Mark Fidrych in the 10th round and Bob Sykes in the 19th.

"Jack Deutch spotted Lance at Walnut High School in California for us," Lajoie recalls. "Deutch had coached Gary Carter in a summer league, and had let Carter slip by us. He was determined not to let it happen again. We may have caught a little luck, because Lance had broken his finger and was playing third base his senior year. We knew he could catch, so it was a matter of drafting him and then moving him back to his natural position."

Lance was also a football star and had a scholarship offer at UCLA. But baseball was his first love, and his senior year was devoted to positioning himself to be drafted by one of the California teams. But it never materialized.

"In my senior year," Lance recalls, "I had been asked to work out for a number of different teams. I worked out for the Padres, the Phillies, the Reds and the Angels. In fact, I was convinced that the Angels were going to draft me, and I was pumped up about that because they were right down the street from my house.

"I went to Anaheim Stadium and took batting practice, and I remember thinking that day that I hit as well as I could possibly hit. I hit balls out all over the stadium. They had me run and I ran a little bit better back in those days. And, of course, they had me put the gear on and throw from behind the plate.

"The guy standing there with the stopwatch said, 'If you throw the ball down to second base in less than two seconds, you can throw out anybody in the league.' And I was in the 1.8s and 1.9s consistently, so I'm figuring to myself when the workouts were over, 'I'm in! I'm in. They're drafting me, I know it.'"

The Angels had the No.10 overall pick that year, so Lance was fairly confident no one would jump in before that and ruin his California baseball aspirations.

"I do know that the Tigers came to scout me the rest of my senior year," he said. "I got hurt after that. I took a foul tip that split my middle finger at the top knuckle and I played with stitches in my finger. One game [playing third base] I got three balls in a row and threw 'em all into the top row of the stands because I couldn't grip the ball right. It was ridiculous."

But Lajoie's scouting team understood and was pleased their prospect was making a poor impression for scouts who may have come late to the party. When the Tigers' spot came up at No. 16 in the first round, Parrish was still on the board, a day that still stands out in Lance's memory.

"My high school coach pulled me out of class and brought me out in the hallway and stuck his hand out," Parrish recalls, his voice re-creating the confusion he felt that day. He said, 'Congratulations, you're the number one pick of the Detroit Tigers.' I said, 'Detroit Tigers? I don't know anything about the Detroit Tigers.' It wasn't like today where everything is on TV. I didn't know the first thing about the Tigers. I was a Southern California guy who listened to the Dodgers and Angels and occasionally watched *This Week in Baseball.*

"I didn't know anybody on the Tigers or anything about the Tigers. I also remember going into our athletic clubhouse and our athletic director came up to me and said, 'So what do you think about the chances of playing for Ralph Houk?' I just gave him a blank stare and he's looking at me for a reaction, and I go, 'Who's Ralph Houk?' He went crazy and made fun of me for ten minutes in front of everybody. I didn't follow baseball that closely and I didn't know who the hell Ralph Houk was. Gimme a break. I was disappointed and confused."

The Angels, with their pick in the 10th slot, six places in front of Detroit, took Mike Miley, a shortstop from Louisiana State University. Miley played parts of just two seasons in the majors, hitting .176 in 262 at bats before dying in a car crash. Not many years after the '74 draft, it was the Angels who were confused and disappointed that they had failed to take the player right under their noses who wanted nothing more than to play for them.

The other part of the '74 draft that Lajoie used to his benefit was a terrific deal he made in trading his 19th-round pick, Bob Sykes, a left-handed starter, and minor-leaguer Jack Murphy for Aurelio Lopez and Jerry Morales in 1978. Sykes won just 12 games in three years for the Cardinals before leaving baseball, while Lopez gave Detroit seven very good years and was 10-1 for the '84 champs. Moreover, had Fidrych's career not been tragically cut short by an arm injury, 1974 would have been an even more fabulous draft year for Lajoie.

In '75, Lajoie got three major-leaguers and three members of the '84 team by making these picks: first round, Tom Brookens; fourth round, Dave Rozema; fourth round, Jason Thompson; fifth round, Lou Whitaker. Thompson could have easily stuck around until '84 and been the fourth from that draft class, but Sparky didn't approve of his lack of speed and also wanted him to become a pull hitter.

But Thompson continued to spray the ball and they dispatched him to the Angels in May 1980 for outfielder Al Cowens. It was a significant trade because Thompson was only 25 at the time, was a two-time All-Star and had hit 94 homers in his first four years in the big leagues. He also had some fine years after he left Detroit, hitting 31 homers and becoming an All-Star with the Pirates in '82. Cowens could also hit, batting .312 and finishing second to Rod Carew in the '77 MVP balloting while playing for Kansas City.

But Sparky soured on Cowens within a year. On top of that, Cowens had the audacity to publicly attack Sparky by complaining about playing time, saying, "Play me or trade me." The Tigers sold Cowens' contract to Seattle in the spring of '82.

At the same time, Sparky replaced Cowens by trading Mike Chris, a first-round pick in '77, plus Dan Schatzeder, to San Francisco for Larry Herndon. What a great trade that turned out to be. While Herndon had some terrific years in Detroit, Chris never won a game the rest of his career, and Schatzeder took the next 10 years to win a total of 33 games.

Obviously, Whitaker was the gem of '75. Lajoie never saw him play before drafting him, but relied on others. "There was an old-time scout named Billy Jurges who worked for the scouting bureau," Lajoie recalls. "Lou also pitched in high school in Martinsville, Virginia, and in his scouting reports, Jurges turned him in as both a pitcher and an infielder and kept a weekly running account on him. Jurges was so big on Lou that we just decided we had to have this kid."

A master like Lajoie would learn to capitalize on the nuances of how the bureau scouts wrote. Those scouts pooled their reports for the use of many teams, and Lajoie could tell if the report was in the scout's words or had been watered down or edited by the bureau.

"When you know the scout and you talk to him," Lajoie explains, "you know by their voice and in their written words what strong convictions they may have about a guy. To me, that's the part of baseball that's missing today in the scouting of players. You have to be trained in reading reports and know the people who are writing them.

"I was always very careful to see if the writing was the scout's writing or if somebody at the bureau had cleaned it up. When those reports are edited and cleaned up by others, it can be very different than the scout's actual words. The cleaned-up ones don't do me any good."

Whitaker was the best second baseman of his era, played 19 years in Detroit and has Hall of Fame credentials, though it's unlikely he'll ever make it in. Lajoie lights up when talking about Whitaker. "I go sign him in Virginia in June '75 and he's just turned

18. I pick him up in Martinsville and I drive him over to Bristol, which was our farm club in Double A until the early eighties.

"I tell Lou that there are things that you're going to have to learn how to do, and I'll help ya, like open a bank account so you got a place to put your check. He just looked at me and said, 'Mr. Lajoie, I was born to play ball. You don't have to worry about me at all.' I mean, Christ almighty, I'll never forget Lou saying that!"

Dave Rozema and Tom Brookens were the other two '75 draftees who played a part in '84. Brookens played for Mansfield State College in Pennsylvania and then played summer ball in the Shenandoah Valley league.

"I had no contact with anyone from any big-league team," Brookens recounts. "A guy named Ralph DeFranco was a local scout who worked for Lajoie, and he showed up at school and said that the Tigers had drafted me. When I heard I was number one, I couldn't believe it. I was tickled.

"They offered me $5,000, but I turned their offer down a coupla times. I enrolled at school again and then DeFranco came a few weeks later and upped it to $12,000. I buckled and signed with DeFranco in my college apartment in Mansfield. I had to go back to school to do it, but it worked. I met Rozema and Whitaker [two other '75 draftees] at spring training. I remember thinking when Rozy showed up with real long hair and white shoes, 'Who in the heck is this cuckoo guy?'"

Imagine getting three cornerstones like Alan Trammell, Dan Petry and Jack Morris in one draft, and ultimately creating four starting players on a championship team from one amateur draft year. That's what Lajoie accomplished in '76. Steve Kemp, drafted number one in '76, was traded for Chet Lemon in 1981, supplying the fourth cornerstone. And the trade of draftee Dave Tobik for John Grubb in 1983 also gave the Tigers an outstanding part-time player. Grubb's game-winning, two-run, 11th-inning double in Game Two of the playoffs may have been the most important hit of the '84 season.

Unlike Parrish, Fidrych and others, Lajoie didn't see Petry, Trammell or Morris play in person before drafting them. His West Coast scout was Dick Wiencek.

"Wiencek had Morris at Brigham Young and Petry and Trammell in California," Lajoie remembers. "Dick saw Jack come down to Riverside, California, to play in a tournament and Dick really liked him there.

"I never saw Jack or Dan pitch before I drafted them. Wiencek and a bureau scout named Dick Lakey were the two guys on Jack. Wiencek liked Petry, and for Trammell, besides Wiencek, I sent Hoot Evers [Tigers' farm director] and Rick Ferrell to see him on several occasions. When Hoot or Rick went out, it was just like me going out. We also used the scouting bureau to keep tabs on these guys."

Like Parrish, Petry was taken aback by the Tigers' interest in him.

"I thought I was going to be picked by the Angels," Petry smiles as he reminisces. "They picked a few spots behind the Tigers and I thought they were going to take me. They were right in my back yard and had been scouting me pretty heavy. Dick Wiencek also scouted Tram, and he was a top-notch scout back then. But I didn't know Tram and had no idea that the Tigers were after me.

"When I was drafted," Petry continues, "it isn't like it is now where you sit in front of a TV set and watch it happen. It took place out east, so it was still the morning in California. I remember my mom coming in and waking me up. Our high school season in Palo Alto hadn't ended yet, and she said, 'Dan, you were drafted by the Tigers in the fourth round.'

"And if you would have said, 'OK Dan, point to Michigan on a map,' I don't know if I could have! That doesn't say a whole lotta good things about the school system in California, but I said, 'What, Detroit? Where the heck is Detroit?' I was 17 and only thinking about the Angels. So, out of the blue, and boom, there you are thrust into this situation.

"Maybe a day later, Wiencek came over and met with my family and made a presentation and gave us an offer. Now, I had signed a letter of intent to go to Cal State Fullerton, which was a great baseball school. It was a powerhouse back then and still is. The Tigers made their offer and my dad said, 'Geez, he's only 17 and he's got college all set.'

"So my dad refused the initial offer by Wiencek and said to me, 'Go to college. I want you to study and have something to fall back on.' Well, the next day I get home from school and my dad says, 'I thought about it overnight and I'm going to call Wiencek back.'

"He called up Wiencek the next day and made no counteroffer, no nothing. He just took the deal and said, 'Dan, you've been wanting to do this your entire life and you're going to do it.' He didn't say to Wiencek, give us more money, or anything.

"It was an $18,000 bonus and incentives for each rung of the minor-league ladder. I got $500 a month to go to Bristol. After taxes you'd get $400 a month. You gotta understand that my dad had never let me work because he always said I should be out running or working out. It was my first job and I thought it was more money than God. And it was just for the two and a half months of the season in Bristol. I didn't know any better. I thought I had all kinds of money."

Trammell, unbeknownst to Petry, was even higher on the Tigers' '76 wish list. Playing to the south in San Diego, Alan was also a basketball star in high school. And unlike Lance and Dan, Alan was a sports fan of the highest order. When Wiencek came by to sign him, there were no mysteries about the team that had sought his services.

"I knew all about the Tigers," Alan recalls with a knowing smile. "I knew all about baseball. I had a good friend who loved Mickey Lolich and was a major Tigers fan. But I knew every team and I wasn't disappointed at all to be taken by Detroit. I just wanted to play and it didn't matter at all. If I would've had my druthers I'd say, sure, I'd like to play for San Diego, because that's all I knew.

"The only thing that bothered me was that when I signed I had to go to Bristol, Virginia, and being from San Diego, it was quite a shock. I hadn't been out of Southern California my entire life, and to go that far away was pretty big at the time. It would have been a shock anyway because baseball became totally different from two games a week in high school to, boom, playing six, seven games a week."

Trammell, just 18, was brutally lonely in Bristol in '76. Before spring training in '78, he married Barbara, his high school sweetheart. (The Trammells celebrated their 25th anniversary in March 2003, as he began his tour as Tigers manager.)

From '74 to '76, with Whitaker, Trammell, Morris and Parrish, Lajoie drafted four players who would get Hall of Fame consideration. And Petry would win 37 games in '83 and '84 combined.

The fifth year of Lajoie's amazing draft run was 1978, a draft that yielded Kirk Gibson, a story for a later chapter.

As for Lajoie's use of other draft picks, Doug Bair was a steal for Dave Rucker. Rucker won 10 games total the rest of his career while Bair was a stalwart and an unsung hero in '84, pitching in 47 games.

With Glenn Wilson, his first-round pick in '81, Lajoie reaped the greatest bounty of all—one of baseball's most-prized gems—an invincible closer.

Chapter 6

The Trade

I remember thinking, "How can they trade them two guys and get these two guys?" I learned a lesson there—you never know nothing, so you're better off just keeping your mouth shut. But I thought, "Wow, what a mistake. . .that's a dumb deal."

— Tom Brookens on the March 24, 1984 trade of
Glenn Wilson and John Wockenfuss for Willie
Hernandez and Dave Bergman

Going into the '84 season, Aurelio Lopez was established as the Tigers closer. But Sparky Anderson, Roger Craig and Bill Lajoie weren't comfortable with him. Lopez was 35 years old in the spring of '84, and although he still had a lively arm and could pitch as often as needed, he had been plagued by gout since the middle of the '83 season. His hand would swell and he was ineffective from July on.

They knew that he'd have to change his eating habits and cut way back on his beer consumption, and they trusted him to do that. But with a team so clearly on the cusp of greatness, they all agreed it was vitally important to add some left-handed bullpen help.

Aurelio was extremely sensitive, and that was another concern. He had retired briefly in '81 after being raked for four homers in a rare starting assignment. It had embarrassed him greatly, and Craig reasoned that by walking away, Aurelio was hoping that they'd trade him, rather than have to come back and face Tigers fans.

He also spent part of '82 in Evansville recovering from arm trouble, and even though he had pitched in 57 games and performed well in '83 prior to the bout with gout, they still had their doubts about him. 1984 would be Lopez's 18th professional season, and the fear that all the wear and tear might catch up to him made the decision to look for insurance an easy one.

With this backdrop, Sparky went to work as a radio analyst for the 1983 National League postseason. The Phillies closer and the National League Fireman of the Year was Al Holland. His set-up man, Willie Hernandez, was never used in the National League Championship Series as the Phillies beat the Dodgers three games to one. But Sparky and Lajoie attended the World Series and it was there that Hernandez blew 'em away. He pitched in three games, and in four innings of work, allowed no hits and struck out four.

Glenn Wilson

John Wockenfuss

Willie Hernandez

Dave Bergman

With the screwball tailing away from righties, Hernandez had become extremely effective. Sparky watched him like a hawk and was head-over-heels in wanting him badly for the Tigers.

After the '82 season, Hernandez learned how to throw the screwball from former Oriole Mike Cuellar, and had come into his own that year. The Cubs had traded him to the Phillies in May for Dick Ruthven and he wound up appearing in 74 games for the two teams in 1983.

Roger Craig had influenced Sparky in appreciating macho pitchers, and Willie had a way of strutting around the mound that also turned Sparky on. When he and Lajoie observed this firsthand in October '83, the deal that would tip the scales in '84 was well into its incubation stage.

Sparky was always bugging Lajoie about trades he'd like to make. In spring training, he would slip notes under Lajoie's door at night suggesting one wacko deal after another. Sparky would sit in his room at night in Lakeland poring over rosters in order to come up with stuff to run past him.

Lajoie appreciated that Sparky was completely dedicated to making the club better, so he indulged Sparky's periodic unsolicited suggestions of, "Whaddya say we get this guy and this guy for that guy and that guy?" In the Hernandez case, Sparky knew he had Lajoie hooked and wouldn't let go of his obsession to get his man one way or another. He kept the pressure on, continuing to stress to Lajoie, "We gotta get Willie."

What also fueled Sparky's hopes was that a Phillies scout, Ray Shore, had been probing Sparky about a young outfielder of his named Glenn Wilson.

Lajoie had drafted Wilson in the first round in 1980 as a third baseman out of Sam Houston State University in Texas. The Tigers switched him to outfield in '81 because he had a rocket arm and, going into '84, Wilson was a pretty hot property. He was still just 25 years old and had displayed impressive tools in his first season and a half in the majors. He hit 12 homers in 322 at bats as a rookie in '82 and set a club rookie record with a 19-game hitting streak. He followed that in '83 with 11 homers and 65 RBIs.

But Wilson didn't run well and, at Craig's urging, Sparky had already decided to let Gibson have the right-field job in '84. By the end of '83, Gibson had finally emerged from nearly two years in Sparky's doghouse, and had come to camp in '84 much better prepared and hungrier than ever before.

As it turned out, Wilson knocked in 102 runs and became a National League All-Star in '85, but other than that, never lived up to the promise he'd shown in Detroit. Sparky had a sixth sense about players and correctly believed that Gibson had a far greater upside than Wilson did. It had to be one or the other, and when that decision was made early in spring training, Wilson became bloody bait to enticingly toss into the baseball trade waters.

The '84 outfield was set: Larry Herndon was entrenched in left, Chet Lemon would be the regular in center, and they'd take whatever they could get from Gibson in right. As it was, Kirk had played all three outfield positions and had been brutal everywhere they put him. Hell, Sparky figured, Gibson had even gotten hit on the head by a ball he lost in the right-field sun in the '81 home opener.

But this was the year to gamble and see if Gibson could recapture his early promise. Whatever the result, they'd live with it, and it would come at Wilson's expense.

Wilson felt anxious and alienated right from the start of spring training. Sparky didn't feel the need to patronize anybody once he had dismissed him from his plans, and he all but threw Wilson in the Dumpster by assigning him a role in his perennial spring training third-base derby.

Sparky's lack of subtlety continued when he complained about Wilson's fielding after Wilson made an error in his spring debut at third. By mid-March, Wilson was already beside himself, feeling completely iced out. He implored Lajoie to tell him whether this blatant mistreatment meant that he was going to be traded.

Lajoie really liked Wilson and felt uncomfortable about the situation. At the same time, the fans up north were quick to seize upon Sparky's handling of Wilson. Wilson was a charming kid with a Texas twang and had been a good ballplayer and a good citizen.

"I can't figure out what Glenn Wilson has done to deserve such shabby treatment from Sparky Anderson and the Tiger organization," wrote a disgruntled fan to the *Detroit Free Press.* Another impassioned fan letter said, "Sparky blasts him mercilessly after the first spring game and he must feel as low as an inchworm knowing his bosses are trying to get rid of him before the season starts."

By March 17, with about two weeks left in Florida, Wilson went to Lajoie and asked to be taken out of his misery by being traded.

While Wilson was hurt and confused, the older and wiser John Wockenfuss was angry. At 35, John Bilton Wockenfuss, the man his teammates and fans affectionately referred to as "Johnny B" was both an experienced player and a veteran of 10 years of Jim Campbell's tightwad policies. He had his own reasons for being upset, and Wockenfuss was more bullish than Wilson in openly trying to force a trade. His name had been floated with Wilson's as being targeted for the Phillies, and Wockenfuss was diligent in ripping just about everybody who mattered. If he bitched everybody out, he figured, they'd have no choice but to get rid of him.

Wockenfuss had proved himself to be the ultimate jack-of-all-trades. He caught, played first, third and the outfield, and was an outstanding pinch hitter with seven game-winning hits in '83. Up until then, he had been an uncomplaining and wonderfully versatile utility man for the team.

Now, in the twilight of his career, Wockenfuss was finally demanding respect and money. For the first time, he was railing publicly about his situation and was obviously fearless of any recrimination. He knew he was out and was ready to be done with the cheapskate Campbell. "If a trade happens, I'll be happy," Wockenfuss told reporters.

Over the winter, Wockenfuss had committed contractual suicide by self-negotiating a two-year deal with Campbell for about $200,000 a year. Campbell had ground him down with his standard negotiating mantra, "We just don't have any more money."

"All they say is, we don't have the cash," Wockenfuss sneered. He had later come to realize that the average Tigers salary was about $265,000, and then when Morris, Petry and free agent Darrell Evans each signed long-term deals worth between $800,000 and $900,000 a year, Wockenfuss felt that he had been lied to and taken to the cleaners. Soon, he'd cap his "get me outta here" dialogue with the words that would clinch the deal.

After hitting a two-run homer off Steve Carlton for the Tigers' lone runs in a 7-2 loss to the Phillies, and with reporters encircled as he stood outside the Tigers clubhouse, Wockenfuss unleashed this fateful diatribe: "As soon as I signed after last year, they started giving these clowns $800,000. I took them for their word and they turned around and dumped on me. All they say is 'they don't have the cash.' Monaghan buys the club for 50 million (dollars) and he's worth 150 million. Please."

As for the homer, he added, "I was hoping I'd do that. I thought I'd add some fuel to the fire." Oh yeah, the fire was stoked all right. It would be another 12 days before he was set free, and they weren't easy days for Wockenfuss to survive. His quotes made it to the Detroit papers and then surfaced back in Lakeland a day later. It's one thing to take on management; your teammates will support you all day when you do that. But when you also lump them into your vitriol, watch out.

Tigers players immediately started referring to each other as "clown." Pitchers in the bullpen would be heard joking to each other,

"Pick up the ball, clown." Wockenfuss had now insulted Campbell, Monaghan, Lajoie and his higher-paid teammates. Sparky attempted levity by saying, "That's just John; he loves to talk." A columnist wrote, "If Johnny B gets traded soon it won't be because he can't play. It will be because he can't shut up."

Critical side notes in the March 12 game against the Phillies were Wilson's error at third and his three solid hits. It was all coming together. The Phillies knew that Wilson was a hard-hitting outfielder miscast at third, and that both he and Wockenfuss were expendable.

But in talks the day before, the Tigers hadn't thrown Wilson into the mix yet, and the Phils weren't going to part with the 29-year-old Hernandez for just Wockenfuss. The two teams had another game scheduled in Clearwater a few days later, and after the hitting display both players had just put on, Lajoie felt he could go for the jugular. He went to Sparky to lay out the sting.

"I told him," Lajoie recalls, "that we play the Phillies next week and we've got to take Glenn with us. We bring the best batting practice pitcher we have and let Glenn pound the fences for 'em again." Lajoie is emphatic now with the delicious recollection: "This is no BS, this is true. So Glenn goes over there and he puts on a show and now I know I've got 'em by the ass because now I can get another player.

"After BP we put him in center to give 'em an even better look. You know that Wilson had a helluva arm and he's throwing bullets to the infield and they just go gaga. So they said. 'OK, we want Wockenfuss and Wilson for Hernandez, and I came back with, 'We need a guy to play first when Darrell plays third or whatever.' They said, 'Who do you want, we'll get you the player.'

"I could tell that they really wanted Wilson now, so I said, 'There's a guy, Dave Bergman, over in San Francisco that we can use.' And they said, 'Oh, we can get Bergman.' I said, 'Get him and the deal is done.'"

Lajoie had drafted Wilson and had great affection for him and his wife. Wilson had made the majors in '82, done quite well and came to town that November because his brother was trying out for the Detroit Panthers, the new United States Football League team. Lajoie says, "We were in the car and Glenn said, 'I know it's dark, but can you take me up to the stadium so I can take another look? I just feel like it.'

"We got there and in the moonlight, he looked at center field with the 440 sign and said, 'Man, that's really a long way, isn't it? Anybody ever hit it up there?' I said, 'Two guys did in the '71 All-Star Game here, Bench and Clemente, or maybe Killebrew, I think.' And you know what he said to me? He said, 'This year, I'm gonna hit a ball up there.' And in the first fucking game of the year he hit a ball into the center-field stands. True story!"

Like the affable Wilson, Tigers fans had long appreciated Wockenfuss for his versatility and wacky batting stance, where he tightly closed his feet and wiggled his fingers on the bat as the pitcher wound up. But the two guys they were traded for were unknowns in Detroit, and that made the trade all the more confusing and easy to question, or even condemn.

Dave Bergman, 30, had emerged as a premier utility player for Frank Robinson's Giants in '83. Bergman batted .355 as a pinch hitter that year, was nearing free-agency qualification and wanted to be paid accordingly. But Giants General Manager Tom Haller was pushing back, and as Bergman went through his spring drills in Arizona, his mindset was akin to Wockenfuss's. Bergman felt frustrated and under-appreciated when, out of the blue, he was traded to Philly for Al Sanchez, and minutes later shipped to Detroit.

Bergman remembers it this way: "The Giants and I were talking about a multiyear contract that spring and I had felt like I had been mistreated terribly by Tom Haller, who wouldn't be on the top of my list of people I respected in the game. We were doing drills in spring training, pitchers covering first base. The pitchers have their hats on backwards, doing things half-assed, and I came unglued during practice. I kind of keep my mouth shut, as you know, but I lost it. I said, 'You no-good son of a bitches, this is why we lost last year. We lost two games because you guys couldn't catch a ball at first base.'

"Vida Blue comes over and settles me down and escorts me into the locker room. That's how crazy I got. So the combination of the contracts and going off on everybody precipitated me being somebody that maybe they needed to get out of there.

"I found out later that Sparky had talked to [Cardinals manager] Whitey Herzog and Whitey was the one who told Sparky that, 'This is somebody who could really help your ballclub,' and that's how it took place.

"Sparky saw me in Cincinnati because I was with Houston earlier in my career and I'd come off '83 where every ball I hit that year was right on the button. It was one of those magical years, probably my best in the big leagues, and my manager, Frank Robinson, appreciated me for that. And that's also when I realized how valuable a utility-type player could be with a manager who appreciated that type of player. I had thought that utility guys were scrubeenies who just weren't good enough to play. Frank Robinson was the guy who made me feel appreciated as a player."

On March 24, the Tigers lost, 3-2, to the Dodgers in Lakeland. As rumors about an impending announcement swirled and spread,

Wilson talked with his wife through the fence that separated the bullpen from the stands. When the game ended, Sparky called Wilson and Wockenfuss into his office to meet with him and Lajoie and tell them that the deed was done.

Reporters waited outside along with Wockenfus's eight-year-old son, Jeremy. It didn't take long for the media to get the gist. Wockenfuss saw Jeremy, put his hand on his head and said, "Dad's done here. I don't play for Detroit anymore." Wilson said, "This is the best thing that could happen to me. I am bitter about a few things, but my momma always told me, 'Don't say nothin' bad if you don't have nothin' nice to say.'"

Skeptical Tigers fans didn't seem to think it was necessary to heed momma's advice. Letters to the papers shot holes through the deal. One fan from Royal Oak wrote, "It's time for Tom Anonymous (Monaghan) to take control of the Tigers before the great con-man (Sparky) destroys them. I refer to the trade of a promising young player with a super attitude, Glenn Wilson, for a journeyman National League pitcher who happens to be left-handed."

Another from Trenton railed, "Sparky is a bum! He sat there like a vulture watching every move Glenn Wilson made, looking for the negative. Why didn't he do the same last year to Kirk Gibson, who did nothing right all season?…Sparky is the one who should be traded."

A guy from Southfield said, "I have been a Tigers fan for 40 years. Sparky is the worst manager we've had."

Most of the Tigers players also took poorly to the move. Lance Parrish probably took it the hardest, saying years later, "When they made the trade I was pissed off because they traded Glenn Wilson, who was a good friend of mine. I was also upset because they released Rick Leach that day and I was good friends with him also.

"The whole spring got off on the wrong foot for me. I thought it was unjust to let Rick go, because he was playing through a bad shoulder. He sucked it up time and again in order to make the team and that hurt him in the long run. It made me very upset when they let him go and traded Glenn all in the same morning, but you come to realize that those things happen. You never like it when your friends get traded, but the old saying is, 'Be happy it wasn't you.' It was just Wilson's time."

Parrish's response is typical of most players. They don't like trades. Friends leave and trades starkly reveal the unsettling uncertainties of the business.

Leach, the former Michigan quarterback, was 26 and had been signed out of college in 1979. He had given up football to pursue his destiny with the Tigers and had also grown up with the core of players Lajoie had drafted. Leach felt that after five years of paying dues he deserved to be part of the Tigers' future.

The day the trade was made they coldly cut him and he was shocked. He said, "Things are going a hundred miles an hour. I'm not sure what's happening." As Leach looked in the stands for his wife, Angie, to pass along the bad news that fateful day, the Tigers were already marching toward the World Series without him.

Tom Brookens was used to being jerked around and had been lumped in with Wilson as part of the third-base derby that spring.

"As a player, I just kept my mouth shut," Brookens reflects 20 years later. "Whatever the organization wanted I went along with, but I remember thinking, 'How can they trade them two guys and get these two guys?' I'm thinking 'That could be the worst mistake we ever made,' and then it turned out to be the best thing that ever happened. I learned a lesson there—you never know nothing, so you're better off keeping your mouth shut. But I thought, 'Wow, what a mistake...' I thought, 'That's a dumb deal.'"

I was in Detroit covering the Pistons that day and center Bill Laimbeer, a baseball fan as well, was aghast. When I informed him of the deal, he said, "Willie Hernandez? You've got to be kidding. He's terrible. I'm telling you right now, he will give up homers and get booed out of Detroit."

Bill had followed Hernandez when Hernandez was with the Cubs as Bruce Sutter's set-up man, and Bill was convinced that the Tigers would be badly burned by this one. Bill was a fan and fans form opinions. But even Sparky and Lajoie couldn't have imagined just how incredible Hernandez would turn out to be in 1984.

Also, no one would have had reason to expect that the all-but-anonymous Bergman would make such an impact. Sparky loved players like Bergman, who could come off the bench and were capable of playing multiple positions. As it turned out, Bergman stayed with the Tigers longer than all members of the '84 team, save Trammell and Whitaker.

Hernandez became just the third pitcher to ever win both the MVP Award and Cy Young Award in the same season and just the second Tiger to win the Cy Young Award. The trade stood far and above all others as the transaction of the year in baseball, and was one of the stronger parts of the case for Lajoie's selection as Major League Baseball Executive of the Year.

Hernandez became an instant success, enabling Tigers fans to just as quickly forgive the departures of Wilson and Wockenfuss. Although it was Sparky's diligence, scouting and insistence that paved the way, he gave all praise to Lajoie on the day the deal was made by saying, "Lajoie accomplished his two goals. He got us a power hitter at first in Evans and a left-handed reliever in Hernandez. I don't know how you can do much better than that." True enough, you couldn't.

Seeing as the Tigers dealt players they no longer needed, the trade was brilliantly conceived, transacted with stunning effectiveness, and applied perfectly to the ballclub's needs.

Years later, as Sparky reflected back on the genesis of the trade, he gave Lajoie credit for being the driving force, while Lajoie credited Sparky.

"Bill's being generous," Sparky says, "But I did say this. I said, 'Bill, the one thing I see here is that the people we're giving up are not, in any way, going to affect our ballclub. With Lopez on the right side, if we can get Hernandez for that left side, we're in.' I said, 'Bill, in my honest opinion, I'll stick out my neck and say that I know we can win with him [Hernandez].' I knew how I set up with pitching and I knew with Lopez, oh my God, he could go five days a week, and I knew that in making Hernandez a specialist, we could really have something.

"And everybody forgets Doug Bair. Doug Bair was our long guy who threw hard. Bill [Lajoie] had a way of picking off a guy that maybe wasn't having a great year the year before, or getting somebody who maybe was a coupla years older than you'd like, but he knew where that guy would fit. The one thing Bill Lajoie knew, he knew where players fit and that's a big difference. A lotta people just get players but they don't know where they're gonna fit 'em. He knew that."

The '84 team was set. A week later they headed north toward record-setting destiny. Wilson and Wockenfuss were well back in the rearview mirror, and Hernandez and Bergman were on their way to becoming household names in their new town and new league.

Chapter 7

April:
The Meteoric Rise

*It's the best month I've ever been in as a player, coach or manager.
It's too bad they don't let you play just one month and end it.*

— Sparky Anderson, April 30, 1984

The Tigers arrived in Minnesota on April 2, primed to start the season the following day. Their Florida record of 11-17, just a .393 percentage, was their worst in 15 years—since the '68 champions had sloshed through at 9-16.

It had been a turbulent spring for a number of reasons, and the big trade with the Phillies was still producing minor shock waves a week later. Lance Parrish agreed that Willie Hernandez had strengthened the team, but still pined for Wilson, saying, "I think they gave up on him too fast." But Sparky still insisted that they not only had gotten him "for free" but had picked up speed and balance also. "I've never seen a club balanced like this—ten right-handed hitters and seven lefties." He was also high on two rookies. "[Barbaro] Garbey can hit, you can bet your house on it, and the ball jumps off Rod Allen's bat."

On March 19, Sparky had said that Howard Johnson and Marty Castillo would platoon at third. But as the season opened, he altered that to a Johnson–Tom Brookens platoon, with

April 1984

April Record: 18-2

Highlights:
9-game win streak to start year
7-game win streak, 4/20–4/26
8-0 on the road

Stars:
Morris: 5-0, 1.98 ERA, no-hitter; wins AL pitcher of month
Petry: 3-1, 2.06
Trammell: .403 BA, 31-77; wins AL player of month
Garbey: .444 BA, 16-36

Key Games:
4/07: **4-0 win** @ Chicago; Morris no-hitter
4/10: **5-1 win** vs. Texas; home opener
4/13: **13-9 win** @ Boston; crazy 1st inning
4/24: **6-5, 4-3** vs. Minnesota: Doubleheader drama
4/29: **6-1 win** vs. Cleveland; Petry near no-hitter

Tom Monaghan

Garbey and Evans to also get some action there. Considering Sparky's spotty track record in settling on a third baseman, it was no surprise that when '84 was said and done, HoJo was out of the mix altogether.

Despite the poor spring record, there was still ample excitement after the 92-win, second-place finish behind Baltimore the year before. And the additions of Darrell Evans and Dave Bergman gave the opening-day lineup a fresh look.

Along with Hernandez, Bergman, Evans and veteran defensive replacement Rusty Kuntz, there were three rookies for a total of seven new Tigers. Catcher Dwight Lowry joined Garbey and Allen as the third rookie.

Garbey, a Cuban star who had escaped on the so-called "Freedom Flotilla," had been signed in a refugee camp by Tigers Latin scout Orlando Pena. Garbey was a curiosity item for that reason, as well as for admitting that he had been part of a Cuban League run-shaving scandal to earn money for his family. His jaw had been broken when he was hit by a pitch at Double A Birmingham, Alabama, in '81, but he had risen above it all by hitting .321 at Evansville, Indiana, and Sparky saw multiple uses for him. Allen had been a minor-leaguer for six years with the Mariners before they released him in October '83, and Lowry was making the jump from Double A ball to back up Parrish.

The new look included the new general manager, Bill Lajoie. Also, new owner Tom Monaghan added some innocence to the equation. Unlike the 83-year-old John Fetzer, the television executive who had been rarely seen or heard from, Monaghan, 47, was a self-described fan fulfilling a lifelong dream. He had even put on a uniform in spring training and played catch with Al Kaline. Talk about paying for your thrills.

Monaghan's mantra, seeing as he really knew nothing about the game, was to repeat, "This is a good team." Correctly concerned about not putting his foot in his mouth, he stayed in the background, chatted amiably with the players, but offered no meaningful analysis.

GAMES 1 & 2 @ MINNESOTA—Jack Morris predictably and easily beat the Twins in the opener, 8-1, raising his lifetime record to 12-2 against his hometown team. The Tigers built a 5-1 lead off Al Williams, who found baseball to be a relaxing respite from his last job: He was a freedom fighter in Nicaragua; a former Sandinista guerrilla!

Parrish's two-run single finished Williams in the sixth. In the seventh, Evans hit a three-run homer off a lefty named Keith Comstock, who was making a soon-to-be forgettable major-league debut.

On April 5, two days later, the Tigers won again, 7-3, for Dan Petry, and there were some omens of what the season would become. Kirk Gibson hit his first homer, a three-run shot off Twins ace Frank Viola. Alan Trammell went 4-4 and Hernandez pitched two innings of spotless relief.

GAMES 3, 4 & 5 @ CHICAGO—The team flew over to Chicago and pushed the record to 3-0 on Friday, April 6, before almost 43,000 fans. Milt Wilcox pitched seven innings of one-run ball, beating Rich Dotson, who had won 22 games in '83. That brought them to the year's first national telecast, the Saturday matchup of Morris vs. tough Sox lefty Floyd Bannister. It was a typical blustery spring day in the Windy City, where a very atypical outcome awaited nearly 25,000 fans and the many millions more watching around the country.

Gibson's power keeps Tigers perfect, 7-3

◆*Game 4: Jack's Gem*

Where:	**Comiskey Park**
Result:	**4-0 Tigers**
Record:	**4-0**
WP:	**Morris, 2-0**
LP:	**Bannister, 0-1**
Standing:	**First, ½ ahead**
Attendance:	**24,616**

Jack Morris remembers:

I wasn't aware of having a no-hitter until I looked up at the scoreboard after the fifth. As it is, I didn't have my best stuff. And I've always said that the real difference between a two-hitter and a no-hitter might just be the attention. I don't remember a whole lot about the game, especially the early parts. Anyway, this guy sitting behind our dugout was leaning over around the fifth or sixth inning trying to jinx me saying, "Hey Morris, you got a no-hitter." No shit.

GAME #4   April 7

Tigers 4, Sox 0

DETROIT	AB	R	H	BI	CHICAGO	AB	R	H	BI
Whitaker 2b	4	0	1	1	Law R cf	3	0	0	0
Trammell ss	4	0	1	0	Dybzinski ss	0	0	0	0
Garbey 1b	3	0	0	0	Fisk c	3	0	0	0
Bergman 1b	1	0	0	0	Baines rf	3	0	0	0
Parrish c	3	1	0	0	Luzinski dh	2	0	0	0
Herndon lf	4	0	0	0	Stegman pr	0	0	0	0
Allen dh	3	0	0	0	Kittle lf	4	0	0	0
Grubb ph	1	0	0	0	Paciorek 1b	3	0	0	0
Lemon cf	4	2	2	2	Law V 3b	1	0	0	0
Gibson rf	1	1	1	1	Walker ph	1	0	0	0
Brookens 3b	2	0	0	0	Hulett 3b	0	0	0	0
					Fletcher ss	2	0	0	0
					Hairston ph-cf	1	0	0	0
					Cruz 2b	3	0	0	0
Totals	**30**	**4**	**5**	**4**		**26**	**0**	**0**	**0**

Detroit	020	020	000	--	4
Chicago	000	000	000	--	0

Game winning RBI -- none, DP -- Detroit 1, Chicago 1, LOB --Detroit 3, Chicago 5, 2B -- Lemon, Gibson, HR -- Lemon, SB -- Law, Trammell, CS -- Whitaker, SH -- Brookens

Detroit	IP	H	R	ER	BB	SO
Morris (W)	9.0	0	0	0	6	8
Chicago						
Bannister (L)	6.0	4	4	4	2	3
Brennan	2.0	1	0	0	1	3
Barojas	1.0	0	0	0	0	1

T -- 2:44 A -- 24,616

Of course, the guys on our bench, superstitious baseball people, wouldn't say anything about it. The guy in the stands wouldn't shut up and he was really getting drunk.

So in the eighth, I literally stood up in the dugout, faced him, and said, "Enjoy yourself because I'm gonna get the next six guys out and you're gonna watch something special." Roger Craig, old school that he was, was looking at me with his eyes bugged out because I acknowledged the damn no-hitter.

I always laughed at people in baseball who were superstitious. Boggs would eat his chicken and Sparky never changed undershirts during winning streaks and had his little dance around the third-base foul line. Dan Petry had a line dance of his own, and I would purposely step on the line and look back at Petry and show him that this is all bullshit and you gotta learn that this is not part of the game.

The only thing that I felt, and it was for my whole career, was that I felt anxious before I pitched. I wanted to get it going. I hated sitting around for the three-four hours of pre-game stuff. I wanted to pitch when I got out of bed, and as far as I'm concerned, superstitions go hand in hand with anxiety and people want to make something happen that they're not able to. Imagine if I was superstitious and let some drunk "jinx" my damn no-hitter.

I walked five or six that day, but what really bothered me was (umpire) Durwood Merrill screwing up the next to last guy in the ninth. Carlton Fisk grounded out and Harold Baines dribbled back to me for the second out. I was pumping now and rushed my body and actually fell down on one pitch to Greg Luzinski.

But I'll go to my grave and Durwood will still argue 'til he can't argue anymore about the fact that I had Luzinski struck out and he didn't punch him out. He called ball four on the 3-2 pitch and it was a strike, obviously a strike, so I had to throw to one extra guy, and that's what I remember more than anything else. Dave Stegman, my former teammate, came in to run for Luzinski and I smiled at him and told him he wasn't going anywhere. Then I got Kittle to end the game.

I suppose the other thing is that some guys who weren't known for great defense, like Gibby making a great play in right and Bergie, who was an excellent fielder, made a coupla great plays at first. I had walked Luzinski at some point and because he was so slow, Bergie didn't hold him on and was able to go in the hole and make a diving grab to save a hit. So I remember thinking this is meant to be because balls that typically would have been base hits weren't becoming base hits.

It wasn't near the significance of playing in playoffs or Series, but for a pitcher to have something very gratifying happen in a regular-season game, then it was that. It was special for me but overall it was just another win, and, to this day, I thank God for all those wins.

Jack Morris defies baseball superstition to no-hit Chicago and revels in the moment with Lance Parrish.

Morris walked six on that cold and windy Chicago Saturday afternoon. As it turned out, the Tigers managed only five hits, with Chet Lemon's two-run double helping to give Jack his four runs by midgame. Jack handled the attention for just the fifth no-hitter in Tigers history and the first in 26 years since Jim Bunning's in 1958 with appropriate and sincere modesty. With his performance featured on national television, and his team off to a perfect 5-0 start by Sunday evening, Jack was invited to appear on *Good Morning America* Monday morning.

But the best sidebar story of the no-hitter is one that hasn't been told. Lance Parrish guided and steadied Jack through the minefield of Merrill's umpiring, the six walks and the overall emotional drama that is a part of any brush with baseball immortality. The following is how Lance recalls the aftermath on that chilly Chicago Saturday afternoon:

Morris no-hits Sox, only 5th in franchise history

Lance Parrish remembers:

After Jack jumped into my arms and when we were done congratulating each other out on the field, Jack stayed out there to be interviewed by Joe Garagiola. It was the first TV Game of the Week for the year, so Garagiola was out there waiting to talk to Jack and we all went in the clubhouse.

It was wild in there and we were all high fivin' and jabbering and one of the clubhouse kids came up to me and said, "You have a phone call in the manager's office." I didn't know who it was and certainly wasn't expecting a call. So I went in there, picked it up and said, "Hello," and the voice on the other end said, "Hey," and was very excited and I could tell it was Jim Campbell. I knew his voice. He was raving about what a great game, what a great performance and blah, blah, and "You did such a great job," and I'm saying "thanks" because I'm excited too at the time. I go, "Thanks, I appreciate it," and he goes, "There's gonna be a little something in this for you, a little extra, we'll make a little contribution because you did so well today," and I go "Man, thanks, that's great."

So, in the course of this whole deal as we're going back and forth, and then he said something about a pitch that I had thrown and it kind of startled me, and I went, "Wait a minute, who do you think you're talking to?" And then he got quiet for a second and then he goes, "Well, who is this?" And I said, "This is Lance," and he yells back, "I didn't want to talk to you, get the hell off the phone." And I wait a second because I'm confused and go, "What about that bonus?" And then even louder, he says, "Get the hell off the phone and get Jack in there." Here I thought he was complimenting me because I was just as much a part of that no-hitter and he was going to give me a little something extra and he just blew me off.

With Saturday's drama still fresh in mind, Dave Rozema and Aurelio Lopez spoiled Tom Seaver's White Sox debut with a 7-3 win on Sunday, April 8, and the Tigers came to Detroit two days later on Tuesday to face the Rangers in the home opener.

GAMES 6 & 7 vs. TEXAS
◆ *Game 6: Evans-ville*

GAME #6	April 10

Tigers 5, Rangers 1

TEXAS	AB	R	H	BI	DETROIT	AB	R	H	BI
Sample lf	4	0	0	0	Whitaker 2b	3	1	0	0
Bell 3b	4	1	1	0	Trammell ss	3	1	1	0
Wright cf	4	0	0	0	Evans dh	4	1	1	3
Parrish dh	4	0	1	1	Parrish c	4	0	0	0
Ward rf	3	0	2	0	Gibson rf	4	1	1	0
O'Brien 1b	3	0	0	0	Herndon lf	2	1	1	0
Yost c	3	0	0	0	Bergman 1b	4	0	1	1
Foley c	1	0	0	0	Lemon cf	2	0	0	0
Tolleson 2b	2	0	0	0	Johnson 3b	1	0	0	1
Wilkerson ss	2	0	0	0	Brookens 3b	0	0	0	0
Jones ph	1	0	0	0					
Anderson ss	0	0	0	0					
Totals	**31**	**1**	**4**	**1**		**27**	**5**	**5**	**5**

Texas	100	000	000	--	1
Detroit	401	000	00X	--	5

Game winning RBI -- none, LOB -- Texas 6, Detroit 6, 2B -- Herndon, HR -- Evans, SB -- Herndon, CS -- Bergman, Trammell, HBP -- by Henke (Lemon), WP -- Henke, PB -- Yost

Texas	IP	H	R	ER	BB	SO
Stewart (L)	0.2	2	4	4	5	0
Schmidt	4.1	2	1	1	0	3
Henke	2.0	1	0	0	1	1
Bibby	1.0	0	0	0	1	1
Detroit						
Petry (W)	9.0	4	1	1	3	7

T -- 2:32 A -- 51,238

Where:	Tiger Stadium
Result:	5-1 Tigers
Record:	6-0
WP:	Petry, 2-0
LP:	Stewart, 0-2
Standing:	First, 2 ahead
Attendance:	51,238

Darrell Evans remembers:

You have to remember, I'd played for almost 15 years in Atlanta and San Francisco, and then I come to a place where the money they gave me was more money than I ever thought was in the world. I put pressure on myself to come in and impress people and make 'em feel like I was worth it. In spring training it had been insinuated that I might be platooned because I was getting older—I'd be 37 in May—and Sparky had some other guys to play.

In the opener in Minnesota, I hit the three-run homer off lefty Keith Comstock and gosh, I don't know how you describe doing that. Man, you kinda put it in the back of your mind that maybe something like this would be great to have happen, but most of the time those things just don't come true. When I hit that homer in Minnesota— that's when I really felt a part of things.

We had opened on the road our first five games and I was looking forward to playing in Tiger Stadium. It was a fantasy come true that I was getting to play in the great American League parks like Tiger Stadium, Yankee and Fenway. Opening-day crowds are always great and there was already such excitement for all the things that had happened, like a 5-0 record and Jack's no-hitter. This team was expected to do well—just missing out the year before, and my coming to be another piece to be put into place to help win—what a scenario! Gosh, I was soaking up everything—and the fans were going crazy. I'd heard so many things about them anyway.

First time I'd seen the stadium was in December after signing, but there was snow on the ground so I hadn't gone on the field. I had just taken batting practice that day for the first time and had gotten a feel for how far the fence was.

Texas scored a run on Petry in the top of the first. We came up and it was pretty clear that Dave Stewart was struggling. Lou walked and got to second on a passed ball and then Stewart walked Tram. He wasn't the Dave Stewart that we ended up seeing as the Cy Young Award winner years later—I'd faced him in Los Angeles with the Dodgers and he was kind of a fastball guy that hadn't had great command of his pitches.

He got behind me 2-0 and I'm hoping I get a good pitch to hit. Gosh, I can still see that ball go. He gave me a fastball down the middle and as soon as I hit it I knew it was gone. You run around the bases and it's this surreal thing where you're saying "This can't be happening," because you want to impress and, shoot, the first time up you hit a home run in the first inning in front of 52,000 new fans.

The Tigers line up before a sellout crowd for the home opener.

Looking back, you say you did something that no one at the same time could've done—someone else could've hit a home run in the same situation, but that made me a Detroiter, I guess.

My wife was in the stands, and that morning she told me that I'd hit a homer my first time up. I tugged on my ear as I rounded third to show her I was thinking about her and I found out that by that time she was hugging everybody around her in the stands.

It was a pretty quiet game after that. Petry went the distance. I'd known he'd been successful so far in his career, but I didn't really know what kind of pitcher he was. He told me later he wanted to locker next to me and talk baseball, so we talked a lot as the year went on.

Dan was always kind of in the background of Jack. I thought he had as good stuff as Jack had—his slider was as good as there was in baseball. Players on other teams I'd talked to had told me that the difference between Jack and Dan at that time was confidence. Dan was probably more consistent during that year than Jack was.

Evans HR off Stewart blows away Texas in home opener.

It was just six games in but already we'd had 10 or 12 guys play important roles. It spoke of how important it was for all the players to be involved—not just the stars. I had been in the National League so I was about to find out how good Tram and Lou and Gibby and Lance and Jack and Peaches already were. Nobody on that club really needed to be the star and that's not always true in baseball.

Anyway, it was a great day for me—one of my biggest in baseball, and I played a lot of years.

And from the lilting prose of Ernie Harwell, when Darrell hit the homer, Ernie said, "Welcome to Evans-ville."

On Thursday, April 12, Morris beat the Rangers and Frank Tanana, 9-4. Jack went seven innings and both of the runs off him were unearned. Just seven games into the new season, Morris was 3-0 with an 0.39 ERA. In the pantheon of meaningless stats, the 7-0 start broke the team record of 6-0 set in 1911. Sparky admitted that he was excited, and as he visibly revealed his excitement to the assembled reporters, he said, in classic Sparky doublespeak, "I'll never show I'm excited. It's not fair to other clubs." Whatever.

They headed out to Boston for an ill-fated three-game series that would be largely washed out by bad weather. The only one of the three that was played took place on Friday the 13th. For those who harbored superstitions—and, aside from Jack, that included most everybody—this one just affirmed their beliefs.

◆Game 8: Lucky 13

Where:	**Fenway Park**
Result:	**13-9 Tigers**
Record:	**8-0**
WP:	**Bair, 1-0**
LP:	**Hurst, 1-2**
Standing:	**First, 3½ ahead**
Attendance:	**35,151**

Rod Allen remembers:

Rod Allen

They signed me February 14, 1984, after Seattle had released me. And for a guy who'd previously had only two big-league hits, just making this team was unbelievable. Everything I'd hit that spring was a rocket somewhere and I had become the talk of the early camp and Sparky took a liking to me.

On March 30, as camp was ending, he announced that there would be three rookies: Barbaro, Dwight Lowry and me. I had started against Bannister for Morris' no-hitter in Chicago, and when we got back home, I'll never forget the ovation Jack got on opening day at Tiger Stadium. I'd also gotten two hits in the 9-4 win against Texas the day before this one, so things were going very well.

Sparky seemed to like starting me against some left-handers, and we knocked out their starter, Bruce Hurst, with eight off of him in the top of the first. I brought one of 'em in on a well-executed hit-and-run single.

I read the next day the bizarre numbers the sportswriters had put together for us:

- *The game took place on Friday the **13th***
- *We sent **13** men to the plate in the first*
- *All 3 outs were made by Lance, who wore **#13***
- *The Sox got 5 in the bottom half off Wilcox for a total of **13** first-inning runs*
- *We won it **13**-9*
- *Lance scored the **13th** run*
- *Larry Herndon got the winning RBI and he wore **31, 13** backwards*

Unfortunately, I got pulled for Darrell Evans after the first inning because they brought in a righty. Sparky didn't care about how many at bats I got. Evans was his big free agent, so that's how he used me. Same thing happened to Barbaro. They took him out after the first and put Bergman in. After the game I was 4-11, .364, feeling real good about my role. That was the club that Sparky had envisioned having. He had the right people in the right roles and he had platoon players. I believe that I made them feel comfortable about trading Glenn Wilson, who was going to be the right-hand bat off the bench. Only thing he didn't have was a closer. So for them to say, we can use this guy (me) in that role, I think I played a part in us getting Hernandez. That's why even though it didn't last, I'll always feel good about being on that '84 team.

By early June, I was sent to Evansville, replaced by Ruppert Jones. But Ruppert played so well and Rusty Kuntz filled a nice role defensively, so I was just odd man out.

Sure, I felt alienated as they went on to win the World Series. And this isn't a knock on anybody who lives in Evansville, but to go from a team in the big leagues, Motor City—the electricity and excitement we generated everywhere we went with the 35-5—to have to leave that and go to Evansville…I wouldn't wish it on my worst enemy. I thought I had a chance of getting back, but it didn't happen. Still, they gave me a ring, and I've always appreciated that.

GAMES 9 & 10 vs. KANSAS CITY—After the rain-soaked weekend in Boston, the Tigers came home Tuesday to face Kansas City, only to get rained out again, making it four straight days without a game.

But the foul weather couldn't short-circuit the magic. On April 18, a cold Wednesday night with only 12,310 on hand, the Tigers took a 3-0 lead into the eighth when Morris dished up a three-run homer to Jorge Orta. In the 10th, Frank White bobbled a Larry Herndon grounder allowing the winning run to score for a 4-3 victory. Willie Hernandez had pitched a perfect top of the 10th for his first AL victory and they moved to 9-0, two games short of the Oakland A's 1981

GAME #8   April 13

Tigers 13, Sox 9

DETROIT	AB	R	H	BI	BOSTON	AB	R	H	BI
Whitaker 2b	5	2	2	0	Remy 2b	5	1	3	1
Trammell ss	4	2	2	0	Evans rf	3	2	1	1
Garbey 1b	1	1	0	0	Boggs 3b	3	1	0	0
Bergman ph-1b	4	1	2	1	Rice lf	5	1	2	2
Parrish c	5	2	2	2	Easler dh	5	1	4	1
Lowry c	1	0	0	0	Armas cf	4	1	1	0
Herndon lf	4	1	2	2	Gedman c	3	2	1	1
Lemon cf	5	1	2	2	Stapleton 1b	3	0	1	0
Allen dh	1	1	1	1	Hoffman ss	2	0	0	0
Evans p	4	0	0	1	Miller ph	1	0	0	0
Kuntz rf	5	1	1	1	Gutierrez ss	0	0	0	0
Brookens 3b	5	1	2	1	Nichols ph	1	0	1	2
					Jurak ss	0	0	0	0
Totals	**44**	**13**	**16**	**11**		**35**	**9**	**14**	**8**

Detroit	800	100	040	--	13
Boston	510	000	030	--	9

Game winning RBI -- none, E -- Hoffman 2, Gedman, DP -- Detroit 6, Boston 1, LOB -- Detroit 9, Boston 6, 2B -- Brookens, Trammell, Herndon 2, Nichols, Whitaker, Easler, HR -- Gedman, Evans, Parrish, CS -- Trammell, HBP -- by Wilcox (Evans), by Abbott (Armas) WP -- Brown

Detroit	IP	H	R	ER	BB	SO
Wilcox	0.2	4	5	5	1	0
Bair (W)	4.1	3	1	1	1	5
Abbott	2.0	2	0	0	1	0
Hernandez	2.0	5	3	3	2	2
Boston						
Hurst (L)	0.1	3	7	5	3	1
Brown	5.1	7	2	2	1	3
Stanley	2.1	5	4	4	0	2
Clear	1.0	1	0	0	1	1

T -- 3:11 A -- 35,151

American League record of 11 straight wins to start a season.

On Thursday, April 19, in a make-up game for Tuesday's rainout, 20-year-old Bret Saberhagen, who would play a role in several other dramas before '84 was said and done, beat Petry, 5-2, in his major-league debut. White, the goat the night before, hit a two-run homer; Howard Johnson made two errors at third and the 9-1 Tigers fell short of the Oakland A's record.

GAMES 11, 12 & 13 vs. CHICAGO—The White Sox returned for three and were swept again. On Friday night, April 20, umpire Nick Bremigan ruled that Ron Kittle had trapped Parrish's soft fly in the bottom of the ninth that scored Whitaker with the winner. Kittle bitched, "I had it right there," as he futilely pounded his glove after the 3-2 loss.

On Saturday afternoon, Rozema beat Hoyt, 4-1, before almost 35,000.

On Sunday afternoon, April 22, there was an 83-minute, fourth-inning wind and sleet storm that 10,000 brave souls suffered through. But Detroit fans were rewarded when Juan Berenguer, whose spring wildness had cost him a spot in the rotation, was masterful on three weeks' rest. Berenguer threw seven innings of two-hit ball to win, 9-1. They were now 12-1. Gibson hit his fourth homer, a two-run shot in the first, and Sparky was seeing his new-found faith in Gibson justified. "He finally found out that the only way to have horses and boats and money is to play good. There's not a tougher competitor in all of baseball and that's why I've always loved the guy." Loved, or tough-loved, the guy. Sparky had all but broken Gibson's spirit during an awful 1983, but we'll save that for later.

GAMES 14 & 15 vs. MINNESOTA—The Twins came in for a Tuesday, April 24, twinighter and were beaten, 6-5 and 4-3. It would be a night of tension and giddy excitement. Three runs in the ninth won game one. Gibson led off the ninth with a triple and Bergman singled him home. Rusty Kuntz tied it on a Ron Davis wild pitch, and Whitaker singled in Bergman to win it for Morris. As the Tigers mobbed each other at home plate, 21,000 fans went wild.

Morris had pitched poorly, falling behind, 5-1, but was saved by his teammates, and Jack led the charge from the euphoric dugout.

Petry started the nightcap but left in the fourth inning with a stiff elbow. Glenn Abbott won in relief, 4-3, on Parrish's three-run, fifth-inning homer off Frank Viola. Aurelio Lopez pitched three innings of one-hit ball to preserve the win and they were now an amazing 14-1. The fans were dancing in the concourses.

GAME #15   April 24

Tigers 4, Twins 3

MINNESOTA	AB	R	H	BI	DETROIT	AB	R	H	BI
Brown cf	4	0	0	0	Brookens 2b-3b	4	0	0	0
Washington ss	3	0	0	0	Trammell ss	2	2	1	0
Hrbek 1b	3	1	1	2	Garbey 1b	4	1	2	1
Engle c	3	0	1	0	Parrish c	3	1	1	3
Bush dh	4	0	1	1	Lowry c	1	0	1	0
Brunansky rf	4	0	1	0	Herndon lf	4	0	1	0
Gaetti 3b	4	0	0	0	Lemon cf	4	0	1	0
Hatcher lf	1	0	0	0	Allen dh	3	0	1	0
Meier lf	2	1	1	0	Evans ph	1	0	0	0
Teufel 2b	3	1	1	0	Castillo 3b	3	0	0	0
Eisenreich ph	1	0	0	0	Whitaker 2b	0	0	0	0
					Kuntz rf	3	0	1	0
					Gibson ph-rf	1	0	0	0
Totals	32	3	6	3		33	4	9	4

Minnesota	100	020	000	--	3
Detroit	001	030	00X	--	4

Game winning RBI -- none, E -- Castillo, Trammell, Gaetti, DP -- Minnesota 1, Detroit 3, LOB -- Minnesota 7, Detroit 8, 2B -- Lemon, Garbey, HR -- Parrish

Minnesota	IP	H	R	ER	BB	SO
Viola (L)	6.1	9	4	4	2	4
Walters	1.1	0	0	0	1	0
Filson	0.1	0	0	0	0	0
Detroit						
Petry*	3.0	2	1	1	2	1
Abbott (W)	3.0	3	2	2	1	2
Lopez (S)	3.0	1	0	0	2	3

* Pitched to 1 batter in 4th
T -- 2:29 A -- 20,315

Afterwards, someone asked Gibson if the Tigers were a team of destiny. He said, "You guys can write what you want, but we think we are."

GAMES 16 & 17 @ TEXAS—Team of destiny or not, President Jim Campbell was still all about saving a few bucks. He sent the streaking Tigers trudging over to Windsor to take a low-budget DC-9 charter to Texas. Sparky didn't have his ID, causing a delay at the border. The Tigers then drove to the Windsor airport, made it to Texas at 3:30 a.m., slogged through customs again, and arrived at the hotel around 4:30.

That night, they stomped the Rangers, 9-4, for Wilcox. Grubb, Johnson and Parrish homered, Lance with another three-run shot like the one that had beaten the Twins late the night before. They were 15-1, and what a wacko 24 hours it had been.

The Tigers beat the Rangers, 7-5, the next night, Thursday, April 26, with four in the first off Frank Tanana. Trammell got three hits to raise his average to a league-leading .415, and Parrish homered for a third straight game. Doug Bair won in relief of Rozema, who left after four with stiffness in his neck and back. The Tigers were 16-1 and heading back home. A win against Cleveland at Tiger Stadium Friday night would make them 17-1 and tie the '81 A's for the best start in major-league history.

GAMES 18, 19 & 20 vs. CLEVELAND—The players reported to Tiger Stadium at 4 p.m. Friday to shoot for the record after having hit the pillow at about six that morning after returning from Texas. Mercifully, they weren't forced to go through Canada this time.

They played 19 innings that consumed more than 5 hours and 44 minutes and lost, 8-4, to the Indians. They made three errors in the 19th inning, including two mishandled bunts by Glenn Abbott, and Gibson dropped a deep fly. Gibson and Lemon complained that Kirk had dropped it while throwing, but it didn't matter. Case closed. But still, 16-2 was not too shabby.

In a quick turnaround, Morris threw a three-hitter to beat Cleveland, 6-2, Saturday afternoon to push his record to 5-0 and move the team to 17-2. Jack had beaten the system: He was spared the two-day trip to Texas and had gone home in the 10th inning of the previous night's marathon. The red-hot Trammell doubled in two in the second and Whitaker and Lemon each homered. Lemon's blow reached the upper deck in right, a rare feat for a righty. The amazing month would end the next afternoon, on Sunday, April 29.

Tigers smash Rangers, make it 15 of 16

◆Game 20: Divine Intervention

Where:	Tiger Stadium
Result:	6-1 Tigers
Record:	18-2
WP:	Petry, 6-1
LP:	Spillner, 0-1
Standing:	First, 6 ahead
Attendance:	24,853

GAME #20   April 29

Tigers 6, Indians 1

CLEVELAND

	AB	R	H	BI
Butler cf	3	1	0	0
Bernazard 2b	4	0	0	0
Franco ss	4	0	1	1
Thornton dh	4	0	0	0
Tabler 1b	3	0	0	0
Hassey c	3	0	0	0
Jacoby 3b	1	0	0	0
Perkins ph	1	0	0	0
Castillo rf	0	0	0	0
Vukovich rf-lf	3	0	1	0
Nixon lf	2	0	0	0
Hargrove ph	1	0	0	0
Fischlin 3b	0	0	0	0
Totals	29	1	2	1

DETROIT

	AB	R	H	BI
Whitaker 2b	4	1	2	0
Gibson rf	4	1	3	3
Evans dh	3	0	1	0
Parrish c	4	0	1	1
Lowry c	0	0	0	0
Herndon lf	4	0	1	0
Johnson 3b	3	0	0	0
Trammell ss	1	1	1	0
Lemon cf	3	1	0	0
Bergman 1b	4	0	1	1
Brookens ss-3b	3	2	1	1
Totals	33	6	11	6

```
Cleveland----------------------000  000  001  --  1
Detroit-------------------------003  010  02X  --  6
```

Game winning RBI -- none, E -- Franco, Vukovich, DP -- Cleveland 1, LOB -- Cleveland 4, Detroit 7, 2B -- Gibson 2, Parrish, Vukovich, Trammell, Franco, WP -- Petry, Camacho

Cleveland

	IP	H	R	ER	BB	SO
Spillner (L)	5.0	6	4	2	3	2
Camacho	2.0	2	0	0	0	0
Frazier	1.0	3	2	2	1	0

Detroit

	IP	H	R	ER	BB	SO
Petry (W)	8.0	1	0	0	2	7
Hernandez	1.0	1	1	1	1	1

T -- 2:20 A -- 24,853

The lineup card for 4/29. Notice Gibson batting second. Sparky still hadn't settled on him as the number three hitter.

Dan Petry remembers:

My wife and I had lost a baby about three or four days before the game, and it would have been our first child, so I had a lot on my mind that day. Not only that, but I had come off a stiff elbow my last game against Minnesota when I'd taken myself out after four innings. Jim Campbell had called to the dugout that night to say, "What the hell's going on down there?" But Dr. (Robert) Tietge diagnosed it as just muscle stiffness and had cleared me to pitch my next start.

Things started well and I was really sharp against Cleveland; in fact, I had a no-hitter into the eighth. With the kind of season we were having, the wonderful start and with Jack having pitched that no-hitter twenty-two days earlier, I don't want to make it sound like God was looking over me or anything, but as the game went along, I started thinking, "Hey, you've lost the baby and this is a blessed season and maybe this is His way of making up for it." Who knows?

Remember that great poster that year, with the light breaking through the clouds at night over Tiger Stadium? It was like, something's magical, something's going on here. What was also memorable is that Tom Brookens had started the game at short because Tram had a chest cold, and in about the third or fourth, Tony Bernazard hit a liner up the middle and Brookens dove for it behind second and threw him out on an unbelievable play. It really was, and that's when I started thinking about God and the baby and all that mystical stuff.

Tram came in the game in the seventh and they moved Tom to third. Then, in the eighth, Broderick Perkins, I think that's what his name was, hit a bullet down third and Brooky dove towards the bag, caught it like Brooks Robinson and threw him out, and that's when I'm really thinking— you lost the baby and now everything is going right here. I hadn't pitched a no-hitter since I was 15, and I only had four outs to go.

But then George Vukovich hit a pretty good fastball past Chet in the left-center gap for a double that ended the no-hit bid. The crowd gave me a standing ovation, and I was still real emotional and tipped my cap to

the fans. Reporters asked me about it afterwards and I told them that my idol growing up in California was Nolan Ryan, and once when he lost a no-hitter for the Angels, he tipped his hat to the crowd. That's why I did it—because the crowd was so nice to me and it just made sense.

When I got back to the dugout, I was coming off the injury and I was starting to run out of gas a little and sat down in my spot. Sparky came over to me and said he knew I felt bad about losing the no-hitter and then told me that I was gonna feel even worse because he was bringing Willie for the ninth. It didn't bother me at all. It had already been one of my greatest nights in baseball.

Willie gave up a run and we won, 6-1, and by the end of the year my wife was pregnant. Our son, Matt, was born in '85.

Petry's brilliant win raised his record to 6-1. Gibson doubled in a run in the critical three-run third and singled in another in the fifth. The win pushed the Tigers to 18-2, concluding the best month in club history. The team batting average was a league-leading .288, with the team ERA a league-leading 2.50.

Of the record-shattering April, Sparky said it best: "It's the best month I've ever been in as a player, coach or manager. It's too bad they don't allow you to play one month and then end it."

Petry fires away in one-hitting the Indians on April 29.

Month by Month

APRIL 1984

Cumulative statistics as of the end of the month

AL EAST STANDINGS

	W	L	PCT	GB
DETROIT	18	2	.900	---
Toronto	13	9	.591	6
Cleveland	10	9	.526	7½
Milwaukee	9	11	.450	9½
Baltimore	10	13	.435	9½
Boston	9	13	.409	10
New York	8	13	.381	10½

BATTING

	AB	R	H	RBI	2B	3B	HR	BB	SO	SB	E	GW RBI	AVG
Garbey	36	9	16	11	4	0	0	3	4	1	1	1	.444
Trammell	77	21	31	10	6	1	2	13	7	7	2	0	.403
Lemon	75	12	25	16	6	2	4	7	6	1	0	1	.333
Whitaker	83	21	27	7	4	0	3	11	6	1	1	3	.325
Lowry	10	2	3	0	0	0	0	1	0	0	0	0	.300
Gibson	67	10	19	12	4	1	4	10	18	4	2	3	.284
Evans	61	8	17	15	4	0	2	7	11	0	0	3	.279
Allen	22	5	6	2	1	0	0	1	7	0	0	0	.273
Parrish	75	9	18	17	1	0	5	4	16	0	0	0	.240
Johnson	34	2	8	5	1	0	1	5	6	0	2	1	.235
Herndon	72	9	16	5	5	1	0	11	11	2	1	2	.222
Brookens	39	4	8	5	2	1	0	2	5	0	1	0	.205
Bergman	35	4	7	6	1	0	0	4	5	1	1	0	.200
Grubb	16	2	3	1	0	0	1	4	2	1	0	1	.188
Kuntz	11	2	2	1	0	0	0	0	7	0	0	0	.182
Castillo	3	0	0	0	0	0	0	0	0	0	1	0	.000
DH Hitters	77	14	22	15	6	0	3	9	15	0	0	3	.286
PH Hitters	24	1	5	7	2	0	0	4	5	0	0	0	.208
TOTALS	716	120	206	113	39	6	22	83	111	18	14	17	.288

KEY: AB-at bats, R-runs, H-hits, RBI-runs batted in, 2B-doubles, 3B-triples, HR-home runs, BB-walks, SO-strike outs, SB-stolen bases, E-errors, GW RBI-game winning runs batted in, AVG-batting average.

PITCHING

	W	L	G	CG	S	IP	H	R	ER	BB	SO	ERA
Berenguer	1	0	2	0	0	14.2	9	3	1	4	13	0.61
Lopez	2	0	9	0	2	19.1	6	3	3	8	13	1.40
Abbott	1	1	3	0	0	10.0	7	6	2	4	4	1.80
Bair	2	0	3	0	1	9.1	10	2	2	2	9	1.93
Morris	5	0	6	3	0	50.0	31	13	11	15	27	1.98
Petry	3	1	5	1	0	35.0	20	10	8	13	20	2.06
Wilcox	2	0	4	0	0	21.2	22	10	10	10	7	4.15
Rozema	1	0	3	0	0	14.1	14	7	7	3	9	4.40
Hernandez	1	0	11	0	2	16.2	18	9	9	7	15	4.86
TOTALS	18	2	--	4	5	191	137	63	53	66	117	2.50

Totals include players no longer with the team and pitchers' errors. KEY: W-wins, L-losses, G-games pitched in, CG-complete games, S-saves, IP-innings pitched, H-hits allowed, R-runs allowed, ER-earned runs allowed, BB-walks allowed, SO-strike outs, ERA-earned run average.

DAY-BY-DAY

Date	Gm #	Vs.	W/L	Score	Winner	Loser	Rec	GA	Att.
4/3	1	@ Minn	W	8-1	Morris	Williams	1-0	--	34,381
4/5	2	@ Minn	W	7-3	Petry	Viola	2-0	--	8,373
4/6	3	@ Chi	W	3-2	Wilcox	Dotson	3-0	--	42,692
4/7	4	@ Chi	W	4-0	* Morris	Bannister	4-0	½	24,616
4/8	5	@ Chi	W	7-3	† Lopez	Seaver	5-0	1½	20,478
4/10	6	Tex	W	5-1	* Petry	Stewart	6-0	2½	51,238
4/12	7	Tex	W	9-4	Morris	Tanana	7-0	3	19,154
4/13	8	@ Bost	W	13-9	† Bair	Hurst	8-0	3½	35,151
4/18	9	KC	W	4-3 (10)	† Hernandez	Beckwith	9-0	2½	12,310
4/19	10	KC	L	2-5	Saberhagen	Petry	9-1	1½	12,100
4/20	11	Chi	W	3-2	† Lopez	† Reed	10-1	2½	33,554
4/21	12	Chi	W	4-1	Rozema	* Hoyt	11-1	3½	34,395
4/22	13	Chi	W	9-1	Berenguer	Brennan	12-1	4½	10,603
4/24	14	Minn	W	6-5	* Morris	† Davis	13-1	5	20,315
(DH)	15	Minn	W	4-3	† Abbott	Viola	14-1	5½	20,315
4/25	16	@ Tex	W	9-4	Wilcox	Stewart	15-1	5½	25,883
4/26	17	@ Tex	W	7-5	† Bair	Tanana	16-1	5½	13,559
4/27	18	Cle	L	4-8 (19)	† Aponte	† Abbott	16-2	5	34,112
4/28	19	Cle	W	6-2	* Morris	Behenna	17-2	5½	28,253
4/29	20	Cle	W	6-1	Petry	Spillner	18-2	6	24,853

*Complete game   † Decision in relief

Chapter 8

May: Record-Smashing and 35-5

If you dreamt this you wouldn't tell anybody.
It's like telling people about a UFO. They think you're crazy.

> — Darrell Evans (who did once claim to have seen a UFO), after the Tigers beat Oakland on May 20 to raise their record to 32-5

With 18-2 tying the major-league record for the best April ever, Sparky decided to be vigilant regarding gloating or making assumptions about how great this team might yet become. When he was asked if he had learned anything from the start he said, "Yep, keep your mouth shut."

Fat chance. In the next two days he'd say, "Morris and Petry would have won at least 25 a year for me in Cincinnati." Pressed for more hyperbole, he "kept his mouth shut" by saying, "This is the best defensive team I've ever seen." So much for verbal vigilance. But he did add, quite respectfully, "This thing hasn't even begun yet. The real war starts when the (American League) East teams play each other."

The only East teams they played in April were Cleveland, which had won that 19-inning mess in the past week, and the

---

MAY 1984

May Record: 19-7

Highlights:
Won **16 of 17** games from May 4 to May 24
26-4 record, best 30-game start in major-league history
35-5 record, best 40-game start in major-league history
17 straight road wins—breaks AL mark, ties NL mark

Stars:

Hernandez:	1-0, 5 SV, 1.11 ERA
Morris:	5-1, 1.79 ERA
Bergman:	.372, 16-43, 7 RBI
Kuntz:	.538, 14-26; 2 HR, 10 RBI

Key Games:
May 08: Trammell grand slam off Quisenberry wins 5-2
May 11: Beat Angels 8-2 to go 26-4
May 20: Beat A's 4-3 to go 32-5
May 24: Tigers beat Angels 5-1 to go 35-5
May 27: Lose 6-1 in Seattle; are swept for first three-game losing streak

---

one wild game at Boston where Parrish was responsible for all three outs in that eight-run first.

GAMES 21, 22 & 23 vs BOSTON—The Red Sox came to town to start the month featuring '83 American League RBI king Jim Rice (126), and league-leading hitter Wade Boggs (.361). In the opener on Tuesday, May 1, rookie Barbaro Garbey, who hit .444 in April, had four RBIs in an 11-2 win as Milt Wilcox defeated Bruce Hurst.

Berenguer lost, 5-4, on Wednesday, and on a cold Thursday afternoon, May 3, Bob Ojeda out-dueled Morris, 1-0. For the first time, Morris was "the other" pitcher despite a complete game five-hitter while fighting a cold. Dwight Evans' eighth-inning line-drive homer off a Morris fastball just cleared the wall between the 365- and 400-foot marks in left center. Back-to-back one-run losses left the Tigers 19-4.

GAMES 24, 25 & 26 @ CLEVELAND—Coming off their first two-game losing streak of the year, the Tigers went on the road for a weekend series at Cleveland May 4–6. On Friday night before fewer than 9,000 fans, Parrish and Herndon had two RBIs each as Petry won, 9-2.

On Saturday, Lopez relieved Bair in the eighth inning of a 6-5 win. Ahead 6-4 in the ninth, Lopez yielded three singles and a deep sacrifice fly, and then nearly lost it when Broderick Perkins hit a potential game-winning homer that barely went foul down the right-field line. Finally, he fanned Perkins to end it. Gibson later kidded Lopez with, "Way to go, Lopey, make it exciting—give up two to the wall."

Sunday, May 6, was even more dramatic. The Tigers came from five runs down to win, 6-5, in 12 innings. Wilcox left after five, trailing 5-0. The Tigers battled back to tie with four in the eighth off three Indian pitchers. Bert Blyleven, who'd given up a homer to John Grubb in the sixth, gave way to George Frazier and Mike Jeffcoat.

Trammell's sharp single to left scored Bergman, and Gibson's grounder scored Howard Johnson to tie it at five. The winner came four innings later on Lou Whitaker's 12th-inning single off Ernie Camacho, scoring Bergman, who'd led off with a double. The Tigers were 22-4 and off to Kansas City.

The tension of back-to-back 6-5 nail biters had put Sparky in superstitious overdrive. In the dugout at Cleveland, he crossed his legs or put his hand in a certain spot when the Tigers were doing well but would change that body language when things seemed to turn. For a spell on Saturday, he tried spitting twice on each pitch because it seemed to work, but, in an epic departure, got nervous during a

Ojeda outduels Morris, 1-0; Tigers slump continues

late Indians rally and left his spot on the bench to get a drink. He admitted that getting up and moving at a time like that was a major superstition breach. "I never do that," he said in resignation.

GAMES 27, 28 & 29 @ KANSAS CITY—When the Tigers arrived at Kauffman Stadium in Kansas City, they had three hitters in the league's top 10: Trammell at .357, Lemon at .351 and Whitaker at .330. Lemon also had seven homers and 24 RBIs to stand among the league leaders.

Berenguer coasted to a 10-3 win on Monday night, May 7, setting the stage for an '84 classic on Tuesday.

◆Game 28: Tram Slams the Quis

Where:	**Kansas City**
Result:	**5-2 Tigers**
Record:	**24-4**
WP:	**Morris, 6-1**
LP:	**Black, 3-2**
Standing:	**First, 6 ahead**
Attendance:	**14,304**

Alan Trammell remembers:

I do remember that game for a number of reasons. First off, it was our thirteenth consecutive road win and we ended up winning seventeen straight, which set an American League record. Also, it brings a smile to me because '84 was the best season of my career and it was so much fun to win the championship and everything that went with it and what it's meant to my life and career.

It was a tight ball game, and it was also a night where Jack was pouting about lack of run support. He had lost, 1-0, to the Red Sox at Tiger Stadium his last game out [May 3], and here it was in the sixth inning or so and he's trailing, 2-0. I'd had to go to the mound several times to get him to calm down. Jack didn't know this until well after the fact, years down the road, that Sparky used to signal to me from the dugout to go talk to him by making a talking motion with his fingers. We were taught in that era that the shortstop was the captain of the infield and Jack often lost his cool. Lance worked on him that night also.

Anyway, it's 2-0 Royals in the seventh. Chet singled in Larry to make it 2-1. Darrell also got a hit off Bud Black and when Bud walked Lou to

Trammell's grand slam off Quisenberry pushes the Tigers' record to 24-4.

GAME #28   May 8

Tigers 5, Royals 2

DETROIT	AB	R	H	BI	KANSAS CITY	AB	R	H	BI
Whitaker 2b	3	1	0	0	Sheridan cf	4	0	0	0
Trammell ss	4	1	1	4	Motley rf	4	0	1	1
Garbey 1b	3	0	1	0	Orta lf	4	1	2	1
Parrish c	4	0	1	0	McRae dh	4	0	1	0
Herndon lf	4	1	2	0	White 2b	4	0	2	0
Evans dh	4	1	2	0	Balboni 1b	3	0	0	0
Lemon cf	4	1	2	1	Slaught c	3	0	0	0
Gibson rf	4	0	0	0	Ashford 3b	3	0	0	0
Brookens 3b	4	0	0	0	Washington ss	2	1	1	0
Totals	34	5	9	5	Totals	31	2	7	2

Detroit	000	000	500	--	5
Kansas City	000	011	000	--	2

Game winning RBI -- none, DP -- Detroit 1, Kansas City 1, LOB -- Detroit 4, Kansas City 4, 2B -- Washington HR -- Orta, Trammell, SB -- Washington CS -- Garbey , White , Motley, WP -- Morris

Detroit	IP	H	R	ER	BB	SO
Morris (W)	9.0	7	2	2	2	5
Kansas City						
Black (L)	6.2	7	4	4	2	4
Quisenberry	2.1	2	1	1	0	2

T -- 2:35 A -- 14,304

load the bases, they brought in [Dan] Quisenberry. Both Lou and I had faced Dan in the minor leagues a few years before, and he had since become one of the premier closers for a number of years in the AL. In fact, in '83 he had broken John Hiller's save record with 45. I don't know what my career average was off him but I know that the left-handers hit him much better. Gibby and Lou seemed to have much better success against him than I did.

He had that unique side-arm, submarine delivery. He had a sinker and a slider, but I was looking for the sinker every pitch. I watched the first pitch for a strike and he elevated the second pitch just enough. It was middle in and down, and in a sweet spot where I could get a little bit of lift. I hit it over the bullpen in left field; it was a line drive, I knew I hit it well—I thought it was at least off the wall, and as I said that night, "Thank you very much," when it made it over. And whether it was luck or whatever, I hit it so I guess that's all that matters.

Early in my career I hadn't established myself as any kind of power hitter, not in my mind at least, but I'd been playing long enough to know that when I hit it, it was at least over [Darryl] Motley's head. Kansas City was at that time considered a big ballpark, and we didn't hit a lot of homers in that ballpark. It may have just made it over the wall, but you don't get any bonus points for distance, just oohs and ahs. It was big because we were losing, 2-1, and ended up winning, 5-2. It was a significant home run because it won the ball game for us.

I'd worn out a lotta shortstops pounding that sinker into the ground, but that one wasn't as good as most of his. In a newspaper article, Quis cracked, "That's a lot longer ground ball than I'm used to seeing him hit." He was quick-witted and was a wonderful guy, a great competitor who was great for baseball and baseball misses him since he died of that brain tumor some years back.

It might have been the only grand slam Quis gave up in his entire career. I know it was the first and people were mentioning that to me immediately after the game. I just smile in reading the story because it reminds me of the great start we had. Winning that game made us 24-4.

We had swept Cleveland over the weekend on our way to Kansas City. On Sunday, they led us, 5-0, and we beat 'em, 6-5, in 12, and Indians Manager Pat Corrales was upset. When we got to Kansas City Monday and read the papers, Corrales was quoted saying, "The Tigers' record is misleading because they haven't played any teams from the AL East." Sports Illustrated also had an article on us that week that said, "When will the bubble burst?"

Well, guess what? After our 24-4 that night, think of it, we still went 11-1 after that to go 35-5! What I'm trying to say is it was a total team effort, and it was just my night to come up with the big hit. I wasn't the *only one. When you look back to our team, nobody hit 30 home runs, nobody had 100 RBIs, and nobody won 20 games, but we still had a lotta guys who had pretty good years—not great years—but pretty good years. Put it all together and we had a great year. I guess Pat Corrales and everybody else came to realize that the bubble would never burst!*

On May 9, the Tigers completed the sweep of the Royals with a 3-1 win. Lopez took over for Petry the last 2⅓ innings for the save. The Tigers' 25-4 mark tied the '55 Dodgers for the best record at this point of a season. Evans went 3-3, and Trammell 3-4 to raise his average to .378. Curiously, Trammell's two AL rivals at shortstop, Robin Yount and Cal Ripken, had each won an MVP award the last two years as their respective teams had won the AL pennant. Would Alan follow suit?

Saturday's game at Tiger Stadium against the Angels was slated to be the national telecast on NBC, and color analyst Tony Kubek said he liked Trammell's MVP chances. Ironically, the game would be blacked out on Channel 4 in Detroit in favor of a show called *Real People*. Those were the rules network baseball insisted on back then, as antiquated as they seem two decades later.

GAMES 30 & 31 vs CALIFORNIA—On Friday, May 11, the Tigers returned triumphant from Kansas City, having swept the six-game road trip, and then made it seven straight with an 8-2 win over the Angels. Wilcox, now 4-0, beat Mike Witt before 44,187. Gibson hit his fifth homer, Bergman had three RBIs and Hernandez got his fourth save. It raised their record to 26-4, and that had never been done before. Barbaro Garbey was hitting .367, and Warner Communications called his agent with some interest in making a movie about his 1980 float to freedom.

A crowd of 38,516 came out on Saturday for the national telecast that would bypass Detroit, and were disappointed in a 4-2 loss to the Angels. Tommy John, 40, threw a complete game on eight hits. Reggie Jackson, 13 years after his All-Star blast at Tiger Stadium, and helped by a 20-mile-an-hour wind, cleared the roof again for his career 485th homer when he belted a Berenguer fastball with a man on in the fifth. Next time up he grounded back to the box and Berenguer held the ball, forcing Jackson to leg it out.

Sunday's scheduled game was rained out.

GAMES 32, 33 & 34 vs SEATTLE
◆Game 32: The Bench Delivers Again

GAME #32   May 14
Tigers 7, Mariners 5

SEATTLE	AB	R	H	BI	DETROIT	AB	R	H	BI
Perconte 2b	4	0	0	0	Whitaker 2b	5	0	1	1
Henderson dh	4	0	0	0	Trammell ss	5	1	3	2
Thomas lf	5	1	1	0	Garbey 1b-3b	4	0	2	0
Putnam 1b	4	1	2	1	Parrish c	3	1	2	0
Cowens rf	3	2	3	2	Herndon lf	4	0	2	0
Bonnell cf	2	1	0	0	Lemon cf	4	0	1	1
Coles 3b	3	0	0	0	Evans dh	3	1	0	0
Milbourne ph-3b	1	0	1	1	Kuntz rf	4	3	3	1
Kearney c	4	0	0	0	Brookens 3b	2	0	0	1
Owen ss	4	0	2	0	Bergman ph-1b	1	1	1	1
Totals	34	5	9	4		35	7	15	7

```
Seattle----------------- 000  201  020 -- 5
Detroit----------------- 120  110  02X -- 7
```

Game winning RBI -- none, E -- Petry, Owen, Whitaker, DP -- Seattle 2, Detroit 2, LOB -- Seattle 7, Detroit 7, 2B -- Thomas, Kuntz, 3B -- Bergman, HR -- Trammell, Cowens, Kuntz, CS -- Owen, Whitaker, SH -- Bonnell, SF -- Brookens, Balk -- Vande Berg

Seattle	IP	H	R	ER	BB	SO
Vande Berg(L)	7.1	13	6	6	2	1
Beard	0.2	2	1	1	0	1
Detroit						
Petry*	5.0	6	3	3	2	1
Bair+	2.0	1	2	2	2	1
Lopez (W)	2.0	2	0	0	0	2

* Pitched to 3 batters in 6th
\+ Pitched to 2 batters in 8th

T -- 3:05 A -- 18,830

Where:	**Tiger Stadium**
Result:	**7-5 Tigers**
Record:	**27-5**
WP:	**Lopez, 4-0**
LP:	**Vande Berg, 2-2**
Standing:	**First, 8 ahead**
Attendance:	**18,830**

Monday brought the Mariners, and the ninth sweep in 13 series was in the making. This was the opener on Monday, May 14, and utilization of the bench made Sparky look ingenious again. He started Barbaro Garbey at first base, something he wouldn't risk doing later in the year, and Garbey went 2-4 off Ed Vande Berg. Rusty Kuntz started for Gibson against the lefty and went 3-4.

Seattle battled from 3-0 and 5-3 deficits against Petry, Bair and Lopez to tie the game at five with two runs in the top of the eighth.

In the bottom of the inning, Kuntz doubled off Vande Berg with one out. Seattle brought in right-handed reliever Dave Beard, and Sparky countered with pinch hitter Dave Bergman batting for Tom Brookens. With two strikes on him, Bergman ripped a triple into the right-center gap, scoring Kuntz with the eventual game winner. Whitaker then singled Bergman in to make it 7-5.

In making his critical choice in the eighth, Sparky had three left-handed pinch hitters to choose from: Gibson, John Grubb and Bergman. Sparky downplayed having pushed the right button, asking rhetorically, "What has Bergman done the last four years? Pinch hit. That's what he is." Sparky had then inserted Bergman at first base for the Seattle ninth, and moved Garbey to third. "This way, you only have to use one guy."

Bergman had hit .355 as a pinch hitter with the Giants in '83. It was a 47-degree night and he had been getting loose for about 20 minutes before he was called upon. Though Bergman would remain a Tiger well into the dark days of the '90s, Kuntz and Garbey were perfect examples of what journeymen players can accomplish when they find themselves in a positive, supportive, winning atmosphere. Both Garbey and Kuntz were gone after the '85 season. But this was 1984, when heroes sprang up from the most unlikely of places.

This 7-5 victory was just another mini-drama in a season full of them. Again, there was no television for the game. Eighteen of the 27 games in May were not on local television, and only 18,830 ventured out on a chilly evening.

This would become the first victory of a nine-game winning streak. Six of the nine wins, like this one, would be by two runs or less. And when the nine-gamer was over on May 24, the Tigers would be 35-5.

The Tigers beat Seattle again, winning ugly, 6-4, on a chilly Tuesday night. Morris allowed only three hits, but walked five in seven innings and gave up a three-run homer to light-hitting Spike Owen in the seventh. Howard Johnson made another run-producing error, the kind that would eventually cause Sparky to lose trust in him. But he did make a fine play on a hard-hit ball to end the sixth and also singled in two to atone.

On Wednesday, the Tigers scored five in the first off Matt Young in a 10-1 win for Wilcox. With every string he pulled producing results, Sparky's bench was again all over this one. Marty Castillo was flawless at third, and Brookens played short for Trammell, who gladly took the day off, saying, "Whoever we put in there does the job." Grubb, Lowry and Bergman all pinch hit in the eighth, with Grubb delivering a three-run homer.

Kuntz played right and drove in two more. And with fabulous show-biz flair, Kuntz pretended that he caught a foul pop that had landed in a fan's lap. He didn't pull it off, but with everything else around him working so damn well, he figured it was worth a try. Bill McGraw in the *Free Press* wrote of this one, "Everything Anderson does is magic."

Sparky affirmed that by saying, "I never had a team that had bench strength like we got." Now the record was 29-5, with Oakland coming in for the weekend, ready to lure massive crowds eager to see more victories pile up and more records fall. Attendance was up an average 10,000-plus a game and was on pace to top three million in '84.

GAMES 35, 36 & 37 vs OAKLAND—Petry beat the A's, 8-4, in a bizarre, six-inning, rain-shortened game on Friday, May 18. The A's were furious. Nobody had ever seen this before: The rain stopped moments after the grounds crew brought out the tarp, yet the umpires called the game even though it didn't rain for another hour and a half! Umpire Durwood Merrill sheepishly explained that weather officials had told him the rain would continue for another hour, but it never did return. The Tigers were now 30-5, another milestone in pushing toward their best-ever start.

On Saturday, Morris beat the A's, 5-4, before 42,906 to move to 8-1. In '68, by comparison, McLain was only 6-1 on May 20. Interim Manager Dick Tracewski, filling in as Sparky attended his father's

Rusty Kuntz

Barbaro Garbey

A common scene in early '84— fans line up around the block to buy the hottest ticket in baseball.

funeral, called Morris' season "mind-boggling, and he's a much better athlete than Denny." Whitaker and Evans had two RBIs each in beating Steve McCatty. The Tigers were hitting .301, with their pitchers boasting a 2.67 ERA.

Outside the stadium, horns honked. Inside, people ran and screamed through the corridors. The Tigers would end the home stand a day later, looking to make it seven wins in the last eight and stretch their record to 32-5 on the year. Rain was in the forecast again, perhaps the only thing that could slow down this baseball beast.

◆ Game 37: Mrs. Wilcox, you OK?

GAME #37	May 20	

Tigers 4, A's 3

OAKLAND	AB	R	H	BI	DETROIT	AB	R	H	BI
Henderson lf	3	1	0	0	Whitaker 2b	4	0	0	0
Murphy cf	4	0	0	0	Trammell ss	4	0	1	0
Morgan 2b	4	0	0	1	Gibson rf	4	1	1	0
Kingman dh	4	0	0	0	Evans 1b	4	1	1	0
Lansford 3b	4	0	1	0	Bergman 1b	0	0	0	0
Bochte 1b	2	1	1	0	Herndon lf	4	0	2	0
Almon ph-1b	1	0	0	0	Grubb dh	2	1	1	1
Davis rf	2	0	0	0	Parrish ph	1	0	1	0
Essian ph-c	1	0	0	0	Lemon cf	4	0	1	0
Heath c-rf	3	1	2	2	Garbey 3b	3	0	1	1
Phillips ss	2	0	0	0	Brookens 3b	0	0	0	0
Burroughs ph	1	0	0	0	Lowry c	3	1	1	1
Wagner ss	0	0	0	0					
Totals	31	3	4	3		33	4	10	3

Oakland --------------------- 011 000 010 -- 3
Detroit --------------------- 210 100 00X -- 4

Game winning RBI -- none, E -- Trammell, Henderson, DP -- Oakland 1, Detroit 1, LOB -- Oakland 2, Detroit 6, 2B -- Bochte, HR -- Lowry, Heath, SB -- Henderson, CS -- Garbey

Oakland	IP	H	R	ER	BB	SO
Sorensen (L)	6.2	9	4	2	1	3
Conroy	1.0	1	0	0	0	3
Caudill	0.1	0	0	0	0	0
Detroit						
Wilcox (W)	6.0	3	2	2	1	0
Hernandez (S)	3.0	1	1	1	0	2

T -- 2:22 A -- 27,073

Where:	Tiger Stadium
Result:	4-3 Tigers
Record:	32-5
WP:	Wilcox, 6-0
LP:	Sorensen, 1-6
Standing:	First, 8½ ahead
Attendance:	27,073

Milt Wilcox remembers:

It was a rainy Sunday, and we were at the end of an unbelievable home stand. I forget all the records we had going then, but I'd pitched the first game of the home stand and beat the Angels to make us 26-4, breaking the Dodgers' best 30-game start. The crowds were getting really big and that was probably a sellout (44,187) on a Friday night (May 11) and Tiger Stadium was getting really wild by then.

So this was the last game of the home stand, and we were playing Oakland, who Petry and Morris had beaten Friday and Saturday before crowds of well over 40,000. We had another eight- or nine-game winning streak going.

I was in the clubhouse getting ready to go out and warm up and I got a call that my mom was down in the first-aid room, and I'm thinking, "What did my mom do now?" So I went down there and she had one of those big braces around her neck. I asked her what had happened and she said she was getting off the exit at Tiger Stadium and this truck hit her in the side and almost spun her completely around and virtually totaled her car—this little white Mustang I'd bought for her. The roads were slick because of the rain and she had actually skidded into the other guy. A trooper had come along and was nice enough to have taken her to the ballpark.

Dr. [Robert] Tietge and some other people were looking at her and basically telling me that she was all right and hadn't suffered any significant injuries, just some minor whiplash. She didn't want to go to the hospital because she had come to see her little boy pitch and that was that.

The rain delay was almost an hour, and by then I was settled down about my mom. We had a rookie catcher, Dwight Lowry, who was giving Lance a rest that day. He'd had only about 20 at bats in his career so far. Dwight was part black, part native-American, real nice, a quiet, religious kid from North Carolina who drove a pickup truck. I liked Lowry; he gave you a good target and he moved the ball around real well.

I gave up a coupla runs early but we always scored first that year and it was like 3-2 us in the fourth when Dwight came up and hit his first big-league homer off Lary Sorensen to put us ahead, 4-2. It was such a big moment for him and that's what I really remember about that year—not just the big moments for yourself, but also your teammates. Dwight was so damn stunned and excited that he started sprinting after he hit it and didn't slow to a trot 'til he was around second.

I think I won Trixie's [Dick Tracewski] first game as a manager that day. I kid him about it all the time. Sparky was out west because his dad had died and Trixie was filling in. I remember thinking how he'd learned real well from Sparky—six innings and get Wilcox out of the game.

But that was really what it was like for me that year. I didn't pitch a complete game all season because Roger and Sparky were protecting my arm. And with our bullpen, if I had a lead after six, that was it. You bring anybody in and they'd do an excellent job. Willie pitched the last three innings scoreless that day and we won, 4-3, and my record moved to 6-0.

The quote from me in the paper that day was, "It's past the miracle stuff; I think we've shown everybody we have a good team." The other quote from Darrell goes, "If you dreamt this you wouldn't tell anybody. It's like telling people about a UFO. They think you're crazy." It's true. The national media had been implying that there was no way we were as good as our start. Since we had made it look so easy, people around the country weren't ready to give us the respect we deserved. But we did deserve it. And the people in Detroit knew we did.

Rickey Henderson is safe as Darrell Evans leaps for Alan Trammell's throw in Wilcox's May 20 win.

GAMES 38, 39 & 40 @ CALIFORNIA—At 32-5, with the baseball world scurrying for explanations and perspective to try to attach logic to an improbable start, the Tigers flew to California Sunday night with Monday, May 21, a welcome day off to adjust to the time change. The Angels were in first place in the inferior AL West, but at 22-20 had problems of their own. Rod Carew had withdrawn himself from their just-completed series with the Yankees with a .115

batting average over the last three weeks, but was expected to start again. Second baseman Bobby Grich had lost 15 pounds with a stomach flu.

A crowd of 41,253 showed up on Tuesday night, May 22, to see the phenomenal Tigers, who quickly scratched out a run with two out in the first inning. Gibson lined one off Mike Witt's glove and beat the throw after the ball trickled to shortstop Dick Schofield. Gibson stole second, his ninth steal in ten tries for the year, and then took third on Bob Boone's wild throw. Parrish then singled Gibson in with a hard grounder through the box.

Of the many statistical curiosities they were creating, Gibson's run meant that the Tigers had outscored their opponents, 49-18, in the first inning. Carew homered off Berenguer in the bottom half to break his slump, but that was it for the Angels off of Berenguer who, with the crowd chanting, "Reggie, Reggie," fanned Reggie Jackson with two on and two out to end the sixth.

Lopez came on in the seventh to protect a 3-1 lead, which he did when Fred Lynn's drive with a man on in the eighth curved foul deep into the right-field seats. It was Detroit's 15th straight win on the road, just two shy of the New York Giants' all-time record of 17 that had stood since 1916.

More than 41,000 came Wednesday night and saw the Tigers win another low-scoring affair, 4-2, for Dan Petry, who held the Angels to two runs through seven before Hernandez finished with two innings of perfect relief, fanning three in the process. Trammell doubled, Lemon tripled and Parrish hit his sixth homer in defeating Tommy John.

A huge throng of 43,580 came Thursday night, May 24, to see if the Tigers could actually make it 35-5. If they were successful, it would become by far the best 40-game start in major-league history.

◆ Game 40: "35-5"

Morris 9-1, Tigers 35-5.

Where:	Anaheim
Result:	5-1 Tigers
Record:	35-5
WP:	Morris, 9-1
LP:	Slaton, 1-2
Standing:	First, 8½ ahead
Attendance:	43,580

Jack Morris remembers:

I don't remember a lot of details from that game, but I know I pitched real well and there was a sense among the boys that we were doing something real special here. I think I struck out about ten and threw a three- or four-hitter. And we won, 5-1. We got four in the fourth and that was that. Tram hit a two-run homer and we got some more hits and a few more runs that inning.

Of course, what really stands out is that it was our seventeenth straight on the road that set the American League record and tied an ancient National League record and it was sorta brought to our attention that, "Hey, you guys are doing something that hasn't been done much in baseball." I also remember thinking about the confidence level that we had for a buncha guys who, at that time at least, had no superstar names, unless you want to count Rusty Kuntz and Barbaro Garbey!

In the locker room after the game, the boys were talking a whole buncha crap. It really wasn't out of line, it was just a lot of ecstatic energy from guys who had never gone through anything like that and we were just expressing our flat-out joy. As I watched and participated in all of this elation we were all feeling, I wondered if we were getting to a point where we were getting too excited about all of this. Think about it. We got a group of guys on this team who have never won anything in their lives. That was cool and I'm very grateful for it as I look back on it today.

For the record, the 17th straight on the road broke the previous American League record of 16 set by the 1912 Washington Senators. Seventeen straight tied the existing major-league mark set by the 1916 New York Giants. Both of those teams had failed to win the pennant, and as the Tigers dealt with sellout crowds and legions of national media jumping in to join their chase, they were made well aware of their predecessors' disappointments.

GAMES 41, 42 & 43 @ SEATTLE—With the nearly incomprehensible numbers 35-5 dancing in their heads, the Tigers flew up the coast to meet the Mariners. Seattle's Ed Vande Berg beat Wilcox, 7-3, on Friday, May 25, as the Mariners scored six runs in less than five innings. On Saturday, 41,342 came to the Kingdome on Free Cap Day to see the Mariners get four off Berenguer in the first, enroute to a 9-5 win for Mike Moore. Gibson and Kuntz homered, but three Tiger runs in the ninth still fell way short.

The Tigers were feeble once again on Sunday in a 6-1 loss. Petry fell behind, 4-1, after allowing nine hits and a walk in four innings. Matt Young, whom they'd embarrassed with five in the first in a 10-1 win in Detroit back on May 16, got the win. It was their first

Gibson ended May with a ninth-inning, game-winning HR at Oakland. His flair for the spectactular surfaced often in '84.

three-game losing streak of the year and Sparky calmly intoned, "I'm not alarmed. I told you times like these were going to come—and this weekend, they did."

GAMES 44, 45 & 46 @ OAKLAND—The Tigers would finish the month with three games in Oakland before coming home to start June with a key two-week stretch that would feature 14 games in 13 days against second-place Toronto and third-place Baltimore.

They quickly put the Seattle experience behind them by winning the first and last against the A's. Morris beat Oakland, 6-2, with a six-hitter in front of 46,238 on Memorial Day to move his mark to 10-1 with a 1.79 ERA. Jack was 5-0 in April, lost 1-0 to the Red Sox in early May, and now had reeled off another five straight in May.

The A's beat Wilcox, 8-5, on Tuesday, May 29, leading the Tigers, 8-1, after four innings. But on Wednesday the Tigers finished May and the road trip with a dramatic 2-1 win when Gibson blasted a ninth-inning homer 400 feet off Steve McCatty to break the 1-1 tie. In a bit of a bullpen role reversal, Hernandez picked up after Berenguer and pitched three scoreless innings for the win, with Lopez getting the A's in the bottom of the ninth for the save.

The Tigers were 19-7 in May for a 37-9 overall record. But the Blue Jays were only 5½ back, posting a 32-15 mark that in any other year would have been dominant. And now the Jays would be getting seven cracks at Detroit in the next 13 days, in what would produce some of the best drama of the entire season.

Month by Month

MAY 1984

Cumulative statistics as of the end of the month

AL EAST STANDINGS

	W	L	PCT	GB
DETROIT	37	9	.804	---
Toronto	32	15	.681	5½
Baltimore	28	21	.571	10½
Milwaukee	22	24	.478	15
Boston	21	26	.447	16½
New York	20	27	.426	17½
Cleveland	17	28	.378	19½

BATTING

	AB	R	H	RBI	2B	3B	HR	BB	SO	SB	E	GW RBI	AVG
Kuntz	37	14	16	11	6	0	2	4	8	1	0	2	.432
Trammell	184	39	64	26	15	2	6	25	18	12	5	3	.348
Garbey	109	18	36	22	6	1	1	6	14	2	4	1	.330
Grubb	41	7	13	7	1	0	3	11	9	1	0	3	.317
Lemon	167	26	53	36	9	3	9	19	26	3	0	2	.317
Castillo	26	1	8	5	1	0	0	1	4	1	1	0	.308
Whitaker	180	33	55	15	6	0	4	21	18	2	6	5	.306
Allen	27	6	8	3	1	0	0	2	8	1	0	0	.296
Bergman	78	12	23	13	3	2	0	8	8	2	1	2	.295
Evans	139	22	39	25	5	0	4	22	17	1	0	4	.281
Gibson	150	29	42	23	8	3	7	17	29	10	3	4	.280
Johnson	58	6	16	13	2	0	2	10	13	1	4	2	.276
Parrish	157	19	43	26	2	1	8	9	33	1	1	4	.274
Herndon	157	16	38	12	9	1	0	16	28	3	1	2	.242
Lowry	25	5	6	2	3	0	1	2	5	0	0	0	.240
Brookens	77	5	12	6	2	1	0	5	9	1	3	0	.156
DH Hitters	167	31	51	29	8	1	4	28	21	3	0	5	.305
PH Hitters	40	4	15	14	3	0	1	5	7	0	0	1	.375
TOTALS	1612	258	472	245	79	14	45	175	249	42	35	35	.293

KEY: AB-at bats, R-runs, H-hits, RBI-runs batted in, 2B-doubles, 3B-triples, HR-home runs, BB-walks, SO-strike outs, SB-stolen bases, E-errors, GW RBI-game winning runs batted in, AVG-batting average.

PITCHING

	W	L	G	CG	S	IP	H	R	ER	BB	SO	ERA
Lopez	4	0	20	0	7	41.2	25	8	8	12	31	1.73
Morris	10	1	12	7	0	100.1	64	26	21	32	68	1.88
Bair	2	0	11	0	2	25	22	7	7	6	21	2.52
Hernandez	2	0	22	0	7	41	33	12	12	11	34	2.63
Petry	7	2	11	2	0	68	60	26	22	30	44	2.91
Rozema	1	0	7	0	0	21.1	19	9	8	6	13	3.38
Berenguer	3	3	8	0	0	45	40	20	17	24	35	3.40
Abbott	2	1	6	0	0	17.1	16	12	8	5	5	4.15
Wilcox	6	2	11	0	0	60.2	66	33	30	22	30	4.45
TOTALS	37	9	--	9	16	421	343	123	133	148	280	2.84

Totals include players no longer with the team and pitchers' errors.
KEY: W-wins, L-losses, G-games pitched in, CG-complete games, S-saves, IP-innings pitched, H-hits allowed, R-runs allowed, ER-earned runs allowed, BB-walks allowed, SO-strike outs, ERA-earned run average.

DAY-BY-DAY

Date	Gm #	Vs.	W/L	Score	Winner	Loser	Rec	GA	Att.
5/1	21	Bos	W	11-2	Wilcox	Hurst	19-2	6½	17,495
5/2	22	Bos	L	4-5	Brown	Berenguer	19-3	5½	23,085
5/3	23	Bos	L	0-1	* Ojeda	* Morris	19-4	5	22,617
5/4	24	@ Cle	W	9-2	Petry	Spillner	20-4	5	8,497
5/5	25	@ Cle	W	6-5	Abbott	Heaton	21-4	5	9,282
5/6	26	@ Cle	W	6-5 (12)	† Lopez	† Camacho	22-4	5	16,125
5/7	27	@ KC	W	10-3	Berenguer	Gubicza	23-4	5½	19,474
5/8	28	@ KC	W	5-2	* Morris	Black	24-4	6	14,304
5/9	29	@ KC	W	3-1	Petry	Jackson	25-4	7½	15,709
5/11	30	Cal	W	8-2	Wilcox	Witt	26-4	7½	44,187
5/12	31	Cal	L	2-4	* John	Berenguer	26-5	7½	38,516
5/14	32	Sea	W	7-5	† Lopez	Vande Berg	27-5	8	18,830
5/15	33	Sea	W	6-4	Morris	Thomas	28-5	8	21,782
5/16	34	Sea	W	10-1	Wilcox	Young	29-5	8	22,001
5/18	35	Oak	W	8-4 (6)	* Petry	Krueger	30-5	7½	41,136
5/19	36	Oak	W	5-4	Morris	McCatty	31-5	7½	42,906
5/20	37	Oak	W	4-3	Wilcox	Sorensen	32-5	8½	27,073
5/22	38	@ Cal	W	3-1	Berenguer	Witt	33-5	8	41,253
5/23	39	@ Cal	W	4-2	Petry	LaCorte	34-5	8	41,205
5/24	40	@ Cal	W	5-1	* Morris	Slaton	35-5	8½	43,580
5/25	41	@ Sea	L	3-7	Vande Berg	Wilcox	35-6	7½	15,722
5/26	42	@ Sea	L	5-9	Moore	Berenguer	35-7	6½	41,342
5/27	43	@ Sea	L	1-6	Young	Petry	35-8	5	12,755
5/28	44	@ Oak	W	6-2	* Morris	Codiroli	36-8	5½	46,238
5/29	45	@ Oak	L	5-8	Krueger	Wilcox	36-9	5½	22,499
5/30	46	@ Oak	W	2-1	† Hernandez	McCatty	37-9	5½	15,224

*Complete game   † Decision in relief

Chapter 9

Sparks Are Flyin'

"I want you guys to look to your right," and we did. "I want you to look to your left," which we all did. "Is there any guy here in this locker room that you wouldn't want to be in a foxhole with?" I looked around and said to myself, "There isn't a guy in this locker room that I wouldn't want to be in a foxhole with." He said, "We got a team, boys. We got something special here. It's not gonna be a honeymoon, but it's gonna be a team because you guys will die for each other." And he was right that year.

— Dave Bergman, recalling Sparky Anderson's
speech on opening night, April 3, 1984, in Minnesota

By 1984, much of the hard work was done. The Tigers were grown up and had some pennant-race experience. They had been tied for first as late as August 12, 1983, and the arduous building process that had begun a decade earlier was about to pay its grand dividend. Sparky had taught the final few courses in big-league finishing school, and was confident that this was now a championship-caliber team. He had the full support of Jim Campbell and had used it to establish his way as the only way. His core stars believed in him and understood what was expected of them as citizens, teammates and professionals. The wild bucks had been broken and reprogrammed, and bought into his vision of how the game should be played.

Jack Morris had been Sparky's ace since he arrived for the third and final time from Evansville on May 9, 1979, five weeks before Sparky was named manager. By 1984, Sparky and Jack had built a powerful alliance.

"Not everybody liked Sparky," Jack recalls, "and there were times when I hated him myself. But I hated him like I'd hate my own brother or dad. The relationship that we had was almost too close for a healthy baseball relationship, the way you see it today. He had an open-door policy with anybody on his team and there were a few of us who took advantage of that—mostly Tram, Gibby, Lance and me. At any time you could speak your mind, and when you went in there you knew you better hold on because you might get it right back in your face."

Morris may have availed himself of Sparky's open-door policy, but for players without Jack's moxie, the "open door" was an entry portal to be avoided.

"I was very intimidated by him," Dan Petry emphasizes, "and shortly after I came up I talked to Roger Craig about it. I never ever wanted to be around Sparky. Never. Because I felt that if I was around him, it meant that something wrong was going on. He wasn't gonna call you in to say, 'Hey, you're doing a good job.' You were expected to do that. He'd say, 'Your reward is your paycheck. I don't need to pat you on the back, you're grown men and get paid good money to do this.' The more I could stay away from Sparky, the better, because that means I'm doing OK."

As a reporter, I wasn't sure if the Tigers players just tolerated Sparky or truly liked him. Years later, I came to realize Jack's point: They fought having to toe the line but otherwise had great regard for the "tough little bastard," whom they learned from, tolerated and ultimately won for. Sparky, like all veteran managers, knew that if the star players are lined up behind you, you are in control. And Sparky knew no other way than to always be in control.

"I can't say enough about what Sparky meant to our team," Morris continues. "There would be other guys who might say, 'All he did was piss us off and we won it despite him.' I didn't see it that way. I knew that he had control. I knew the things he did to motivate us and if that included pissing us off, it's all part of motivation. It's a technique that probably isn't used anymore because of the character of the people playing the game today, but it worked at the time.

"He had the front office's support, and he knew that he could bench a guy or sit a guy out. With the front office knowing that what he did was going to be a temporary thing, he could say to the boys upstairs, 'Trust me, I'm gonna piss this guy off for a few days, but he's gonna come back and he's gonna play hard.' And I'm not sure that works in the baseball world today."

Dave Bergman was an established baseball survivor when he arrived in '84. "Sparky didn't teach me anything about the game of baseball," says Bergman, "but he taught us all how to be men, how

George "Sparky" Anderson lives up to his nickname in getting tossed May 12 vs California.

to respect people, how to respect one another, how to live with guys. We went through the '84 season and everything in the locker room wasn't hugs and kisses. He would tell us that if you got into an argument with your wife you still had to go to work and strap it on and that it was the same with your teammates. He taught us how to be professional athletes. You saw how we looked when we traveled and how we conducted ourselves.

"We had our moments. I remember Gibby going crazy on a bus in Boston one time because the air conditioning wasn't working. But stuff like that wasn't really important. Sparky knew how to handle everything and had total control of the ballclub. And he had a knack of nipping things in the bud quickly. There were personal issues that we had that would never get out of the locker room. He would protect us and we would protect him and that's the true sign of family. He wouldn't allow team meetings without him being present. He'd say, 'I am the captain of this ship and there will be no meetings without me. If you have something to say you come into my office and we will address it. But I will be the emcee of the meetings.' I trusted him."

The man who laid down the irrevocable threat, "My way or the highway," was maybe 5'8", 160 pounds. But the "tough bastard" that Bergman, Morris and others now affectionately refer to had a distinct flip side that was closer to his true nature. Sparky was never wishy-washy with players or people; he knew exactly what he believed in and you had no trouble knowing where he stood.

His philosophy was simple: He knew what was right, he trusted what he saw, and there was no wavering from that. His father, LeRoy, was a house painter in South Dakota who moved his family to Southern California in the early '40s when Sparky was seven or eight. His father taught him to be kind and have respect for people. LeRoy Anderson died at age 76, while the Tigers were putting the finishing touches on their 35-5 start.

Mention LeRoy and Sparky instantly says, "May 17, my father died. He was so marvelous. He had a third-grade education and I've said this many times, he's smarter than any Harvard lawyer I've ever known. He taught me that every man, every mother and every father, wants the same things. They want their children to be healthy, to go to school, to eat good food. Everyone in the world wants that. And then he told me, 'Just remember always, it will never cost you one single dime to be nice. Never a dime. It's the only thing you'll get in your lifetime that is going to be free.'

"Just prior to his passing away, we had gotten off to such a good start and he said, 'Georgie, it looks like you might have something here.' He loved the game so much. Because of what my dad taught me, I always respected people. That didn't mean I didn't get angry or mad at some. But I still always respected 'em. As for ballplayers, I never could accept some of the behavior. Why can't you be a star and be a kind person? Why not? People say [about a star], 'Well, he changed.' No, he didn't change, he was a skunk in his mamma's womb but he didn't have the chance to show you. You can't change. Athletes think that the adulation they get as ballplayers means they don't have to be a good person, and it doesn't."

Tigers General Manager Bill Lajoie worked closely with Sparky for more than a decade. "He was two different guys," Lajoie says. "Say the winter meetings for example. We'd have to go through the lobby and he'd say, 'Bill, I'm gonna walk behind you and don't stop for anything,' because he was kind of shy. And it wasn't because he was ducking autographs. He just wasn't comfortable being 'on' all the time. But then, when it was time for the camera to be on him, he could be another person. He was brilliant with the press, you knew that. The guy could handle the press and handle his team. That's why he was around for so many years."

As for autographs, Sparky gave thousands of them and, best any of us could tell, never griped as so many others have. Petry says that the way Sparky handled his autograph-seekers should have been a lesson to all of the players.

"He was very humble," Petry notes, "and I still to this day follow his example. Somebody would come up to Sparky and ask him for his autograph and he'd sign it and they'd say, 'Thank you,' and then he'd look at them and say, 'No, thank *you*. Thank you for asking for my autograph.' Now, here's a Hall of Fame manager thanking people for approaching him. He was very humble."

When Trammell took over as Tigers manager in 2003 and was asked his philosophy of managing, he continually reiterated, "Sparky taught us how to play the game, how to be professionals."

Sparky distills it into stark, black-and-white terms: "All sports don't have three things—there's no middle ground in sports," he methodically begins. "There's no gray area. There is bad and there is good and there is nothing in the middle. You either teach it right or you let 'em do it wrong. It's very simple and it's a shame when people say, 'Everybody does it (manages) different.'

"No—everybody doesn't do it different. If anybody does it different they're wrong! When you got a man on second base and you got no outs, when you're done hitting he either scores or he's on third. You're getting that ball over to the right side. When you're asked to bunt, you bunt him over. Don't come back and tell me you messed up. I don't have to have you tell me you messed up, I can see it.

"Like I always told 'em: Don't come back and say, 'Oh, I'm sorry,' to a pitcher when you've made an error. Does he come back and say he's sorry when he threw one up in the seats? No, baseball isn't made for 'sorries' and 'my fault.' I don't hear 'my fault' on this club. I know whose fault it is, I'm sitting here with two eyes. If it's your fault then you shouldn't have done it."

Sparky was unfailingly determined to never let success, celebrity or money cloud his view of where he came from and what he was really all about. If he felt himself slipping, he'd catch himself and verbalize his insignificance in the big scope of things. He felt it was imperative that those he cared about or, at the very least, those that he let get near him, wouldn't misunderstand the difference between humble "George" and his public alter ego, the big cheese the world knew as "Sparky."

He viewed the institution of baseball with great reverence. He wouldn't allow himself—for even a moment—to take for granted that he, of so little baseball talent and from such modest roots, could achieve a lofty position in the game that had been his life. The position he attained in baseball was a blessing of immeasurable magnitude and he would never want LeRoy to think that Georgie was taking himself too seriously.

"He would say," Bergman recalls, 'no matter how good any of you become and even if you make it to the Hall of Fame, you will never be bigger than the game.' He would say to us, 'Sparky will never be bigger than the game. The Detroit Tigers will never be bigger than the game. Major League Baseball will never be bigger than the game of baseball.' He put things in perspective in his own infinite wisdom and we would call them 'Sparkyisms.'

"Many times we would hear him talk to the press for twenty minutes and after it was over we'd think, 'What did he just say?' He would keep your attention for twenty minutes and you guys would walk out and be asking each other, 'What did you get out of that?' and spend another fifteen minutes trying to figure out what he was saying and realize there wasn't really anything there. So he just wasted forty minutes of your time and was also protecting us from having to talk to you (the media)."

The man who created "Sparkyisms" had taken years to even get to like the nickname that became his indelible mark. As a 20-year-old Texas League shortstop in the mid-'50s, with no arm and a weak bat, he knew that he had to make up for physical shortcomings with intensity.

In 1955, his third year in the minors, an announcer for his Fort Worth team in the Texas League began describing his arguments with umpires by saying, "Sparks are flying, here comes old Sparky again." It followed him to Montreal in '56 and, natural self-marketer that he was, he decided not to fight his dislike for "Sparky," but rather began to appreciate the value of a distinctive moniker.

Sparky would become a failure as a major-league ballplayer. He struggled six years in the minors in the Dodgers chain. At some point he switched to second base in order to overcome his inability to throw. He was traded to Philadelphia after the '58 season and finally got major-league exposure with the pitiful, last-place '59 Phillies.

As a big-leaguer for the first and last time, he hit .218 in 477 at bats, the only major-league at bats he would ever get. Demoted to Toronto, Sparky played four more years before taking over as manager there in 1964 at age 30. He managed Toronto for five years until '69 when an old pal, Preston Gomez, hired him as a coach for the Padres. Before the '70 season, he cashed in another chip with one of his minor-league cronies, Lefty Phillips, who was managing the Angels.

But before he even got to put on a uniform as Angels coach, opportunity all but knocked down his door. Reds General Manager Bob Howsam had come to appreciate how the demanding little man who could make sparks fly could also get talented players to play to the best of their abilities. Only 24 hours after Phillips had made him an Angels coach, Sparky became manager of the Reds at age 35.

He was replacing Dave Bristol as Reds manager. The '69 Reds had won 89 games and led the NL in runs while finishing four games back of the division-winning Braves. But the Reds felt that Bristol's leadership was lacking. Sure enough, as soon as Sparky showed up in spring training he started running all those future Hall of Famers 'til their tongues drooped. By then, he knew the importance of immediately establishing control and then never allowing players to stray from a strict code of conduct.

"I had them do everything but pick rocks out of the infield," he says. After pushing Pete Rose, Johnny Bench and the boys all that spring of '70, the Reds won 70 of their first 100 games. They went on to win 102 and swept the Pirates in the National League playoffs, only to lose the World Series in five games to Earl Weaver's Orioles.

Sparky knew how to rally his troops, how to build camaraderie and how to control players of all ages and abilities. Part of that stemmed from his fearlessness. Bergman played against him in the National League, and then on his team for nine years in Detroit.

"If I had to say just one thing about Sparky, it would be that he was never afraid of a confrontation with anybody, physically or verbally," Bergman recalls. "And when the benches would clear, he'd be out there with the boys. One of his favorite phrases was, 'We're going to war together.'

"One of the best speeches I ever heard in nineteen years in pro ball was in Minnesota when we started the season there in April (1984). We had an off day after the opener. He came in the locker room, and this is the genius part of Sparky. He said, 'I want you guys to look to your right,' and we did. 'I want you to look to your left,' which we all did. 'I want you gaze across the room. Is there any guy here in this locker room that you wouldn't want to be in a foxhole with?'

"I looked around and said to myself, 'There isn't a guy in this locker room that I wouldn't want to be in a foxhole with.' He said, 'We got a team, boys. We got something special here. It's not gonna be a honeymoon, but it's gonna be a team because you guys will die for each other.' And he was right that year."

Sparky remembers that speech because it was another distillation of his philosophy. "Baseball to me is like a war," he begins the analogy. "I told 'em, 'It's very simple. Nobody in their dugout over there, or their foxhole I call it, can beat us. Here's what happens, gentlemen. In our foxhole we can beat ourselves. Isn't that amazing? They can't beat us, but we can beat ourselves. So when we're in our foxhole, let's fire our heavy artillery into their foxhole.'

"And I said, 'I want no looking back when the thing is over. I don't want nobody disappearing out of this foxhole because we're all here together whether we like it or whether we dislike it, we are together. I can't straighten out all the things people do above this concrete [dugout]. But I promise you this: As long as you're in my foxhole, under my concrete, you'll be protected.'"

When Alan Trammell requested that Sparky visit his first spring training in 2003, Sparky had some doubts about how comfortable he would be. But those doubts were quickly dispelled.

"I was away from managing for seven years," says Sparky, still aglow with the memory, "and I told my wife, 'Honey, I sat down on the bench in Lakeland, Florida, and there it was—it was like a picture. Like I had never left at all. I always believe that if you look at a forest and there's a tree out of place, you better know that the tree's out of place, just by looking. If you can't do those things, I can't teach you. You'll never learn.'"

Trammell, whom Sparky calls "Huckleberry Finn" for the mischievousness that most are unaware of, was one of the "good people" that Sparky always insisted would play for him. "Bad people," those who were insincere and selfish—people you wouldn't want in your foxhole—were quickly weeded out.

"My definition of a good person, my definition is kind of funny," Sparky explains. "For instance, I loved David Wells. I loved Kirk Gibson, I loved Jack Morris. Everybody said, 'Boy, they give you trouble. Boy, they can be jerks.' I said, 'Just a minute. Those people are great individuals. They have, like all of us, the sides about them that you might not like.' There was a lotta sides people didn't like about me.

"People thought I was very arrogant and very cocky. I was! 'Cuz I knew in my heart that I knew everything that I had to know when I walked into that dugout. Nobody was gonna trick me. There was no tricks for me. I knew everything that could happen.

"And that's why to me, a definition of a good person is a person who goes to war. In other words, if I rolled the ball on the clubhouse floor—

and I said it many times—if I roll that ball, Jack Morris is gonna grab it. I don't have to worry. I don't have to worry about where Kirk Gibson is gonna be when the game is on the line. David Wells calls here at my house when they come to Anaheim. And if I'm not here he'll say to my wife, 'I wanna talk to Daddy.'

"People don't understand, a good person is not a person that's an angel. George Sherger, my great, great coach that I had with me at Cincinnati who was also my first manager, I can't even tell you how much I love him. He's eighty-something years old and he always told me this: 'George, whatever you do, don't you round you up a bunch of milk-shake drinkers.'"

But even though Sparky tolerated no "milk-shake drinkers," players who might back off in "war," he was still insistent on respecting others and acting professionally. Sparky's players were always required to wear coats and ties on plane flights when representing the organization.

"People would say to me that I would tell them how to act," Sparky says emphatically. "No. How to act means you know how to treat people. People have a right to be treated with respect. One day on the charter, the stewardesses said, 'Mr. Anderson, we'd just like to tell you this is the very best team we have ever had. They are so nice.' I said, 'Thank you very much, but may I ask you a question? Isn't that the way they're supposed to be?'

"I always told my players this: 'You don't have to like one single person in this room, including me. But, for this club to be a good baseball team, you have to do one thing or it will never work, I promise you. You must learn to tolerate each other and tolerate me and I must tolerate you. Toleration is totally different than liking. You must tolerate people. We are not above anyone. We don't know what that other man is going through in his mind and in his heart. But I know this, we'll tolerate him because he's with us. That's the whole thing. All that matters is that we are dedicated to the same cause.'"

Sparky's Reds lost the World Series to the Orioles in '70, and came in fourth in '71, winning only 79 games, the only time he finished lower than second place during his nine years in Cincinnati. Over the next five years, '72 through '76, his Reds never won fewer than 95 games. He won the National League title in '72, but lost four one-run games to Dick Williams' A's in the '72 Series. However, in the '75 Series he beat the Red Sox in seven, and in the '76 Series, swept the Yanks. But two second-place finishes in '77 and '78 finished him in Cincinnati.

Dick Wagner, the new team president, became impatient. Five division championships, four pennants and two World Series titles in nine years with a substandard pitching staff wasn't enough. On November

28, 1978, Sparky was called to a meeting at a Los Angeles hotel and was fired. The loyalty that he treasured so dearly in those who he loved and worked with had been shattered. Sparky vowed to resurface and restore his reputation. In June 1979, with the Tigers of Les Moss muddling along at 27-26, the call would come from Jim Campbell.

It took Sparky five years to establish himself as a baseball genius in Detroit. Despite all the success he had with the Reds, Tigers fans had a hard time believing in him. They had seen a decade of pretty pathetic baseball under his predecessor, Ralph Houk, who had won three straight pennants and two World Series with the Yankees, but had proven in his Tigers experience that without the players, there really wasn't a whole helluva lot you could do.

Sparky was getting more out of Houk's maturing pups than Houk had, but people still weren't ready to just jump on the Sparky bandwagon. Sparky, like Houk, had been victimized by winning with great players. It was a classic "Catch 22." If you won with Mickey Mantle and Roger Maris you were supposed to. Same with Rose, Bench and Morgan. But if you didn't win, then it must be your fault. Sparky, in the popular view, appeared to be over-managing.

Although for the most part he would manage "by the book," like the righty versus lefty stuff known by any baseball fan, he also pulled pitchers quickly, and that tended to make many of his decisions appear capricious and arbitrary.

By '84, Milt Wilcox had played a total of nine years for Sparky in Cincinnati and Detroit, and that gave him a unique perspective on how the two situations differed.

"We had had some bad teams here and we were rebuilding," Wilcox says. "So Sparky came in and wanted to build the team himself. He didn't get to build the team in Cincinnati, but he got to build this Tigers team, and the first thing he said was, 'My way or the highway,' and a lot of us guys didn't like that at all. Cutting our hair and not allowing facial hair was another thing. He wanted to let it be known who was in control, like, 'This is my team, and if you fucking don't like it, you're outta here.'

"And that's what he did," Wilcox continues. "He got rid of Jason Thompson, Steve Kemp and Ron Leflore, although Leflore for different reasons. Phil Mankowski, Milt May, guys like that didn't fit what Sparky thought they should be. Not that they weren't good ballplayers. But if you're left-handed and you play in Detroit, you better be a pull hitter and take advantage of the right-field fence.

"Kemp and Thompson hit as many homers to left as right. But Sparky thinks certain players should do certain things. One of the first things he did was try to make Alan Trammell become an opposite-field hitter. But Alan has always been a pull hitter. He wasn't a home run hitter, and Sparky wanted him to hit the ball the opposite way. It took him time to get over some of this stuff and we went through some growing pains with Sparky."

As for the "hair" thing, Sparky scoffs at the accepted notion that his dictates regarding long hair and facial hair revealed a conservative side to his personality or were based on his need to control his players.

"In Cincinnati, we were number one, the Reds, the kings," he says with a chuckle. "Now in Oakland, Finley pays 'em $300 each to grow mustaches. So the guys came and asked, 'Skip, can we grow mustaches and get with the fashion?' We had a meeting and just so we were on level ground with this, I said, 'We are the number one team in America. If we would've started the mustaches, we'd wear 'em. But we ain't taking a back seat to nobody!' And that's all it was. I had not a thing against mustaches, but we weren't going to be number two."

Parrish had spent four years in the minors, longer than some of the others, remembering, "When I first came up, they made some trades where I just shook my head like, wow. Jason Thompson, Kemper to Chicago for Lemon. I thought, 'Here's some guys, some of our better hitters, and geez they traded Jason and Kemp? It's like nobody's safe around here.'"

"When Sparky came over," Lance recalls, "I was upset because they got rid of Les Moss. I didn't care who Sparky was. I liked Les. Les was my manager in Double A and Triple A and if it wasn't for Les, I probably wouldn't have made it to the major leagues because he worked so diligently with me in the minors. After a while it became evident that Sparky had quite a bit of pull as far as players coming and going, especially going, because he made it very clear to everybody that he wouldn't put up with certain things."

The players Wilcox mentioned, with the possible exceptions of Kemp and Thompson, never did much anywhere else after leaving Detroit. But Kemp and Thompson had been popular here, and people took note of that. Sparky had also ridden into town and gotten Les Moss fired. As Parrish said, Moss had paid his dues and many fans were also skeptical of the need to abruptly fire such a loyal man.

So be it. After a chance meeting with Sparky, Campbell's quick decision to jettison Moss proved to be one of Campbell's best moves ever. Moss wasn't skillful in dealing with the media and was essentially boring and colorless. Mix those characteristics with a team that still wasn't ready to win, and it's understandable why Campbell couldn't resist making the dramatic change.

Letters to the sports pages in Sparky's early years in Detroit often referred to Sparky as a con man. Besides his "lack of loyalty" to

Steve Kemp, a fine player who didn't fit into Sparky's plan.

players like Kemp and Thompson, fans also processed some of the colorful quotes he gave the media as disingenuous rather than the "good copy" that the reporters so enjoyed getting from him. In the spring of '84, Sparky joked about Tigers fans' outright contempt, saying, "Last year I'd stick my hat out of the dugout and wave it. If there weren't any bullet holes in it, I knew it was safe to go out to the mound."

At his opening news conference in '79, Sparky promised a championship in five years. Well, here it was five years later, and damn if the little con man wasn't delivering in a powerful manner. Maybe he wasn't merely a passenger back in his heyday, just riding the Big Red Machine. Was there something to be said for his ability to deal firmly with players and demand a professional attitude? Had all the doublespeak simply masked a solid talent evaluator and motivational master? Maybe the reckless quote machine was all part of his managerial genius?

As for his five-year prediction, Sparky would later reveal that Campbell had presented him a five-year contract so he simply predicted a championship in five years. Seemed to make sense to him at the time. He knew he was good, but when he hit the jackpot in '84, he also knew how lucky he really was. The five-year prediction had been no more than a sound bite based on a shot in the dark.

It was around 1984, when the media attention was growing exponentially and Sparky was again the hottest manager in the sport, that he felt it was important to drive home the conceptual difference between his given name, "George," and his baseball name, "Sparky."

"George" was the man with the lower-class upbringing who met his wife, Carol, in the fifth grade and had been deeply devoted to her ever since. "George" was the man who, during the season, shared their condo with his bench coach and boyhood baseball buddy, Billy Consolo. "Sparky," contrastingly, was the well-honed baseball and media act, and it was important that he knew that you knew that this "Sparky" role, in some ways, defied his true self.

Sparky also knew that we knew he was as dumb as a fox. I always suspected that's why he clung to those laughable double negatives. He probably could have cleaned up the grammar, but why bother? It was part of the "wink-and-nod" Sparky act. It provided a homespun style that he used to great advantage. Sprinkled within the "ain't nobody nevers," he would drop genuine pearls of wisdom about life and baseball. This way, he could be smart and savvy without sounding pompous, something that the pride he felt in his working-class roots would not allow him to do.

It partly explains how he was such a master in dealing with the media. His only other Detroit coaching contemporary even remotely in his class was Pistons Head Coach Chuck Daly. Like Chuck, Sparky also knew exactly what the media was looking for. And he would give you all you needed and usually more, in exchange for your vigilance in protecting his image and position.

Sparky never openly said, "Don't burn me," because he didn't need to. Reporters already knew that the payoff for watching his back was so good. Merely pointing the microphone at him guaranteed two days of good material, so a reporter would have to be crazy not to spare him undue criticism and cheap shots.

The media's unwritten pact with Sparky allowed us to poke fun at the absurdity of some of the things he said, but never to question his worth as a manager. And nobody ever really went after him. After all, when he was capable of making it so good for us, we were also justifiably fearful of having it pulled away. Except for occasionally questioning a strategical decision, no one messed with him on a regular basis.

Al Ackerman at Channel 4, who developed a close relationship with him, affectionately called him "Fifth-place Sparky." From '74 to '82, the Tigers never finished higher than fourth overall. During Sparky's first four years, '79–'82, the Tigers finished fifth, fifth, fourth and fourth, even though they were over .500 every season.

In '83, the Tigers finished second behind Baltimore, and people should have somewhat anticipated what was to occur in '84, but Tigers fans had been disappointed too many times and weren't yet ready to believe. Don't forget, Sparky was the guy who had called Gibson "the next Mickey Mantle," and going into '84, Gibson had played well in only the strike-shortened 1981 season.

Enjoying a moment with the master of dealing with the media.

Here's one example, among dozens, of why people thought Sparky was the ultimate bullshitter: In June '84, Sparky sent veteran spot-starter Glenn Abbott to Evansville and called up a 23-year-old rookie pitcher named Carl Willis.

After a decent relief outing or two, Sparky offered to a group of writers around him, "Carl Willis will become the next Rollie Fingers." Seven weeks later, Willis was traded to the Reds and never heard from again; Fingers would make the Hall of Fame. But on a slow night in June, Sparky had come through for the media and, best I can recall, no one dared bring up later what a crock that had been.

Another rap on Sparky was that he didn't do well with young players. Houk had been the shepherd for the future championship core that the Tigers began developing in the mid to late '70s. It was Houk who provided the guiding hand for Parrish, Trammell, Lou Whitaker, Dave Rozema, Tom Brookens, Petry and Morris.

Wilcox was just 20 when he made the '70 Reds, and played for Sparky in '70 and '71 before being traded to Cleveland for outfielder Ted Uhlaender, who was 10 years older than Milt, prior to the '72 season. "I was a young ballplayer of his," Wilcox remembers. "Sparky never really developed any good young ballplayers. Bobby Tolan was young [and Sparky admitted in later years that he had mishandled him]. Don Gullet, he worked well with Gullet. But Howard Johnson over here in Detroit, he never really helped develop Howard and guys like him.

"That's one of the downfalls of Sparky. He wanted the veterans. He knew that veteran players knew how to handle themselves. When Cincinnati went through the rebuilding stage later in his time there, he didn't get along well with young players."

Sparky disputes that vehemently. In the spring of 1970, his first year with the Reds, he replaced 15 nonperforming Reds veterans and stocked the team with young players like Dave Concepcion, Hal McRae and, yes, 20-year-old Milt Wilcox!

Fourteen years later, it was a different situation. Sparky surrounded the veteran core the Tigers had in '84 with more veterans: Darrell Evans, Larry Herndon, Dave Bergman and Willie Hernandez. Ruppert Jones came in June. Even Rusty Kuntz was 29 and well-traveled. When parts of the Tigers core started dissipating, and the farm system didn't provide talented replacements, the team began slipping into a long hibernation that would extend into the 21st century.

By 1990, Morris couldn't take any more. "The year Sparky took a sabbatical, '89," Jack soberly reflects, "I could talk about that forever but I don't think it's important for anybody else to know what Sparky and I know about that year. But the bottom line is, I recognized that he wasn't doing that. [Morris is referring to what he said earlier about knowing just when to pat players on the back or kick them in the ass.] I confronted him about that and he didn't have anything to say, almost like he was in his own little world at the time.

"I knew there were outside things happening, his family situations that he had to deal with, and he had to get away. But the way I saw it, was that the (control) and character he had for so many years, our winning years, had sort of vanished. He was getting the kind of players who absolutely infuriated some of us. In earlier years he was able to think that Gibby and Jack and Lance and Tram and Lou would carry the team no matter what. But he got some players who were absolutely pathetic, and that's all there is to it."

In '89, just two years removed from a division title, the Tigers lost 103 games. The losses, coupled with family problems that suddenly cropped up, affected Sparky deeply. He didn't cope well, and Tigers physician Clarence Livingood ordered him home to California for a few weeks of rest. On sabbatical, Sparky decided that he needed to separate his ego from the results. He returned after getting treatment, and for the rest of his career was able to cope with losing in a healthier manner.

Beneath the signature white mane and the endearing double negatives, beneath the ruddy, sun-creased skin, and beneath the show biz bluster, lived an utterly self-effacing man who determinedly held on to a deep appreciation of what life had given him.

Sparky had a sign in his office that read, "Every 24 hours the world turns over on somebody who was on top." He knew that his time would be coming. It came in 1995, yet his demise as Tigers manager ironically remains the greatest testament to his character and convictions.

The owners had threatened to use replacement players, scab workers, in the event of a '95 player strike. Sparky was the only manager in baseball who took a stand against it, refusing to fall in line. He publicly declared that utilizing players of less than major-league quality was reprehensible and an affront to the game he so deeply respected, and that he would not manage them under any circumstance.

The labor issue was settled about a month into the season, and replacements were never used, but his relationship with Tigers ownership was fractured beyond repair. By mutual decision with Mike Ilitch, he resigned after the '95 season, and when he went into the Hall of Fame five years later, he entered as a Cincinnati Red. True to his principles, Sparky has never spoken badly of the Detroit organization. But he has no statue at Comerica Park, and his number 11, the number worn by the winningest manager in Tigers history, has yet be retired by the team.

Chapter 10

Country Boy

We were all young and there were lots of good things going on in the music world and we were stuck listening to the organ at Tiger Stadium…I said so many times to people, it would be so awesome if they would put a new sound system in here and play some current music. These people would go crazy…But it was just the same old organ, and Campbell could care less. I thought, "This guy is unbelievable."

— Lance Parrish on Tiger Stadium's unbelievably
bad public address system

A round the middle of May, with the Tigers beating everybody and leaving fast-start records in their wake, *Detroit Free Press* columnist Mike Downey wrote a tongue-in-cheek column complaining that with the Tigers playing so incredibly well, there was nothing to complain about. He could uncover no controversy whatsoever, and it was frustrating him. So Downey started a controversy and struck a chord at the same time—that he was sick and tired of hearing John Denver's "Thank God I'm a Country Boy," which blared at mid-game as the grounds crew raked the infield.

Grounds crew member Herbie Redmond, whose broom position was in the middle of the sweeping crew, had at least managed to popularize an otherwise innocuous nightly ritual by dancing, gyrating and waving his cap to a growing legion of adoring fans. While the other five crew members walked in step with their brooms neatly trailing behind, Herbie would create dance steps and play to the crowd. Herbie gave "Country Boy" some life, but after five years of repeated play, night in and night out, Downey was saying, "Enough already!"

"Country Boy" grated on Downey, so he claimed, because Denver had revealed himself to be a serious Orioles fan, which added fuel to the song's sudden "controversial" presence. Downey revealed three problems with the song. He wrote: "It's a hick tune in a hip town; it's sung by an acknowledged Orioles fan; it even turns the stomachs of the players, including the ones with big stomachs."

To many of the players, an "unhip" song like "Thank God I'm a Country Boy" also paralleled Tiger Stadium's antiquated sound system, and the boring and old-fashioned song selection condoned by team President and CEO Jim Campbell.

This was all part of the "generation gap"—more like a chasm—that separated an authority figure like Campbell from baby-boomer players, fans and other assorted modern-day realities. In '84, Campbell had several times reinforced his reputation as a killjoy by cutting off beer sales in the seventh inning and by ripping bleachers fans for foul language and for tossing beach balls on the field. And, of course, Campbell was responsible for insisting on playing embarrassingly old-fashioned organ music over the public address system. So, it was no surprise that Campbell scoffed when Downey, soon to be backed by avid fan support, called for the elimination of "Country Boy."

"I'm a baseball man, not a stage-show manager," was Campbell's flippant, but revealing quote. He had at first tried to stonewall the flap, but the media wasn't going to let this one slip away. On May 20, with the team surging toward 35-5 and with fans flocking to the ballpark like never before, the *Free Press* initiated a phone poll to read the pulse of Tigers fans on this issue.

Now under some pressure, Campbell instructed WJR-AM radio icon J.P. McCarthy to field requests from his listeners with one proviso. Campbell said, "I'll change the tune. As long as it isn't rock 'n' roll." In other words, he was saying that he didn't really care what Tigers fans wanted; it was his role to repress any attempt to modernize the presentation of Tigers baseball or—perish the thought—to actually cater to Tigers fans' desires. This may have been the 1980s, 30 years into the rock 'n' roll era, but there would be none of that head-banging garbage in his ballpark.

That was Jim Campbell—an old baseball man who acted as if pop culture had made no worthwhile innovations since the '40s, and to recognize that there had been would constitute an affront to decent people everywhere. He would preserve the purity of baseball, and it was of no consequence to him that rock 'n' roll just so happened to be the most listened-to radio format.

Campbell's belated concession was also laughable, and revealed a critical blind spot in an otherwise warm and understanding man. On May 23, the *Free Press* revealed that 2,200 readers had called in, and 66 percent wanted "Country Boy" out.

"In the late seventies," Milt Wilcox recalls, "they used to play a song, 'Doggy in the Window.' They had an organist and they'd play songs like these and we'd be in the outfield before the game and we're almost going to sleep. We'd go into Anaheim, Texas and Boston and they're playing the music that was hip at that time and you'd get a better feeling. We'd play the stuff that we liked in our clubhouse, but then you'd go out on the field and hear 'Doggy in the Window.' Crazy. Oh yeah, and 'Thank God I'm a Country Boy,' also."

At the same time, the rampaging Tigers had gotten some creative juices flowing. In May, radio play-by-play legend Ernie Harwell and local songwriter Dan Yessian wrote a song called "Tiger, Tiger" that went:

(Chorus)
Tiger, Tiger baseball team, reaching for that pennant dream
Tiger, Tiger baseball team, reaching for that pennant dream
C'mon Tigers, Detroit Tigers, my baseball team.
(1st verse)
Soon we'll hear the cheers or boos,
Telling us if they win or lose.
Know for certain when they score,
We're gonna hear those Tigers roar.
(Chorus)
(2nd verse)
They got tradition on their side,
Fantastic fans and home town pride,
Greenberg, Cobb and Kaline too,
Tiger heroes who come through.
(Chorus)

Harwell had also written "Maestro of the Mound" in '68 to honor former star pitcher Denny McLain. The line, "Denny McLain, Denny McLain, there's never been any like Denny McLain," had remained in Tigers lore.

There was also a suggestion to bring back the '68 ditty, "We're all behind our baseball team, Go Get 'em Tigers!"

At the same time, the popular "Morning Crew" on FM radio's WRIF, which featured George Baier as a "Dick the Bruiser" character, had written a Tigers tribute song, "Every Swing You Take," as a takeoff on "Every Move You Make," by the rock group The Police.

Tom Monaghan, who was taking a look-and-see approach in his first year as owner, quickly backpedaled away from the music flap. He said he didn't want the responsibility of replacing the song. He begged off by saying, "I'd pick something by Bing Crosby, and the whole team might rebel." Mayor Coleman Young put in a bid for Sammy Davis's "Hello Detroit."

John Denver, who was watching the Orioles play in California while on tour, heard about the controversy and said, "If they don't like the fact that I'm an Orioles fan, then the deciding factor on a new song should be what the players want."

The Orioles had been using "Country Boy" during their seventh-inning stretch for the past nine years, ever since the song's composer,

John Martin Sommers, an avowed Orioles fan, had introduced the team to John Denver after a Baltimore-area concert. Denver had also sung the national anthem before the first World Series game in '83 while wearing an Orioles jacket, and then sang "Country Boy" live in the seventh inning. Ugh. Denver was due at Pine Knob, an outdoor concert venue, in early June and said he would have something special for Detroiters when he sang "Country Boy."

For several years, Jack Morris had been sniping at Campbell for refusing to upgrade Tiger Stadium's antiquated sound equipment, as well as his embarrassingly bad music menu. Parrish shakes his head when he recalls his frustration.

"There were so many comments made about our sound system, or lack of," he says. "We were all young and there were lots of good things going on in the music world and we were stuck listening to the organ at Tiger Stadium. We'd go around the American League and hear such good stuff in other stadiums. I said so many times to people, it would be so awesome if they would put a new sound system in here and play some current music. These people would go crazy.

Tigers fans enjoying the Wave, which debuted in '84.

"Our fans were vocal and got into the game so much that I knew this would be a great addition to this stadium. They'd be that much more entertained and fired up during the break times in games," Parrish continues. "But it was just the same old organ, and Campbell could care less. I thought, 'This guy is unbelievable.'" Morris bitched constantly but Campbell refused to budge. "He was either too cheap to invest or was actually satisfied with what he had. Or both. He still played organ music, laughable as that was in the modern age."

Campbell correctly knew that there were much more serious problems with fans. Back in June 1980, he had closed the bleachers for the duration of a home stand, an emphatic statement that he would not tolerate rowdiness. Now, 1984 brought him a new set of problems. Sparky was really bothered by the "Wave," which had debuted at Michigan Stadium in '83 and Sparky felt was childish.

By mid-May, Tigers fans had gotten very loud and creative with it. When Michigan quarterback Steve Smith had trouble having his signals heard against Iowa, coach Bo Schembechler had turned to the crowd and shook his fist to make them stop. They did. Bo had threatened to play games without fans if it persisted. Michigan fans then went to the silent Wave and whispered a collective "Shhhh" while doing it. All of these Wave variations were practiced and enjoyed by the hundreds of thousands of fans pouring into Tiger Stadium.

Knocking beach balls around the bleachers had also become a real bother, as many of the balls would reach the field and interrupt play. The excitement of winning had also induced more beer drinking, and rowdiness was again becoming a legitimate stadium issue.

While the "Country Boy" controversy was picking up steam, the Tigers were out west, completing the 35-5 start and set to return for a seven-game home stand against chief AL East rivals Toronto and Baltimore. They were 37-9, but had achieved most of it against the decidedly weaker AL West, commonly referred to back then as the "AL Worst."

Crowds of 40,000-plus were expected for the Tigers' June return, and management was concerned about crowd control. There was talk of raising the bleacher fence from 6 feet to 12 or 14 feet to contain the beach balls. To solve this and other potential problems, Campbell pulled an old card from his deck: He would reduce portable beer stands by 50 percent, and the number of spigots at the concession stands would come down 10 percent. Bill Haase, Tigers executive VP, said, "Hopefully, we will give the fans a fair shot at policing themselves, helping them help themselves."

Obviously, this policy would also prevent well-behaved fans from getting a beer, but perfect solutions to the rowdiness and ugly behavior weren't easily found. Fans who tried to self-police the rowdies

Tigers fans adored dancing Herbie Redmond, who made sweeping the infield entertaining.

faced retribution, and Haase argued that additional ushers and security personnel sometimes caused the rowdies to test the enforcers more than they otherwise would. There was even talk from the league office about threatening the Tigers with a forfeit if the beach balls caused too many delays.

The Tigers' return home was much anticipated: June featured fourteen straight games against the Jays and Orioles, seven at home, then seven on the road, soon to be followed by six games with the Yankees. To help, the Detroit newspapers provided viewing guides for the initial home stand, three vs. Baltimore and four vs. Toronto, which trailed by only 5½ games despite the Tigers' staggeringly successful start.

PASS had Friday's broadcast, and there was that option. PASS, (Pro and Amateur Sports Systems), a cable TV entity in its first year of existence, offered very few programming choices and had yet to attract a subscriber base of more than a few thousand homes. PASS was also expensive, costing about $12 a month. Some area bars offered it, but it wasn't a viable option for the majority of Tigers fans.

NBC was back for Saturday's game, the Tigers' third national telecast of the year. Channel 4, which also aired the *Game of the Week,* would have Sunday's game.

When the Jays came in Monday, ABC was bringing Howard Cosell and crew to air it on *Monday Night Baseball.* Tuesday, Wednesday and Thursday were all on PASS, and this was a big problem for home viewers and a big bonanza for PASS. PASS had set a goal of 20,000 statewide subscribers by season's end and would get some help reaching it with this series.

But the best thing was simply to be there, and nearly a quarter-million Michiganders would choose that option. After a slow start, the Orioles were 28-21, in third place, on a five-game winning streak, and 10½ games behind Detroit. Had the Orioles been playing in the AL West, they'd be leading by three. If the Tigers were out west, they'd be up by a whopping 13½.

Sparky still had some concerns. Larry Herndon was hitting .242, Tom Brookens .154, and Milt Wilcox, Juan Berenguer and Dan Petry had been erratic the past few weeks.

Chapter 11

June: Big Crowds, Double-Digit Leads

Some of this insanity is out of control.

— Dan Petry, June 5, 1984

The fairy tale continues. I'm the happiest person in the world.

— Rusty Kuntz, on June 19, after his two-run
single in the eighth off Ron Guidry beat the
Yankees 7-6

June 1 was an amazing night. A crowd of 47,252 came to the ballpark and saw the Tigers slam the Orioles, 14-2. The Tigers led, 9-0, after three innings. In a six-run second off Scott McGregor, Kirk Gibson got hit by a pitch with the bases loaded and looked menacingly at McGregor; Rusty Kuntz had a two-run single and Alan Trammell a two-run homer. Chet Lemon hit a three-run homer in the third off reliever Bill Swaggerty. Petry pitched six scoreless innings and Doug Bair cleaned up.

Meanwhile, the press box was jammed. There were some 50 national media members in town to cover the hottest team in memory—about 49 more than usual. There were curious correspondents from New York to Philadelphia, from *Sports Illustrated* to *Time* to *Newsweek.* Larry Guest of the *Orlando Sentinel* wrote, "Captain Whitehead says his Tigers have had more media exposure in two months than his Cincinnati 'Big Red Machine' of the '70s received in a whole season."

"It doesn't bother me, but I don't play," Sparky said. "When you've got to give interviews for an hour and a half before a game, it's tough for a player to keep his concentration."

Mark Whicker of the *Philadelphia Daily News* wrote: "The Tigers creamed Baltimore...47,402 fans endlessly performed 'The

JUNE 1984

June Record: 18-12

Stars:

Hernandez:	15 APP. 7 SV, 2-0, 30 IP, 1.50 ERA
Brookens:	.366, 15-41
Whitaker:	.314, 32-102
Rozema:	3-0, 2.89 ERA

Key Games:

June 04: Johnson and Bergman hit 3-run HRs to beat Toronto 6-3 in 10
June 10: Petry shuts out Orioles 8-0 as Tigers sweep DH
June 11: Whitaker's 2-run homer beats Toronto 5-4 for Rozema
June 20: Johnson's 3-run HR in 13th beats Yankees 9-6
June 26: Parrish's 2-run HR in 10th beats Yankees 9-7

Wave.'...then the right field bleachers would yell, 'Tastes Great,' and the left field bleachers would reply, 'Less Filling'...Said Baltimore pitching coach Ray Miller, 'I don't know about the Tigers, but these damn fans may collapse from exhaustion.'"

Unbeknownst to the media and fans, Campbell had replaced "Country Boy" with an end-run that would get stopped for a big loss. He still so clearly didn't get it, that it made his attempt to appease the fans look lamer than ever. He had conspired with WJR to choose "Tiger Rag," a song written in 1917. "Tiger Rag," with the chorus, "Hold that Tiger, hold that Tiger," had been popular when Woodrow Wilson was president and Hall of Famer Ty Cobb was tearing up shortstops with his sharpened spikes.

Chet Lemon is greeted at home after his three-run third-inning HR puts the Tigers up 9-0 before more than 47,000 fans on June 1.

The result was predictable: Many booed the song, many held their thumbs down, and many couldn't hear it because the sound system still stank. Even Herbie Redmond, despite being fearful of angering his bosses, said, "I can't get into it. I don't like that music."

Morris, never missing a chance to tweak Campbell, said, "With the speaker system here, it doesn't matter what they play. The system in Baltimore is so superior that even John Denver sounds good there."

WJR had sponsored a pep rally at Hart Plaza Friday afternoon, and 2,500 people showed up. They played "Tiger Rag," and Herbie attempted, somewhat unsuccessfully, to dance to it. They also introduced the Martha Reeves rendition of her classic, now renamed:

"Dancin' in the Seats."

...All we need is Lou, sweet, sweet Lou
And Grubb and Berenguer.
There'll be Lemon, Herndon, Gibson and Bergman,
Dancin' in the seats.

I had a dilemma that Friday night, June 1, that prevented me from appearing in public. Al Ackerman, our sports director at WDIV, was furious with the station's management because he had been told that I would be replacing him on the 11 o'clock news. Al had been on at 6 and 11 since the 1960s at both Channel 7 and twice at Channel 4. He had come back to WDIV five years earlier with a campaign called "Old irascible Al is back."

Now old irascible Al was angry about being demoted, and he wasn't taking kindly to having his stripes torn off. He had coined "Bless You Boys," which he had worked hard to make into an '84

Tigers rallying cry. I didn't blame him. Nobody likes it when people in charge run roughshod over your career. What I did blame him for was getting me caught in the crossfire at Channel 4.

Our third man, Jim Berk, was on vacation. In those days, I had a lot going on with two morning radio shows as well as being Al's street reporter and anchoring the 5:30 p.m. news. Our sports producer, Tim Larson, had tipped me off that Al was going to call in sick after the 6 o'clock news with knee problems. He would later win a $500,000 settlement with a local hospital for a botched operation, so he really did have knee problems. He also had knee problems when they were convenient, and this would be one of those nights.

I wasn't going to get caught between the station and an unhappy coworker. This was the pre-cell-phone era, and I bolted after the early news and laid low, refusing to answer my phone as the station called frantically.

On one of the biggest local sports nights of the year, the leading news station and Tigers rights-holder had no sportscaster for its 11 o'clock broadcast. Mort Crim—a great guy and a great anchor who was also virtually a sports illiterate—struggled unsuccessfully through the game highlights. Joe Lapointe followed the story in the *Free Press* on Saturday morning.

The next two days didn't go well for the Tigers. A throng of 40,292 saw 22-year-old Storm Davis beat Morris, 5-0, on a three-hitter. All five runs came early, including two-run homers by Ken Singleton in

Ackerman skips TV

Al Ackerman was missing from the WDIV newscast Friday night when the Tigers played Baltimore.

News producer Tim Larson said that Ackerman had injured his knee and "his doctor advised him not to come to work." Larson said that Channel 4 didn't have a substitute because "Jim Berk is on vacation and Eli (Zaret) couldn't be reached."

Asked whether Ackerman was angry over speculation that Zaret would replace him on the prestigious 11 p.m. sports anchor spot, assistant news director Mark Effron said: "It's not a valid question. It's a question I couldn't answer."

Channel 4 was told in the late afternoon that Ackerman wouldn't be at work Friday night, Effron said.

Anchorman Mort Crim said after the newscast late Friday night, "I know he (Ackerman) has had some back problems."

Asked why he didn't mention the absence of Ackerman on the air, Crim said it "was not scripted."

Isn't that unusual? "It strikes me that way," Crim said.

—Joe Lapointe

Al Ackerman

Al Michaels, Howard Cosell and Earl Weaver.

the second and Wayne Gross in the third. Jack fell to 10-2, and spoke at length afterwards. "I stunk. We stunk. We lost." Jack had a knack for getting his point across with great economy.

On Sunday, Mike Flanagan beat Wilcox, 2-1, on a seven-hitter. The Tigers went a total of 15 innings over two games without a run until Brookens homered to right in the seventh. Overall, they had lost six of nine since the 35-5 start.

GAMES 50, 51, 52 & 53 vs TORONTO—Toronto was only 4½ back and was coming to town for four games starting the next night. It would be Howard Cosell, Al Michaels and Earl Weaver for the nationally televised Monday night game on ABC, and it would provide one of the most exciting events of 1984.

◆ *Game 50: 13 Pitches*

GAME #50   June 4

Tigers 6, Jays 3

TORONTO	AB	R	H	BI	DETROIT	AB	R	H	BI
Garcia 2b	5	0	2	0	Whitaker 2b	4	0	2	0
Collins lf	5	0	1	0	Trammell ss	5	0	1	0
Moseby cf	5	0	1	0	Gibson rf	3	0	0	0
Upshaw 1b	5	2	2	1	Herndon ph-lf	1	0	0	0
Aikens dh	3	0	0	0	Parrish c	4	1	2	0
Johnson ph	2	0	0	0	Evans dh	3	0	0	0
Bell rf	3	1	2	2	Grubb lf	4	0	1	0
Mulliniks 3b	2	0	1	0	Kuntz pr-lf-rf	1	0	0	0
Barfield ph	1	0	0	0	Lemon cf	3	2	0	0
Iorg 3b	0	0	0	0	Bergman 1b	4	2	2	3
Whitt c	2	0	0	0	Johnson 3b	3	1	1	3
Fernandez ph	1	0	0	0	Brookens 3b	0	0	0	0
Martinez c	0	0	0	0					
Griffin ss	4	0	1	0					
Totals	**38**	**3**	**10**	**3**		**35**	**6**	**9**	**6**

Toronto---------------- 010 002 000 0 -- 3
Detroit----------------- 000 000 300 3 -- 6
2 outs when winning run was scored.

Game winning RBI -- none, DP -- Toronto 2, Detroit 1, LOB -- Toronto 8, Detroit 9, 2B -- Whitaker, Parrish, Garcia, Moseby, HR -- Upshaw, Bell, Johnson, Bergman, SB -- Bell, Whitaker, CS -- Collins, Griffin, SH -- Brookens, Evans, HBP -- by Stieb (Parrish), by Stieb (Lemon), PB -- Whitt, Parrish

Toronto	IP	H	R	ER	BB	SO
Stieb	6.2	6	3	3	2	3
Lamp	2.0	1	0	0	2	1
Key (L)	0.2	1	1	1	0	0
Jackson	0.1	1	2	2	1	0
Detroit						
Berenguer	6.2	8	3	3	2	7
Hernandez	3.0	2	0	0	1	3
Lopez (W)	0.1	0	0	0	0	0

T -- 3:30 A -- 26,733

Where:	Tiger Stadium
Result:	6-3 Tigers in 10 innings
Record:	39-11
WP:	Lopez, 5-0
LP:	Key, 2-3
Standing:	First, 5½ ahead
Attendance:	26,733

Dave Bergman remembers:

Even though we had the greatest start in baseball history, if you remember, it was just a week or so later and we still weren't really shaking Toronto. What was the lead, maybe four or five games? But when it was really time to strap it on and go to war, we knew how to do it.

That game in early June, with Howard Cosell and the national television guys in for Monday Night Baseball, is the game that's made me so well received in Michigan. Fans don't remember the ground balls I've booted or the times I struck out with the bases loaded. But that game, where I had the 13-pitch at bat and fouled off seven pitches from Roy Lee Jackson, all with two strikes, proves again that it's better to be lucky than good. I had a blue-collar, lunch-bucket kind of career, but that at bat has lived with me ever since.

The seventh inning was the real key that night, and [Toronto pitcher] Dave Stieb had a 3-0 lead on us when we came up in the bottom half. Our ballclub was so strong that our order that night had John Grubb hitting sixth, Chet Lemon seventh, me eighth and Howard Johnson ninth. Stieb

plunked Lemon, who was on first with one out in the seventh. Stieb was the toughest right-hander we faced back then, but we also knew he'd have brain farts during the game. If he threw his slider and fastball all game, he was unhittable, but he always tried to embarrass you by tricking you with a changeup.

He had made me look foolish earlier in the game, but in the seventh, I sat on the changeup and I managed to single to right. I figured, I can't hit his fastball and slider, and if he had thrown three fastballs, I was gone. With Chet and me on, Howard Johnson was up next. Hojo hit a bomb that was just foul, and then Stieb got one over the plate and HoJo hit a three-run homer off the foul pole. That was the key hit of the game to tie it at three after seven.

The Tigers battled often with Jay's ace righty Dave Stieb.

I can't remember exactly when it happened, but I pulled a groin late in the game and I told Pio DiSalvo, our fabulous trainer, that he had to do something because I'm not coming out of this game. Pio had a military background and was a great ad-libber in solving problems. It was probably about the eighth inning that he took me back in the clubhouse and wrapped me up. He was all over the place, going around and lifting up and then brought it around my waist and I was fine for the rest of the game. So if Pio's not the trainer, I may be out of that game before I could deliver the biggest hit of my career.

In the tenth, Lance singled to right off reliever Jimmy Key, and Darrell sacrificed him to second. That brought in Roy Lee Jackson, their ace reliever, and he got Rusty to bounce back to him for the second out. Roy Lee walked Chet to set up the force and make it first and second, two out, and I just said to myself, go up there and slash and have a good time.

Little did I know.

He gave me some real good pitches to hit out of the ballpark and I only fouled 'em off, but my forte as a hitter is that if you throw me a slider down and in, you better get it in because I can golf it out of the ballpark. I got a break because there was a pitch at one and two—an outside fastball—that truly was outside. And in my career I was rung up on pitches much more outside than that one, but [umpire] Terry Cooney spared me that time. On the thirteenth pitch, Roy Lee threw me a slider way low and in, that I golfed out for the 6-3 win.

Bergman hits his dramatic game-winning "golf shot" homer off Jackson, providing one of the most memorable moments of 1984.

The next day, [Jays manager] Bobby Cox, who had been my minor-league manager, was throwing batting practice for his team. I was talking with guys near the cage and, as a sign of recognition that I'd got him the night before, he threw one at my back. Then he smiled and said, "Nice job last night."

Several postgame comments that night stand out. Brookens, the number nine hitter, who was due up after Bergman and batting .159, joked, "You knew they were going after him hard when they saw me on deck." It was a good one-liner by Brookens, but with two outs, why didn't Cox walk Bergman to set up a righty-righty matchup with Roy Lee Jackson and Brookens?

Pitching coach Roger Craig commented on the classic Bergman-Jackson at bat, "That's as good a job as I've ever seen of any pitcher battling any batter."

Although Bergman didn't mention it in his recollection, it was his first Tigers homer. Of his seven that year, he also hit a three-run shot off Ron Musselman in another big win in early September when the Tigers went to Toronto and would sweep the Jays to wrap up the pennant race.

The next two days went poorly. More than 74,000 fans came to the stadium to see the Jays narrow the lead to 3½ with an 8-4 win on Tuesday, June 5, followed by a 6-3 win on Wednesday.

In the latter, Petry was roughed up in a loss to Luis Leal, and Bergman's dramatic homer just two nights earlier had already faded from view. Tigers beat writer Bill McGraw wrote in the *Free Press,* "The party might be over for Sparky and our gang. It seems like a lifetime ago when the Tigers were national news with the 35-5 start." A lifetime, or a 4-8 record in the 12 games that followed the 35-5.

Still, 39-13 was looking amply superhuman; it's just that those determined Jays had 36 wins and had also won 18 of their last 23.

Fortunately, Morris beat Jim Clancey, 5-3, before 40,879 on a muggy Thursday night to end the four-game set on a positive note. Jack went to 11-2 with his eighth complete game of the year, and Ruppert Jones—up from Evansville in place of Rod Allen—hit a three-run homer off Clancy in the sixth to break a 1-1 tie.

The Tigers locker room was virtually incapable of handling postgame scenes like the one that night. It was ludicrous, really. Even under nonpennant-race conditions, with no national media covering the Tigers story, the locker room was cramped and woefully undersized. Twenty-five players and half a dozen coaches had to fit into a space no bigger than eight or nine hundred square feet. There was also a buffet table, card table, an equipment area and a mirror where players would blow-dry their hair. The Tigers locker room was a relative closet compared to spacious, modern locker rooms that feature large, adjacent training and weight rooms, as well as separate coaches' and managerial quarters.

Jones had filled in for Chet Lemon that game in his first full day with the team. While a huge throng of reporters surrounded Jones to talk to him about his game-winning blow, Lemon emerged from the shower and saw the unwieldy swarm of reporters spilling into his locker space. One guy was even standing on Lemon's stool in a desperate lean to get his microphone near Jones. I was in that scrum and noticed Chet's dismayed look as he stood there wearing only a towel. Not only did Lemon patiently wait 10 minutes for the crowd to clear, but when it did clear, he then politely told many of the same reporters how pleased he was to see Jones perform well and how glad he was to have him as a teammate.

The Tigers were off to play the same two teams again—first to Baltimore and then Toronto to complete the 14-games-in-13-days showdown with their top rivals. The Tigers also demoted rookie catcher Dwight Lowry and brought up rookie reliever Carl Willis from Evansville.

On the music scene, Campbell had scrapped "Tiger Rag" after a torrent of negative feedback and had the organist play a slow version of the Beach Boys' "Fun Fun Fun" to accompany the fifth-inning base path sweeping. Predictably, it was booed. And the now-pouting broomsman, Herbie, was a no-show. Campbell had barred him from dancing on the just-completed home stand, and whether he would allow him to dance again upon their return remained in doubt.

Dr. Bernard Miller, a dentist from Huntington Woods, Michigan, had threatened Campbell with a 200-man kazoo band behind first base to blow "Dancin' in the Seats" as a guerilla tactic. Miller claimed he'd gotten through to Campbell on the phone with the threat before Campbell quickly hung up on him.

With the Jays hot on the Tigers' heels and the national media looking for an angle, *Chicago Sun Times* reporter Ron Rappaport, a Detroit native who had attended the home stand, spoke the fears of many Tigers fans: "What I am really afraid of is Detroit may one day look back on this team as one of the great unfulfilled promises in its history, a civic disaster to go down with the Battle of River Rouge and the creation of the Toyota Celica. I'm worried about the young boys who are having their first fling with the Tigers, who have not been made cautious by years of defeat. There may not be enough Vernor's ginger ale in the world to make them smile again."

GAMES 54, 55, 56 & 57 @ BALTIMORE—But smile they did in Baltimore Friday night, June 8, when Wilcox beat Davis, 3-2, before 50,361 on Johnson's seventh-inning homer, his second big blast that week. Willie Hernandez was brilliant, as usual, in killing an eighth-inning threat to save Wilcox and disappoint the massive Orioles crowd.

GAME #57   June 10

Tigers 8, Orioles 0

DETROIT	AB	R	H	BI	BALTIMORE	AB	R	H	BI
Whitaker 2b	3	1	0	1	Bumbry lf	4	0	0	0
Trammell ss	5	1	3	0	Shelby cf	4	0	0	0
Gibson rf	5	0	3	2	Ripken ss	3	0	1	0
Parrish c	5	0	0	0	Murray 1b	3	0	0	0
Evans 1b	3	0	0	0	Gross 3b	2	0	1	0
Kuntz lf	1	1	1	1	Singleton dh	3	0	0	0
Grubb dh	1	0	0	1	Young rf	3	0	0	0
Herndon ph	3	1	1	0	Sakata 2b	3	0	0	0
Garbey lf-1b	4	1	1	1	Rayford c	3	0	1	0
Jones cf	2	0	0	0					
Lemon ph-cf	2	1	0	0					
Johnson 3b	3	1	3	2					
Brookens 3b	1	1	1	1					
Totals	38	8	13	8		28	0	3	0

```
Detroit----------------------------------- 003  001  031  --  8
Baltimore-------------------------------- 000  000  000  --  0
```

Game winning RBI -- none, E -- Ripken, DP -- Detroit 2, Baltimore 1, LOB -- Detroit 9, Baltimore 2, 2B -- Gibson, Gross, Garbey, Rayford, HR -- Johnson, CS -- Trammell, SF -- Whitaker, HBP -- by Martinez, (Grubb), WP -- Martinez

Detroit	IP	H	R	ER	BB	SO
Petry (W)	9.0	3	0	0	1	5
Baltimore						
Martinez (L)	5.0	6	3	3	2	2
Underwood	0.2	3	1	1	1	0
Swaggerty	2.0	2	3	1	1	0
Martinez	1.1	2	1	1	0	2

T -- 2:44 A -- 51,764

Mike Flanagan shut out the Tigers, 4-0, on Saturday, June 9, in 98-degree heat. In the sixth inning, Berenguer got hit behind the ear by an Al Bumbry liner that had deflected off Berenguer's glove. The game was on national television, and Berenguer was visibly upset when Craig came out and pulled him. Berenguer apologized after the game but had made his point, seeing as Lopez gave up a couple of runs in relief.

Sunday, the Tigers swept a doubleheader, 10-4 and 8-0, as Petry spun a shutout in the nightcap. With more than 51,000 on hand again, the Orioles had drawn nearly 150,000 for a three-date, four-game series.

Sparky would later cite this doubleheader as two of the five most important wins of the regular season. They had been reeling at a 6-9 pace since the 35-5 start. In getting 18 runs in the doubleheader, Gibson had six RBIs, HoJo had five hits and another homer, and Whitaker scored five runs in the first game with Trammell knocking in four.

The lead was back to seven games over the Jays as the Tigers headed to Canada for another ABC national telecast on Monday night, June 11. Before flying out, they gave up on inconsistent pitcher Glenn Abbott and bought Sid Monge from the Padres as a lefty reliever. Dave Rozema would return to the rotation and get the nod to start another big series with Toronto.

◆ Game 58: Rozy's Return

Dave Rozema

Where:	**Toronto**
Result:	**5-4 Tigers**
Record:	**44-14**
WP:	**Rozema, 2-0**
LP:	**Leal, 6-1**
Standing:	**First, 8 ahead**
Attendance:	**35,062**

Dave Rozema remembers:

I'd hurt my arm in a start at Texas near the end of April and they had wanted me to rest it a little bit. This was my first start back. I'd got my only "W" against the White Sox in Detroit early in the year [April 21], but that next start, in Texas, I was ahead, 5-2, but felt stiffness and Roger took me out in the fourth inning. He said, "I need you for the season." The Rangers came back and tied it and then Aurelio got the victory that game in relief.

We used to kid Aurelio and call him "The Snake" because of nights like that. You're pitchin' good, they take you out and then he comes in and snakes you out of the "W." The stiffness in my back and shoulder wasn't serious, but it's April, it's early, it's cold and I threw a lotta changeups and I knew the stiffness would go away and I would come back. I'd had some relief appearances in May and early June and had been throwing OK, so it wasn't like I had been totally out of it. But now they went back to the five-man rotation.

We had such a big lead on everybody except Toronto, so here it's Toronto, Monday Night Baseball, national TV and I haven't started since April and I was nervous. No, truth is, I'm scared shitless! It's my first start coming back and it's one of the biggest games we'd played. I was saying to myself, "Just keep the ball down, because they're a good-hitting team."

Between Jack, Peaches, Milt, me and Berenguer, we had like five or six guys who could start. It was a big series, tons of people, and thousands came from Detroit to watch us because I remember that our hotel was f ull and all the banners they would wave at the game.

It was going good—we led, 3-0, in the third. I had good stuff, I was keeping it down and my role was get us to the fifth, sixth or seventh, and the bullpen will do the rest. They got a few guys on [singles by Ernie Whitt and Damaso Garcia], and then I got a little slap-hitter up there, Dave Collins. I thought I could backdoor him with a changeup, but it came too far in and too high and he slapped at it, got it all for a three-run homer right down the line to tie the game up.

Shit. I don't know why, but it seemed that guys like that would always get me. Like Brett Butler. He hit about five homers in his career and got me for a grand slam once on a changeup that floated into him. And with Collins, I just should have kept it down. Hell, I got the two best infielders in the game at short and second [Trammell and Whitaker] and with a guy on first, I just should have gotten the force out. When you throw a stupid pitch in the big leagues, you make a mistake and they get you.

I still knew that with our team, if you can limit 'em to two to four runs you're going to win almost every time. In the fourth inning, it's a tie game now at three, and I'm thinking that something's gonna happen with one of the big boys, Darrell or Lance or Gibby. All of a sudden Lou comes up and Lou rakes one off Luis Leal, two-run job way out in right and I leap out of the dugout. The dugout's about nine foot high and I banged my head on it. I got up for a white boy, at least that night!

I knew I had to shut 'em down now. Roger always said, "OK, you gave up your three runs, so pitch your game. Keep it down, keep it away from left-handers." The ball carried well there. And they had good lefties: [Lloyd] Moseby, [Ernie] Whitt, [Dane] Iorg, all these guys. I got 'em out in the fifth and also got that little shit Collins on a fly to end the inning.

Aurelio, "The Snake"

GAME #58   June 11

Tigers 5, Jays 4

DETROIT	AB	R	H	BI	TORONTO	AB	R	H	BI
Whitaker 2b	4	1	1	2	Garcia 2b	4	1	2	0
Trammell ss	5	1	2	0	Collins lf	4	1	1	3
Gibson dh	3	0	0	1	Moseby cf	4	0	1	1
Parrish c	4	0	1	0	Upshaw 1b	4	0	1	0
Evans 1b	3	1	1	0	Aikens dh	2	0	0	0
Garbey ph-1b	2	0	0	0	Johnson ph	2	0	0	0
Grubb rf	2	1	1	0	Bell rf	4	0	1	0
Kuntz ph-rf	1	0	0	0	Mulliniks 3b	3	0	0	0
Lemon cf	3	0	1	1	Iorg 3b	0	0	0	0
Jones lf	3	0	2	1	Barfield ph	1	0	0	0
Herndon ph-lf	1	0	0	0	Whitt c	3	1	2	0
Johnson 3b	3	1	1	0	Fernandez ph	1	0	0	0
Brookens 3b	0	0	0	0	Griffin ss	3	1	1	0
					Martinez ph	1	0	0	0
Totals	**34**	**5**	**10**	**5**		**36**	**4**	**9**	**4**

Detroit	120	200	000	--	5
Toronto	003	000	100	--	4

Game winning RBI -- none, E -- Whitaker, Trammell, DP -- Detroit 1, LOB -- Detroit 9, Toronto 6, 2B -- Grubb, Jones, Parrish, Whitt, Lemon, 3B -- Trammell, HR -- Collins, Whitaker, SB -- Bell, SH -- Gibson, SF -- Gibson, Lemon, HBP -- by Rozema (Garcia), WP -- Leal

Detroit	IP	H	R	ER	BB	SO
Rozema (W)	5.0	4	3	3	0	2
Monge*	0.0	1	0	0	0	0
Willis	1.2	3	1	1	0	0
Hernandez (S)	2.1	1	0	0	0	3
Toronto						
Leal (L)+	6.0	9	5	5	2	7
Key	1.2	1	0	0	2	2
Lamp	1.1	0	0	0	0	2

* Pitched to 1 batter in 6th
+ Pitched to 1 batter in 7th
T -- 3:04 A -- 35,062

Five innings was what they needed, so I left up, 5-3, and the bullpen took over. We'd just gotten Sid Monge, who had a great side-arm curveball and he pitched the sixth. Carl Willis, another guy we just got, gave up a run in the seventh and Willie came in and finished the game. We won, 5-4, and I was 2-0 and back in business. I pitched well until late July and was 7-1 before Sparky and I had a falling out.

However, the next two days weren't pretty. Collins, who had tormented Rozema on Monday night, gave an impassioned pre-game speech to his teammates on Tuesday, June 12, and then tripled in a run in the first off Morris.

Morris felt a twinge in his pitching elbow while getting battered for six runs in three innings of a 12-3 Blue Jays rout, and this would signal the start of a very strange stretch for Morris, unlike anything he had encountered or would encounter in his career. He also refused to see a team doctor. "They can't tell me anything I don't know," was his defiant stance. "I ain't taking no shots."

Sparky was also temporarily down on Larry Herndon, who was hitting just .243. The recently called up Ruppert Jones would now platoon with him in left. Sparky liked waking players up this way. "He'll (Herndon) have a chance to win it back. Nothing lasts forever."

Stieb beat Wilcox, 7-3, on Wednesday, June 13, reducing the Tigers' lead to six games. Almost 111,000 had attended three games at smallish Exhibition Stadium on a Monday through Wednesday. The Tigers had produced an even split of the 14 games against Toronto and Baltimore. They had entered this stretch against their main foes with a 5½ game lead, and had upped it to six games when it was done.

GAMES 61, 62, & 63 @ MILWAUKEE—The last two weeks of June went extremely well for the Tigers, increasing the lead from six games to ten games by month's end.

On June 15, the same night that Detroiter Tommy Hearns blew out Roberto Duran with three knockdowns in two brutal rounds in Las Vegas, the Tigers pitty-patted their way past Milwaukee, 3-2. The Brewers Gold Glove fielders, Robin Yount and Rick Manning, both made eighth-inning errors, allowing the two unearned runs that decided the game.

Yount butchered an Alan Trammell grounder and Manning dropped a John Grubb fly ball. Sparky Anderson asked cleanup hitter Lance Parrish—who had already homered and doubled—to sacrifice-bunt two runners over in Milwaukee's fateful eighth. Willie Hernandez, as was his habit by now, pitched two scoreless innings

Jack Morris's fabulous season was rudely interrupted when he hurt his elbow in Toronto on June 12.

to save it for Dan Petry. Meanwhile, Evans, while in Toronto, bought a new game called "Trivial Pursuit," Canada's latest contribution to Western civilization. The clubhouse would never be the same.

How captivating were the Tigers? A bulging crowd of 50,395 showed up in Milwaukee on Saturday, June 16, to see the Tigers take on the sub-500, sixth-place "Brew Crew." Juan Berenguer, a fellow Panamanian and longtime Duran friend and fan, delivered his own knockout, pitching a five-hit, complete-game 6-0 shutout. Evans had four RBIs, including a three-run homer off Don Sutton. Morris missed the start with the sore elbow, but at least agreed to see Dr. Tietge after having refused to do so the week before. X-rays revealed no damage, and he was told to miss just one more start.

Rozema beat the Brewers, 7-4, on Sunday, June 17. He pitched better than Lopez, who came in for him and gave up three runs in relief. Chet Lemon doubled and tripled for three RBIs. Meanwhile, the Jays swept Boston to keep pace six games back.

GAMES 64, 65 & 66 vs NEW YORK—The Tigers returned to Detroit Monday, June 18, for a seven-game home stand against the Yankees and Brewers that would average more than 41,000 fans per game. Although they were just 11-12 since the 35-5 start, Tigers Hall of Famer Al Kaline, color man on the ratings-explosive WDIV telecasts, said he thought that this Tigers team was stronger than his was in '68. It was the first admission from any of the '68 champs that baseball greatness was again unfolding in Detroit. But Kaline warned that the '84 team still hadn't proven it could handle adversity.

The Tigers would take two of three from the Yankees. On Monday, June 18, Wilcox lost, 2-1, to Phil Niekro's knuckler. The local television rating for the ABC national telecast was an astronomical, Super Bowl–like 37.5, largest of the year. And 54 percent of all televisions turned on in Detroit were tuned in to the Tigers that night.

◆ *Game 66: HoJo Jolts Yanks*

Where:	**Tiger Stadium**
Result:	**9-6 Tigers in 13 innings**
Record:	**49-17**
WP:	**Bair, 4-0**
LP:	**Rijo, 1-7**
Standing:	**First, 7½ ahead**
Attendance:	**43,972**

The three games against the Yankees drew more than 125,000 fans. Monday's 2-1 loss to Phil Niekro was the Tigers' third straight nationally televised game on ABC's *Monday Night Baseball.* Nobody could get enough of the Tigers, and although the final two games of the series were not on local television, those who jammed Tiger Stadium to near-capacity saw a pair of thrillers.

On Tuesday night, Game 65, with the game tied 4-4 in the eighth, Kuntz delivered a two-run single off Ron Guidry to put the Tigers ahead, 6-4. They extended the lead to 7-4 in the ninth, when Barbaro Garbey, playing first base, booted a grounder. Lopez walked two and gave up two runs to make it extremely tense before Willie Hernandez came on to get the final two outs and save the 7-6 victory.

Hernandez pitched well in all three games in the series and was preceded in the last two by Lopez. At this point in the season, Lopez was aware that he and Hernandez were no longer equals, and he was fighting to accept the same set-up role that had frustrated Hernandez for the first seven years of his career.

Howard Johnson was a 175-pound slugger who hit two big three-run homers in June.

But Kuntz was the story. He was hitting .356, and afterwards, Sparky said, "He's done something to help us in every game he's played." Kuntz said he was "the happiest person in the world," and had every right to be because 1983 had been a disaster for him. He was 29 and had to move five times in the space of a year: from Edmonton, the White Sox Triple A club, he was called up to Chicago, but then he was traded to the Twins in June and immediately sent to Denver. The Twins brought him up for 100 at bats, but gave up on him and traded him to the Tigers in December '83 for pitcher Larry Pashnick. He still had to have a good spring just to make the Tigers.

Now Kuntz was quickly becoming a cult hero. With cameras and reporters in his face after beating the Yankees, he poured his heart out. "I was twenty-nine and everybody was in a panic; I'd just gotten married and my wife, my in-laws, my father, everybody's crying. So when it gets to be three o'clock every afternoon and I drive here, I'm the happiest person in the world."

Wednesday's game was even better. Almost 44,000 at Tiger Stadium saw a game that was tied four times and went 13 innings before Howard Johnson blasted the fourth home run of the evening, a two-out, three-run shot into the upper deck in right center off Jose Rijo, to send the crowd and his teammates into delirium. They mobbed HoJo as he approached home plate, and what made it even more thrilling for Johnson was that his parents and in-laws were on hand to experience it with him.

Johnson was only 23, but felt as if everything to that point had been a struggle. He had exploded in '82 in his first big-league exposure, hitting .347 the last two months of the season. However, he had fought off injuries in a disappointing 1983, and Sparky still didn't feel comfortable with him at third base.

But this game looked like a breakthrough, and it seemed as though Sparky had finally seen the light regarding the powerful, 175-pound HoJo. In fact, Sparky said afterwards, "He's going to be the third baseman in Detroit for many years to come. I'm going to bring him along slowly, but he's come a long way since last year, hasn't he?"

On this night, June 20, after his manager's endorsement and his second critically important three-run homer in two weeks, HoJo's future in Detroit seemed brighter than it had ever been.

But less than two months later, on August 28, in Seattle, HoJo made a costly error on a slow roller. With Tommy Brookens nursing a hamstring problem, Sparky announced that Darrell Evans and Marty Castillo would platoon at third the rest of the year.

For me, the saddest part of the fabulous World Series celebration of 1984 was to see Howard Johnson enjoying it as best he could, even though Sparky had reduced him to little more than a spectator.

After the wildly exciting three-game Yankees series, a Love Letter to the *Free Press* read: "Eli Zaret says the Tigers are going all the way. Al Kaline says the Tigers are going all the way. J.P. McCarthy says the Tigers are going all the way. What do you say?" George Puscas replied: "I say if the Tigers don't go all the way, a lot of guys are going to look stupid. Including the Tigers."

Sports Illustrated had written four articles on the Tigers in recent weeks. In the latest issue, they printed six Tigers-related letters, four of them favorable. But not this one from two guys from Baltimore: "After reading *Sports Illustrated*'s fourth article on the Detroit Tigers within the space of a few weeks, I have come to the conclusion that there is no point in continuing the 1984 season. Since the Tigers seem to have already clinched the World Series, the Cy Young Award, the Manager of the Year and any other award you can name, it would certainly be a waste of time to go on playing through the hot summer

GAME #66   June 20

Tigers 9, Yankees 6

NEW YORK	AB	R	H	BI	DETROIT	AB	R	H	BI
Randolph 2b	7	1	1	0	Kuntz rf	2	1	0	0
Wynegar c	6	1	2	1	Gibson ph-rf	2	1	0	0
Mattingly 1b	6	0	2	1	Trammell ss	5	1	2	2
Winfield rf-cf	6	2	3	2	Garbey 1b	4	1	2	1
Gamble dh	2	0	1	1	Bergman 1b	2	0	0	0
Harrah ph	1	0	0	0	Parrish dh	6	2	2	1
Griffey ph	1	0	1	0	Lemon cf	5	1	4	2
Kemp lf	5	0	1	0	Herndon lf	4	0	0	0
Smalley 3b	5	0	1	0	Grubb ph	0	1	0	0
Moreno cf	2	1	1	0	Brookens 2b	2	0	0	0
Baylor ph	0	0	0	0	Whitaker ph-2b	3	0	0	0
Dayett rf	2	0	0	0	Johnson 3b	5	1	2	3
Meacham ss	6	1	1	1	Castillo c	5	0	0	0
Totals	49	6	14	6		45	9	12	9

New York	220	000	011	000	0	--	6
Detroit	201	001	110	000	3	--	9

Game winning RBI -- none, E -- Bergman, DP -- New York 2, Detroit 3, LOB -- New York 10, Detroit 6, 2B -- Winfield, Meacham, Lemon, Randolph, HR -- Trammell, Parrish, Winfield, Lemon, Johnson, SB -- Moreno, CS -- Trammell, SH -- Kemp, Whitaker, Lemon, PB -- Castillo

NEW YORK	IP	H	R	ER	BB	SO
Shirley*	5.0	7	4	4	2	0
Christiansen+	2.0	3	2	2	2	3
Fontenot	5.0	0	0	0	1	3
Rijo (L)	0.2	2	3	3	1	0
Detroit						
Petry	6.0	9	4	4	2	1
Lopez #	1.0	1	1	1	1	0
Hernandez	4.0	3	1	1	2	4
Bair (W)	2.0	1	0	0	0	2

* Pitched to 1 batter in 6th   + Pitched to 2 batters in 8th   # Pitched to 1 batter in 8th

T -- 3:51 A -- 43,972

months. *SI* should publish its World Series article next week, and then we could have an early start on football season... PS. Should you decide to publish an article on the Tigers' bat boy, or Sparky Anderson's dog...please cancel our subscription."

GAMES 67, 68, 69 & 70 vs MILWAUKEE—On Thursday, June 21, the Brewers' 39-year-old Don Sutton avenged his loss to Berenguer the previous weekend in Milwaukee with a 4-3 win. With another aging and future Hall of Fame pitcher, Phil Niekro, having won on Monday, they'd lost to two pitchers averaging 42 years of age in a four-day span. Larry Herndon's two-run, seventh-inning homer off reliever Rick Waits cut the lead to 4-3. But in the eighth, Ben Oglivie leapt to the top of the fence in center to snatch Kirk Gibson's drive and preserve the win.

The Tigers passed the million mark the earliest in team history in the loss to Sutton. Atypical of Jim Campbell's management style, the Tigers actually made a warm gesture to their fans. Perhaps Campbell was overwhelmed by the fumes of his victory cigars. Tim and Carol Przydzial purchased reserved seats about half an hour before the game. As the one-millionth fans, they were given front-row boxes for the night, season passes for 1985, a radio, a television and an assortment of souvenirs. Tim, a Cadillac Motor Car plant worker, gushed that he had been coming to the ballpark since he was seven years old when his uncle took him. Perfect, huh?

The human interest stories were everywhere. Before the game, the father of a 12-year-old girl spotted Lance Parrish through an open door to the clubhouse and took a chance by shouting to him that his daughter was Parrish's biggest fan. Lance came out and chatted with the family and posed for a picture. When he left, the girl burst into tears and cried to her mom, "He said, 'You're welcome.' To me! Lance Parrish!"

Before huge and adoring crowds the rest of the weekend, the Tigers swept the last three against the Brewers. They drew nearly 165,000 for the four-game series. In the last 19 dates, June 5 through the 24, they drew a total of nearly 900,000, averaging about 45,000 a game.

Dave Rozema went five strong innings to beat Bob McClure, 7-3, before 48,497 on Friday night. Almost 45,000 saw Wilcox beat Chuck Porter, 5-1, Saturday afternoon. Wilcox had fallen from a 6-0 record start to 7-5 before coming around in this one, crediting pitching coach Roger Craig for encouraging him to challenge the hitters again. Howard Johnson slugged yet another three-run homer in the second. Gibson was 3-4 with a steal. One report on the game called

Gibson "The man Detroit loved to hate last summer." Gibby's response: "I'm a lot smarter, I've learned a lot about the game."

◆ *Game 70: Rooftop Rupe*

Where:	**Tiger Stadium**
Result:	**7-1 Tigers**
Record:	**52-18**
WP:	**Morris, 12-3**
LP:	**Haas, 4-6**
Standing:	**First, 8½ ahead**
Attendance:	**39,067**

Let's not lose track of the fact that the stars won it for the Tigers in 1984. If Marty Castillo, Barbaro Garbey, Rusty Kuntz and Ruppert Jones were the core of the team, no number of role players to surround them would have put them over the top.

Jack Morris, Dan Petry, Kirk Gibson, Lance Parrish, Willie Hernandez, Lou Whitaker and Alan Trammell were the stars. But what made 1984 so utterly amazing was that players like Ruppert Jones came from nowhere to succeed to dizzying degrees. Jones had been cut by the Pirates in spring training, and in looking for work had signed a minor-league contract with the Tigers to play at Evansville.

Jones was only 29 and should have been in his prime, but after hitting just .233, the Padres released him after the '83 season. Now the Pirates had also quit on him and things were looking bleak. But Jones was a lefty and had a great glove and the Tigers decided to bring him up on June 5 in place of Rod Allen, who lacked Jones' long-ball power and defensive skill. Two nights later, on June 7, after the Blue Jays had won twice in a row to narrow the Tigers' lead to just 3½ games, Jones hit a three-run, sixth-inning homer just inside the right-field foul pole to break a 1-1 tie and pace a 5-3 Tigers win. Before more than 40,000 fans, Jones emerged from the dugout, waved his cap and made his first curtain call.

Now, two and a half weeks later, Morris was dueling Moose Haas on a Sunday afternoon, leading 1-0, in the sixth. Haas was working on a three-hitter when Gibson opened the sixth by roping a triple into the right-center gap. Parrish promptly singled him in to make it 2-0 Tigers.

Tom Tellman entered the game in relief and yielded a single to Chet Lemon. Tellman then came inside with a fastball and Jones cranked a high, arcing blast near the foul pole that bounced off the roof and then over it. The 17th homer ever hit over the right-field

GAME #70   June 24

Tigers 7, Brewers 1

MILWAUKEE					DETROIT				
	AB	R	H	BI		AB	R	H	BI
James rf	4	0	0	0	Whitaker 2b	4	1	1	0
Gantner 2b	4	0	0	0	Trammell ss	3	1	1	0
Yount ss	4	0	0	0	Gibson rf	3	1	1	2
Cooper 1b	3	0	0	0	Parrish c	4	2	3	2
Oglivie lf	3	0	0	0	Evans dh	4	0	0	0
Simmons dh	3	0	0	0	Grubb lf	1	0	0	0
Clark cf	3	1	1	0	Lemon ph-cf	2	1	1	0
Sundberg c	3	0	1	1	Bergman 1b	2	0	1	0
Romero 3b	3	0	1	0	Garbey ph-1b	2	0	0	0
					Jones cf-lf	4	1	1	3
					Johnson 3b	2	0	0	0
					Castillo 3b	1	0	0	0
Totals	**30**	**1**	**3**	**1**		**32**	**7**	**9**	**7**

Milwaukee ------------------- 000   000   010 -- 1
Detroit ------------------------ 010   006   00x -- 7

Game winning RBI -- none, E -- Bergman, LOB -- Milwaukee 2, Detroit 5, 2B -- Clark, Sundberg, 3B -- Gibson, HR -- Parrish, Jones, CS -- Gibson

New York	IP	H	R	ER	BB	SO
Haas (L)*	5.0	5	5	5	3	3
Waits	0.1	1	1	1	0	1
Tellmann	2.2	3	1	1	1	2
Detroit						
Morris (W)	6.0	1	0	0	0	4
Lopez (S)	3.0	2	1	1	0	0

* Pitched to 4 batters in 6th
T -- 2:32 A -- 39,067

Curtain call! Ruppert Jones' career was briefly resurrected in Detroit in '84.

roof landed on Trumbull Avenue and bounced onto a parked Buick Riviera before clunking into a door on the Checker Cab building. Jones said it was "the hardest I ever pulled a ball." The crowd chanted, "Rupe, Rupe, Rupe," and another '84 hero was confirmed.

Morris had a no-hitter into the sixth before giving up a single at the end of the inning. He had just returned from elbow stiffness, and once Jones' homer sealed the victory, Lopez finished the last three innings.

Ruppert Jones—a quiet, religious type—hit a career-high .284 in 1984, with 12 homers and 37 RBIs in 215 at bats, while fielding all 154 outfield chances flawlessly. He played very little in the postseason, going 0-8, and wasn't asked back for 1985. Instead, the Tigers went with two young outfielders who never amounted to much—Nelson Simmons, who hit .433 in a September call-up, and Jim Weaver, a 25-year-old who hit 15 homers for Triple A Toledo.

Jones played the last three years of his career with the Angels, never hitting more than .245. He retired with a .250 average and proudly wore a World Series ring, symbolizing his contribution to Tigers' history.

The 52-18 Tigers, the fans and the media remained in a state of unabated amazement. Following the heavily attended Brewer series, they had won eight of ten since losing those last two at Toronto when their lead was reduced to six. Now the bulge was back to 8½ as they headed to New York Sunday night following the "Rooftop Rupe" game.

GAMES 71, 72 & 73 @ NEW YORK—The Yankees beat them, 7-3, Monday night, June 25. The Tigers had been 40-0 in games they led after seven, but that ended with Ron Guidry beating Doug Bair in relief of Dan Petry. Sparky walked the floor of the New York Stock Exchange Tuesday morning with Jim Campbell, George Kell and Ernie Harwell. Frantic traders stopped in their tracks, asking for autographs and handshakes. They also put Sparky's name up in lights to announce his presence.

New York Times columnist Dave Anderson took Sparky to breakfast and said to him, "You're leading the league in everything." Sparky's reply was, "Yes we are, and in happiness, too." And that line, "Tigers lead league in happiness," became the headline over the column.

Sparky went on to say, "This is the best bunch of guys I've ever been around. I don't worry about anybody ever doing anything silly on the plane or the bus. We've got no bad people on this club." He went on rave that "Lou Whitaker has the best, most accurate power arm for a second baseman I've ever seen. And he can hit."

As for Trammell, ". . . great hands, great, accurate arm. I don't ever remember a combo with those stats." As for Parrish, "Nobody can throw with him. And he's a power man. He'll hit twenty-five homers and drive in a hundred runs." Completing his assessment of the Tigers "up the middle," he said, "And in center field, it's obnoxious the way Chester Lemon plays. He gets a great jump on the ball. I thought Cesar Geronimo was good until I saw Chester out there every day."

Meanwhile, the Blue Jays were getting swept by the Brewers, while Parrish cracked a two-run, 10th-inning homer Tuesday night, June 26, to beat the Yankees, 9-7, in a wild one. The Tigers blew a four-run lead they'd built off Shane Rawley and Bob Shirley, and then had trailed by three before coming back with two out in the eighth.

Trammell singled in two unearned runs resulting from a Roy Smalley error, and then Evans' pinch-hit single off Clay Christiansen drove in Kuntz with the tying run. Berenguer, Lopez and newly acquired Sid Monge pitched poorly. Still, the win gave the Tigers a 10-game lead, the first time it had reached double digits all year.

With the Jays struggling so badly in Milwaukee, the lead stayed at 10 despite a 5-4 loss Wednesday night. Carl Willis, whom Sparky had incorrectly predicted would be the next Rollie Fingers, gave up three runs in the eighth.

The Tigers would return home to finish the month with four games in three days against the Twins before embarking on an 11-game road trip that would take them through the All-Star Game.

GAMES 74, 75 & 76 vs MINNESOTA—Back home, the Twins met the Tigers, and 44,619 jammed the stadium for a twilight doubleheader on June 29. It started weirdly for Jack Morris, who gave up five runs in less than six innings to fall to 12-4. In the second inning, Randy Bush doubled, Tim Tuefel grounded out, and then someone named Andre David hit a two-run homer into the upper deck in right in his first major-league at bat. Morris said it was "off a hanging forkball right in his eyes."

GAME #72   June 26

Tigers 9, Yankees 7

DETROIT	AB	R	H	BI	NEW YORK	AB	R	H	BI
Kuntz rf	3	2	0	0	Randolph 2b	5	1	1	1
Gibson ph-rf	1	0	0	0	Wynegar c	4	1	1	2
Trammell ss	5	0	2	2	Mattingly 1b	5	1	2	0
Garbey 1b	3	0	2	2	Baylor dh	5	1	2	2
Evans ph-1b	1	1	1	1	Gamble rf	3	1	1	1
Bergman 1b	0	0	0	0	Dayett ph-rf	1	0	0	0
Parrish dh-c	6	1	2	2	Kemp lf	5	0	2	1
Lemon cf	6	0	1	0	Smalley 3b	5	0	0	0
Herndon lf	5	1	2	0	Griffey cf	4	1	1	0
Brookens 2b-3b	5	2	3	0	Meacham ss	4	1	2	0
Castillo c	4	1	2	0					
Grubb ph	0	0	0	0					
Hernandez p	0	0	0	0					
Johnson 3b	4	1	1	0					
Whitaker 2b	1	0	0	0					
Totals	**44**	**9**	**15**	**9**		**41**	**7**	**12**	**7**

Detroit------------------ 040 000 030 2 -- 9
New York---------------- 003 012 100 0 -- 7

Game winning RBI -- none, E -- Smalley, LOB -- Detroit 11, New York 8, 2B -- Garbey, Randolph, Kemp, HR -- Wynegar, Baylor, Parrish, SB -- Johnson 2, Gamble, Brookens, CS -- Garbey, Trammell, SH -- Meacham, WP -- Rawley 2

Detroit	IP	H	R	ER	BB	SO
Berenguer	2.1	5	3	3	1	0
Lopez	3.2	4	3	3	2	5
Monge	1.1	2	1	1	0	2
Hernandez (W)	2.2	1	0	0	0	2
New York						
Rawley	1.2	4	4	4	3	1
Shirley*	5.1	7	2	0	0	2
Fontenot	0.2	0	1	1	1	0
Christiansen (L)	2.1	5	2	2	2	3

* Pitched to 2 batters in 8th

T -- 3:22 A -- 32,301

The Twins went on to win, 5-3. Twins Manager Billy Gardner wondered if Morris' elbow, which had caused him to miss two starts prior to his win over Milwaukee five days ago, was still bothering him. Morris' response: "It felt fine. No excuse. My rhythm stunk and the outcome stunk."

In the *Free Press* that morning, Bill McGraw wrote an article on the platooning of Gibson, with a subtitle that read: "Kirk Gibson wants to play more, but he accepts Sparky's strategy." Gibson hadn't started against any of the three lefties they'd faced in the Yankees series and only got to pinch-hit three times.

He said, "I don't like being a platooned player... when a guy takes you out against left-handers, he's telling you subconsciously, 'You can't hit them.'" He even talked about the possibility of free agency after the '85 season, but concluded with, "Who am I to tell him he's doing wrong? We're 10 games up with his methods. I haven't proven to him I can hit left-handers."

What juicy irony. In game two that very night, by the sixth inning, Sparky had already used his two reserve outfielders, Herndon and Kuntz. Gibson told Rozema on the bench, "I'm locked in...there's nothing Sparky can do. I've got to stay in there."

Gibson had already hit a two-run, first-inning homer off righty starter Mike Smithson. Then, in the ninth inning of a 5-5 tie, he faced lefty reliever Pete Filson with one on and one out—and did it again—another two-run homer to dramatically win the game, 7-5. "I don't like to sit against lefties," was how Gibson again left it with the press before heading home to nearby Grosse Pointe on a breezy Friday night.

More than 48,000 jammed the ballpark on Saturday night, June 30. With the game tied, 3-3, in the eighth, Twins reliever Ron Davis wild-pitched the first batter he faced, Barbaro Garbey, scoring Herndon with the tie-breaker. Out strode Hernandez, who fanned pinch hitter Tim Laudner and got Kirby Puckett to fly out to center to end it. Of Hernandez' 14th save and seventh in June alone, Sparky said in mild amazement, "That's what we brought him over here for, but I never dreamed it would be nothing like this."

Tigers split on Gibson HR

Month by Month

JUNE 1984

Cumulative statistics as of the end of the month

BATTING

	AB	R	H	RBI	2B	3B	HR	BB	SO	SB	E	GW RBI	AVG
Kuntz	74	22	23	15	5	0	2	13	16	1	0	3	.311
Lemon	262	44	81	50	20	4	12	28	39	4	1	2	.309
Trammell	307	55	95	41	18	4	8	34	25	14	7	4	.309
Whitaker	282	47	87	23	9	1	5	32	25	4	8	6	.309
Garbey	170	26	52	32	9	1	2	9	18	3	6	2	.306
Johnson	140	20	41	27	6	0	6	19	30	5	6	4	.293
Bergman	121	19	35	20	4	2	2	14	15	2	5	3	.289
Gibson	244	43	68	43	10	5	11	21	47	15	4	9	.279
Jones	42	6	11	11	2	0	4	1	11	0	0	2	.262
Parrish	276	35	76	43	10	1	14	9	51	1	2	6	.275
Herndon	228	25	58	19	11	2	1	19	41	3	1	3	.254
Grubb	80	10	20	10	4	0	3	18	15	1	0	3	.250
Evans	200	29	49	33	6	0	5	41	31	1	1	4	.245
Brookens	118	12	27	16	6	2	1	9	13	2	5	0	.229
Castillo	60	4	12	5	1	0	0	3	14	1	1	0	.200
DH Hitters	278	44	69	44	11	1	8	38	48	3	0	--	.248
PH Hitters	85	11	25	19	4	1	1	11	16	0	0	2	.294
TOTALS	2657	408	749	391	124	22	77	274	404	59	53	51	.282

KEY: AB-at bats, R-runs, H-hits, RBI-runs batted in, 2B-doubles, 3B-triples, HR-home runs, BB-walks, SO-strike outs, SB-stolen bases, E-errors, GW RBI-game winning runs batted in, AVG-batting average.

AL EAST STANDINGS

	W	L	PCT	GB
DETROIT	55	21	.724	---
Toronto	45	31	.592	10
Baltimore	42	35	.545	13
Boston	36	40	.474	19
Milwaukee	34	42	.447	21
New York	33	41	.446	21
Cleveland	31	42	.425	22½

PITCHING

	W	L	G	CG	S	IP	H	R	ER	BB	SO	ERA
Hernandez	4	0	37	0	14	71	54	17	17	20	62	2.16
Morris	12	4	17	8	0	130	98	45	38	39	82	2.63
Bair	4	1	22	0	3	47⅓	39	16	15	14	36	2.85
Lopez	6	0	32	0	9	65	45	24	22	25	42	3.05
Petry	11	3	18	3	0	114⅔	110	43	39	39	65	3.06
Rozema	4	0	13	0	0	49⅓	39	18	17	12	20	3.10
Monge	0	0	4	0	0	8	10	4	3	2	3	3.38
Berenguer	4	5	13	1	0	73⅔	68	32	29	36	50	3.54
Wilcox	8	5	17	0	0	97⅓	96	49	45	37	52	4.16
Willis	0	1	7	0	0	11⅔	16	8	8	3	3	6.17
TOTALS	55	21	--	12	26	691⅓	604	276	249	233	420	3.24

Totals include players no longer with the team and pitchers' errors. KEY: W-wins, L-losses, G-games pitched in, CG-complete games, S-saves, IP-innings pitched, H-hits allowed, R-runs allowed, ER-earned runs allowed, BB-walks allowed, SO-strike outs, ERA-earned run averages.

DAY-BY-DAY

Date	Gm #	Vs.	W/L	Score	Winner	Loser	Rec	GA	Att.
6/1	47	Bal	W	14-2	Petry	McGregor	38-9	5½	47,252
6/2	48	Bal	L	0-5	* Davis	Morris	38-10	4½	40,292
6/3	49	Bal	L	1-2	* Flanagan	Wilcox	38-11	4½	34,228
6/4	50	Tor	W	6-3 (10)	† Lopez	† Key	39-11	5½	26,733
6/5	51	Tor	L	4-8	† Acker	Abbott	39-12	4½	35,983
6/6	52	Tor	L	3-6	Leal	Petry	39-13	3½	38,167
6/7	53	Tor	W	5-3	* Morris	Clancy	40-13	4½	40,879
6/8	54	@ Bal	W	3-2	Wilcox	Davis	41-13	5½	50,361
6/9	55	@ Bal	L	0-4	* Flanagan	Berenguer	41-14	5½	44,404
6/10	56	@ Bal	W	10-4	† Bair	Boddicker	42-14	6½	
(DH)	57		W	8-0	* Petry	Martinez	43-14	7	51,764
6/11	58	@ Tor	W	5-4	Rozema	Leal	44-14	8	35,062
6/12	59	@ Tor	L	3-12	Clancy	Morris	44-15	7	40,437
6/13	60	@ Tor	L	3-7	Stieb	Wilcox	44-16	6	34,122
6/15	61	@ Mil	W	3-2	Petry	Cocanower	45-16	6	32,074
6/16	62	@ Mil	W	6-0	* Berenguer	Sutton	46-16	6	50,395
6/17	63	@ Mil	W	7-4	Rozema	McClure	47-16	6	44,902
6/18	64	NY	L	1-2	Niekro	Wilcox	47-17	5½	40,315
6/19	65	NY	W	7-6	† Lopez	Guidry	48-17	6½	41,192
6/20	66	NY	W	9-6 (13)	† Bair	† Rijo	49-17	7½	43,972
6/21	67	Mil	L	3-4	Sutton	Berenguer	49-18	6½	32,291
6/22	68	Mil	W	7-3	Rozema	McClure	50-18	7½	48,497
6/23	69	Mil	W	5-1	Wilcox	Porter	51-18	7½	44,680
6/24	70	Mil	W	7-1	Morris	Haas	52-18	8½	39,067
6/25	71	@ NY	L	3-7	Guidry	† Bair	52-19	9	29,237
6/26	72	@ NY	W	9-7 (10)	Hernandez	† Christiansen	53-19	10	32,301
6/27	73	@ NY	L	4-5	† Howell	† Willis	53-20	10	30,428
6/29	74	Minn	L	3-5	Williams	Morris	53-21	9½	
(DH)	75	Minn	W	7-5	† Hernandez	† Filson	54-21	10	44,619
6/30	76	Minn	W	4-3	Petry	Schrom	55-21	10	48,095

*Complete game † Decision in relief

Chapter 12

Screwball

Some year Eddie Murray will hit 50 homers and drive in 180 runs. That's the kind of year Willie had this year. He'll never do it again. He'll have some good years…but he can't ever be expected to do what he did this year.

— Sparky Anderson, on Willie Hernandez during the
'84 World Series

Willie Hernandez agreed with that statement when it was repeated to him in 2003. He's been out of baseball for almost 15 years and is living in his native Puerto Rico. Willie's hair is a little shorter and grayer, and he looks a lot less intimidating than he did on the mound back in 1984.

The vision of him strutting confidently to the mound back then, hitching his pants, digging a hole in front of the pitching rubber with his spikes, adjusting the massive lump of tobacco in his cheek and then staring down the first hitter is an enduring image of the Tigers' championship season. His regal, sneeringly confident, all-powerful demeanor quickly prompted pitching coach Roger Craig to dub him "The King."

"When Sparky said that I'd never have a season like that, he also said that nobody can have a season like me," Willie recalls with a chuckle. "He called me in his office in '85 because I lose two games in a row and I blew a save situation in the same week, so he said, 'Will, you got me scared.' I said, 'Why, Sparky?' He said, 'I'm glad that happened because now I can go to sleep at night. Now I know you are human.'"

Hernandez laughs heartily at the recollection. He also had an excellent season in '85 but never again approached his '84 numbers, and since no one expected him to, it's no knock on his legacy. An experience like he had in 1984 was more than any baseball player could ever hope for. Just to have been a contributing member of the team considered the best of the '80s would be privilege enough. But to also win the MVP and Cy Young awards, and to have been on the mound at the end of games that clinched the division, pennant and World Series, is beyond storybook stuff.

Hernandez pitched in a league-leading 80 games in '84, saved 32 of 33 tries and had a 9-3 record with an ERA of 1.92. Beyond the awards and the adulation of the media and

fans, 1984 provided Hernandez with something much more personally significant, something that ran deeper, something he had vainly
struggled to gain in his previous seven major-league seasons.

Willie desperately wanted to be regarded as a bullpen ace and
to be paid commensurately with the top closers in baseball. Until
'84, he felt he had been disrespected by the heralded closers for
whom he served as set-up man, and by Cubs and Phillies management, which had paid him no more than second-tier money. He felt
as if he was being laughed at, and he vowed that someday they
would all pay for it.

Hernandez was 22 years old when made the Cubs roster in '77 as
a set-up man for Bruce Sutter. Sutter was in his second year and
became an All-Star that year with 31 saves. With Willie preceding
him to the mound, Sutter was an All-Star again in '78. And in '79,
Sutter became a three-time All-Star and also won the Cy Young
Award with 37 saves.

Here are the three-year totals ('77–'79) for Sutter and his set-up
man, Willie Hernandez:

	Games	Innings	Saves	ERA
Sutter:	188	307	95	2.25
Hernandez:	172	249	7	3.37

Sutter was making more than $500,000 a year by the late '70s.
Hernandez made $19,000 his rookie year and just $50,000 in '79. He
certainly wasn't as good as Sutter and he didn't have the split-finger
pitch that made Sutter a superstar. Willie was probably a little below
where he should have been as far as salary and status. He just happened to be on a team that was blessed with the game's top closer.

But what mattered was how Willie perceived it, and to him, it all
added up to a big ball of disrespect.

"Pitching behind Sutter, it was frustration on top of frustration,"
he says. "The front office, they never give me credit. I made Bruce
Sutter 'Fireman of the Year' twice, once the MVP and the Cy Young
Award pitching behind him." (Sutter never was MVP, though he finished in the top 10 each of the years Willie set the table for him.) In
Willie's mind, Sutter was "Mr. Everything," and Willie was perceived
as his butler or valet.

In 1980, he essentially told the Cubs, "Screw this. Make me a
starter." He would no longer accept his thankless set-up role. They
played along, said they would, and he proceeded to go 1-9 as a combination starter-reliever.

"I wanted to be a starter because pitching behind Bruce Sutter,
they never pay me for that. I put my foot in my mouth because I had

a bad season," Willie humbly recalls. They sent him to Iowa in '81 and that woke him up. "I told them I'd be a reliever again and they brought me back up."

By then, Sutter had left for St. Louis and the Cubs had found Lee Smith. In '82, Smith appeared in 72 games and recorded 17 saves. Willie pitched in 75 games and had a career-high 10 saves.

"I was pitching behind Lee Smith, but I was getting more credit because I was getting into more games and they let me get some saves," Willie recalls. He was back on track, getting to close games more often, but was still doomed to pitch behind a star. Smith would eventually become baseball's all-time saves leader.

Dallas Green was running the Phillies in '82, having replaced himself as manager with Pat Corrales. The Phillies had won the World Series in 1980 and finished second in the NL East with 89 wins in '82. For '83, they acquired Al Holland from the Giants to be their closer. But Holland hurt his arm early in the season, and the Phillies were desperate to replace him. On May 22, they pulled the trigger, trading starter Dick Ruthven and pitching prospect Bill Johnson to the Cubs for Hernandez. To Willie, this seemed perfect.

He was on a winner now and accepted being the set-up man when Holland returned to action. But Holland was woefully lacking in baseball etiquette, and the respect and appreciation Hernandez craved and demanded was still not forthcoming.

"Holland got healthy, and when Holland was asked about his set-up men, he didn't want to talk about me, he wanted to talk about himself. So he'd change the subject," Hernandez ruefully recalls. "I was beside him listening (during an interview) and I said to myself, 'This guy is an asshole,' and after the season I said I want myself out of here."

Baseball's bullpen format was clear to him and it was time to move up. There is "The Man," and there are those who set up "The Man." In '83, Holland had pitched 68 times to Willie's 63. Holland had 25 saves, Willie had only seven. Willie vowed that 1984 would be different.

"I went to spring training with the mind that I wanted to get traded," he recalls. "So Sparky make a couple of moves and sent me to heaven."

Still, the Tigers had to beat the competition to get him. In early March, the Blue Jays came hard at the Phillies but couldn't close a deal when the Jays refused to part with young outfielder Jesse Barfield. Barfield had hit 27 homers in just 388 at bats in '83 and was only 24 years old. That's when the Tigers dangled Glenn Wilson in front of them, and the Phillies took the hook.

On March 24, the deal of Hernandez and Dave Bergman for Wilson and John Wockenfuss was completed. Willie jumped in his car and made the 60-minute drive from the Phillies camp to Lakeland.

"When I came from Clearwater to Lakeland, I sent a message to tell Sparky I am here. I got dressed and I was going to meet him in the dugout. He asked me when I got to the dugout, 'Will, how do you want me to pitch you?' I said, 'Every day. You pitch me every day and I guarantee you that we gonna do OK because that's the way I like it. If I pitch every four days, I gotta be a starter because I cannot be the same (as effective). If I pitch every day, I'm gonna be trim and nasty!' I told him that."

The Tigers players were wary. They didn't know much about Willie because he had received little notice despite his 342 appearances in seven seasons. And they were still shaken over the sudden departures of Glenn Wilson and John Wockenfuss, as well as the unceremonious release of Rick Leach.

Wilson had been Lance Parrish's best friend on the team, but Parrish knew his job was to create rapport with the new guy. He sucked it up and went to work.

"Willie came over and I had no idea in spring training that he was gonna be that good," Lance readily admits. "He was just a guy who threw a lotta different pitches, with a pretty good screwball. I wasn't that smart to project that he was going to be as good as he was. He threw the ball well and located his pitches well. I'm always happy when I see that.

"But as the season started to go forward and he kept getting the job done, it was like, 'Wow, this guy's pretty good.' He threw a fastball, breaking ball and screwball, but he threw his breaking ball and his fastball side-arm as well. He threw both pitches on top and both from the side, so it was almost like five different pitches. He'd come from the side on left-hand hitters. It was an awesome pitch, that screwball."

The screwball breaks the opposite way of a normal breaking pitch. When a lefty throws a breaking ball, it moves in on a right-handed hitter. But the screwball spins the opposite way and moves toward the outside on a right-handed hitter. Willie had learned the screwball the winter before the '83 season.

"Before spring training in '83, I worked out for two-three weeks in Puerto Rico," Hernandez relates. "Mike Cuellar lived in the area and he worked out in the same stadium I was working out in." Cuellar, a Cuban living in Puerto Rico, had retired after the '77 season. In a six-year stretch with the Orioles, Cueller had won between 18 and 24 games each year, winning 20 or more four times.

Hernandez says, "Cuellar asked me, 'You wanna work on that pitch?' He told me, 'You have a changeup but the screwball can make a lot of difference.' He said, 'Will, I'm willing to help because this pitch, you can't learn it from one day to the other, you have to work on it a lot because your mechanics change and then everything changes.'

"We start playing catch and in five minutes he took me to the mound. He told me to just open up my body a little bit. So I did and he said, 'That's unbelievable. Nobody can learn that pitch that quick. You got a gift from God.' I learned it in five minutes. Throw the cutter to the right-hand hitters so nobody can dig [in] on the plate looking for the screwball, then they look for the screwball and I throw the cutter on the inside corner. It was amazing."

It's a hard pitch to learn and the rap on it is that the reverse movement a pitcher imparts strains the elbow and shoulder. Willie shrugs that off. "Not hard on the elbow. You throw the pitch with your upper body. You lag your arm and your arm and upper body go down to together, so no strain there. Not your elbow, shoulder, anything, because you throw with the upper body."

Hernandez relishes the chance to recall the genesis of his incredible '84 success. He had almost flamed out in 1980 when his damaged pride had caused him to demand that the Cubs make him a starter. The 1981 season had been horrible for him also, as he spent most of it in the minors attempting to recover from the fall to 1-9 he'd taken the year before. Actually, the screwball was the second new pitch he learned in remaking his career.

Willie Hernandez— the Fireman of the Year poses in his element.

"In '82, Ferguson Jenkins taught me the cutter," Willie adds in continuing to recall the elements of the dramatic rise in his pitching prowess. Jenkins was nearing the end of his Hall of Fame career and took Willie aside for some instruction. The cut fastball from a lefty tends to dive in at right-handed hitters.

"I hadn't been able to dig on right-handed hitters that much because my fastball was sinking a lot," he says. "So now when I started pitching inside with that pitch, it made the difference. One pitch goes one way, the other pitch goes the other way, and that's why I had big success."

Whereas Sutter, Smith and Holland had Willie available as set-up guy so they could waltz in and rack up saves, Willie now needed his set-up guy on the Tigers. Sparky understood Hernandez' need to be "The Man," and for that to happen, Aurelio Lopez would have to accept the role of advance man. By the same token, Willie would be careful not to treat Lopez as he had been treated by the "asshole," Holland.

Hernandez claims that with the roles clearly defined, Lopez was okay with his arrival. "What Sparky did in the beginning of the season was he named the starters, who's gonna be short relief, who's gonna be middle relief, who's gonna be ace. He knows that Aurelio and I can do anything—long, short, anything in between."

Roger Craig decided to let them both pitch often to see how things would shake out. In the Tigers' 35-5 start, Willie came in 17 times for seven saves; Lopez pitched 18 times with six saves, often in the closer's role. Hernandez' dominating stuff eventually pushed him to the forefront, but by that time, Lopez realized that his new friend and teammate deserved it.

Craig was masterful in managing the workloads and egos of both men. In the diary he wrote during the season, Craig said, "Lopez has some problems that stem from Willie's emergence as our No. 1 reliever. Aurelio is a high-strung, emotional person who enjoyed being cast as the No. 1 bullpen artist. As Willie gradually took over as the king of the bullpen, Aurelio's ego was bruised. I'm going to have to help Aurelio understand his role."

When '84 was said and done, Hernandez had pitched 80 times, Lopez 71 times, and they amassed a combined 46 saves (Willie with 32, Aurelio 14), and a combined 19-4 record.

When he would stride in from the bullpen, Hernandez appeared completely relaxed and in charge, as if to say to opposing hitters, "I have a job to do, and this will not be fun for you. And if you get too comfortable with me, I might have to hurt you, too." He had been haunted by past failures, and he realized that the edge he had now gained wouldn't last forever.

"When somebody have success, people want to step on you to try to make you look bad, laughing at you," he claims. "So that nobody can make me look bad, when I came to the mound the only one who's gonna run the show is myself, nobody else."

Yet, Hernandez denies that the macho image he portrayed at the peak of his powers was something he purposely created. He had no prepared act, like Al "The Mad Hungarian" Hrabosky of the

Cardinals, who would turn his back to the hitter and then wheel around and stomp to the rubber. "Because you feel in charge, you look in charge," Willie says in explaining his philosophy. "I didn't try to impress anybody. I don't plan to intimidate anybody. They are intimidated because I like to pitch inside and somebody dig in on the plate too much, I'm gonna dig (pitch inside) a little more and a little more. Nobody's gonna fool around with my food. Pitching on the (inside) corner is how I make a living. If you let guys dig in you'll have no success and you'll be back home before you plan to."

Willie uses the word "dig" to explain a lot about the pitching process. Hitters "dig" in by crowding the plate and challenging him to throw inside, and he "digs" back by moving them off the plate. He also "digs" a hole in front of the rubber with his cleats in order to push off. Willie refers back to a confrontation with the Yankees' Rickey Henderson to explain how he established his turf and evidenced his disdain for hitters.

"Almost every pitcher uses the right side of the rubber," he continues. "But for my screwball I have to pitch on the left side. Almost nobody uses it. Against the Yankees we had a 2-1 lead and the Yankees have men on first and second, ninth inning. I came in from the bullpen, and I had to dig on the left side of the rubber because I had to break the rubber in so I can push on it. I look mean because I gotta see the motivation, the attitude from the hitters. If he looks at me and he's scared, I go right at him. But the guy who tries to intimidate me, I tell you what I do.

"When I came in against the Yankees, Rickey Henderson is the first hitter. When I was kicking the mound to dig in, he was kicking home plate as imitation. People try to fuck with you, intimidate you. I was kicking once, he was kicking twice. Once, twice. He looks at me and I look at him and say, 'Okay, you got it.' So I come fastball in, voom. I push him back. He started kicking at the plate again. 'Okay,' I say, I come in—voom, more closer, ball two. Third pitch, he's still digging, I knock him right on his ass. I yell to him, 'Now you ready.'

"Sparky is watching and angry, waving his arms. I look over at him and he say, 'What are you doin'? 2-1, two men on, you can't put another guy on base. It's 3-0 count now.' He was going crazy in the dugout.

"Lance comes out. 'What are you doing?' I said, 'Fuck this SOB.' He said, 'I know.' So I come back outside with screwball on the black, voom, strike one. Next I give him breaking ball inside corner, voom, strike two. So now Rickey thinks, 'What you gonna do? Which corner you gonna throw it?' I threw a fastball right in the cock [down the middle], voom, he took it for strike three. Ha! When the game ends I went to the foul line by his dugout and yell at him, 'Next time you want to dig in, you dig on your mama's ass.' Everybody was laughing in our dugout.

"I didn't try to intimidate people, but this is business. You show guts. You throw the screwball and breaking ball for strikes to Henderson. He doesn't know what I'm gonna throw next. So I go right down the middle. He's one of the assholes I'm talking about."

Hernandez had another fine year in '85 with 31 saves and a 2.70 ERA. Meanwhile—without Willie—Holland was struggling in Philadelphia and was traded away early in the '85 season. Holland recorded only 15 more saves after '84. But Willie says he took no joy at the demise of Holland and the Phillies, who went from the World Series in '83 with Hernandez to a .500 team in '84, and sub-.500 in '85.

"I feel sorry because they are dumb and they didn't know what a big help I was giving them and they deserve it, but I'm not happy (about Philly's demise)," he says. "Holland had a weak arm and he couldn't handle more than five innings a week. I would take him to two outs in the ninth so he can get a save pitching a third of an inning.

"So when I leave he got worn out. I don't give a damn because the Tigers give me the money. If I had gotten the money in Philadelphia, I would have stayed there. No, I don't feel happy—I feel sorry for those dumb son of a bitches, they didn't appreciate what a big help I was for them."

Hernandez made $335,000 in '84 and had a year left on his contract. He had no agent and was trying to work on an extension with Bill Lajoie. He told Lajoie he either wanted a new deal or he'd exercise his right to demand a trade before the '85 season. In a case of poor timing that also reeked of selfishness, Hernandez made his contract frustration public before Game Three of the World Series.

He revealed that Lajoie had offered him a four-year extension late in the season, but it didn't elevate his salary to the elite level. They eventually settled on a four-year extension worth about $1,150,000 per year that would commence in 1986 and carry him until his career ended after the 1989 season. By then, Holland ('87) and Sutter ('88) were out of baseball. Ironically, Sutter, Holland and Hernandez all pitched until the age of 35.

Though he lives in Puerto Rico, Willie plans on selling his construction business and is looking to get back into baseball. He lives not far from his birthplace of Aguada with his three sons and his wife, Carmen, whom he married in '78. "We're even more in love today," he says of Carmen, and backs that up with the hearty laugh of a prideful man, now fully at peace.

Chapter 13

The Patriarch

He ran the club like it was the '40s and '50s.

— Milt Wilcox on his tightwad boss, Jim Campbell

I could give him a knife, turn my back, and never have to worry.

— Sparky Anderson on his beloved boss, Jim Campbell

You can't write anything comprehensive about the Tigers of the second half of the 20th century without taking into account the dominating influence of Jim Campbell, the general manager from 1963 to 1983. In 1978 he added "team president" to his résumé, and in 1984 he gave up the GM position to add CEO to his nameplate. It was then that he elevated his farm director and assistant GM, Bill Lajoie, to the role of general manager. Lajoie had drafted all the team's key players, had overseen all the major trades and just that spring had pulled the trigger on the fabulously successful trade of Glenn Wilson and John Wockenfuss for Willie Hernandez and Dave Bergman.

On the management side, the Tigers were a three-headed beast. Sparky, the manager and major public persona, was the spokesman and mouthpiece. The relatively reticent Campbell and Lajoie ran the business side and procured the players to suit Sparky's style and vision. But Campbell had final say on everything, and he ruled his Tigers with an old-school propriety and conviction.

Campbell's name and unsmiling visage surfaced several times in '84, but only when he was playing the role of the old-fashioned curmudgeon, which he legitimately was. He was a relic from an era past, a bald, walrus-looking grump, who seemed strangely determined to present the public only his most sourpuss face.

Former owner John Fetzer, a media magnate, and new owner Tom Monaghan, a pizza kingpin, left Campbell alone to watch over the players, the payroll and all aspects pertaining to the bottom line. Fetzer's marching orders to Campbell decades earlier had been to keep the Tigers profitable, and Campbell took great pride in fulfilling that role. The mission of his life was to honor the wishes of the man who had put such faith in him. Fetzer rarely interfered, and Campbell returned that trust with the highest level of dedication and loyalty.

He developed Tiger Town, the vast minor-league complex in Lakeland, and rebuilt the farm system. Under his watch, the 1968 World Champions were developed.

Campbell had just one major blind spot, but it was so blatant and pervasive that it kept him distant from the people who should have meant the most to him—the Tigers players and fans. Simply, Campbell could not adjust to a changing marketplace and steadfastly clung to the past to the point of absurdity.

Committed to the "purity of the game" and whatever that meant to him, Campbell believed that baseball should be presented in an unadorned fashion, and he refused virtually all marketing innovation.

Jim Campbell behind his desk in 1969. As Denny McLain and the other Tigers realized, negotiating with the boss was no picnic.

He was determined to keep the Detroit baseball experience unadulterated by gaudy promotions and special days.

When Campbell did surface to be heard by the public, it was most often to either pooh-pooh a fan-friendly marketing suggestion or to comment in response to another one of his ballplayers bitching about his stinginess.

Milt Wilcox spent more time under Campbell than did any of his Tigers teammates. Campbell had acquired him in 1976 as a sore-armed Cubs castoff. According to Wilcox, "No ballplayer had a relationship with Campbell. When you were invited to see him, you would sit in that office with the cherry wood, and he'd smoke a cigar and it was almost like you were privileged to go into that office and talk to him.

"The only time you went in there was if you were supposed to sign a contract that was for a lot less money than you should be making, or he was going to yell at you for some article in the paper. I don't think any players had any warm feelings for Campbell. The only guys who did were the guys who he'd get to sign for less, like Alan Trammell and Lou Whitaker, who he had snowed over. That's why Jim Campbell was around. He saved John Fetzer lots of money."

He saved Fetzer money, and he had been doing it for a long time.

Denny McLain was paid $30,000 in 1968, the year he won 31 games as well as the MVP and Cy Young awards. The Tigers broke two million in attendance, an increase of 25-plus percent from the best previous attendance in club history.

Denny and I spent five years together on radio and television in the early '90s. This was his most revealing Campbell story:

Prior to the '69 season, Denny was called in to see Campbell to "negotiate" his new contract. Back then, before free agency, players had virtually no bargaining power. Because of the "reserve clause," which was finally shot down in 1976, baseball teams retained players as their exclusive property in perpetuity. A player's only negotiating power was to threaten to deny the team his services, which hurt everybody, including the player.

McLain went into Campbell's office determined to get what he deserved, even though, deep down, he was pretty certain that his bluff would be called. He figured that Campbell would offer him a "generous" $20,000 raise to get him to $50,000 or so, and he didn't want to even let those words flow from Campbell's mouth.

So when he sat down, Denny got right to the point. "Jim, I want a hundred thousand. Mantle, Mays, Williams, Kaline are all hundred-thousand-dollar players, and I just won 31 goddamn games, Jim. You know I'm worth it and I'll make it real simple Jim—I'm not playin' this year unless I get a hundred grand."

Campbell, from behind his desk, looked passively at McLain, whose heart was pounding, his fighting spirit fully engaged. "Denny, you know I can't do that," Campbell gently replied. "I can't give you Kaline money. He's been here since 1953, 10 years longer than you. If I give you a hundred grand, then what's Freehan gonna say? What's Cash, Northrup and all those guys gonna say? They'll be in here wanting their deals tripled. It can't happen, Denny. I've got a ballclub to run, and I won't lose money doing it."

Denny stood his ground even though he knew his gun was all but empty. "That's bullshit, Jim," he said. "That's not my problem, Jim. You can't win without me, and Kaline was hurt half of last year. I want a hundred grand and you know I deserve it."

Still in control as always, Campbell quietly laid down the bottom line. "Denny, I was going to offer you fifty, but here's what I'll do. I'll double what you made last year. I'll give you sixty, against my better judgment. But that's it. Take it or leave it."

McLain had one bullet left: "No, Jim. That's still bullshit. I'm walking out of here. I'll get gigs playing the organ or whatever it takes."

Campbell stared at him from across the desk, starting to show impatience and anger for the first time. "OK, Denny, do what you have to do. But before you walk out, I'll just tell you this. My final offer is sixty, and every minute that goes by that you don't sign, it goes down a thousand dollars."

At that point, the man who had beaten opponents 31 times, and who had bills that needed immediate attention, was himself beaten. He looked at Campbell and meekly said, "OK. Where's the pen?"

There wasn't a lot of mystery to Jim Campbell. You knew exactly what he stood for. Older fans respected that Campbell had built the '68 championship team, and that gave him great credibility. But they also knew that the man was a killjoy who staunchly refused to spruce up the stadium beyond the barest basics, or to willingly add any fun to the experience. He was the nauseatingly dedicated traditionalist who played the role of Fetzer's loyal hatchet man.

Prying Fetzer's cash from Campbell was a frustration that all Tigers players shared. Jack Morris tells a Campbell story that reveals much about Campbell's style and depth. "This is one I haven't told many people, but it exemplifies my relationship with Jim Campbell.

"I went upstairs to see Campbell (at Tiger Stadium) one year, sometime before '84, to negotiate a contract. Lajoie hadn't started doing the negotiating yet, and I went into Campbell's office and it was this classic scene you'd see in a 1920s baseball movie. Here's this bald, a little overweight guy, sitting back in his big leather chair with this beautiful oak desk and he's smoking this huge cigar. He looks at me kinda like I'm a nothing and that I should just be honored to be in his presence and he asked me to sit down.

"I get in the chair and it's real smoky and I asked him, 'Jim, can you open up a window?' and he looks at me crazy and I said, 'I'm sorry, but I've got really small lungs because my heart's so big.' He looked at me and his veins just about popped out and he said, 'Get the hell outta here right now.'

"The next day I went up there again and he laughed about it, but it was just that pecking order that he wanted everybody to know that he was the man. Now, after saying all that, if you don't write this next part, I'll kill you." (OK, Jack. Here's the rest of the story!) "Campbell wrote me a letter the day I retired—one of the only people who ever acknowledged my retirement. He wrote me this nice long letter about what it meant to have a guy like me play for him and how proud he was to be associated with my career."

Campbell took a long and circuitous route to his exalted office. After graduating from high school in 1943, he joined the war effort with the Navy Air Corps. Afterwards, he went to Ohio State, studied some business and played a little outfield for the Buckeyes. Graduating at age 25 in December 1949, he was off and running with his first baseball job as business manager of the Thomasville, Georgia, Tigers of the Class D Georgia-Florida League.

Campbell loved telling about how the night after he reported for duty, the ballpark burned down. He immediately took charge, borrowing uniforms, patching things together on the fly, and had the park quickly rebuilt. This immediately earned him the respect of his superiors. A quarter-century later, in '74, the Tiger Stadium press box burned down, prompting what is perhaps Campbell's greatest one-liner: "Just my luck; the press box burns down and not a single sports writer in it!"

Campbell's management savvy put him on the fast track. In 1950 he was promoted to manage the Tigers' top farm team in Toledo, and by '52 he made the big club as business manager of the Tigers' farm department.

In '56, when John Fetzer bought the team from the Briggs family, Campbell was initially named farm director. And within a matter of months, he was named business manager of the entire organization. He was elevated to vice president in 1959, at age 34, and by the end of 1962, the admiring Fetzer named him general manager. It was then that Fetzer gave him the dictate that would affect every decision Campbell ever made. Fetzer instructed him, "Keep it simple, run it all, make all the decisions. Just keep it in the black and keep the problems off my doorstep." And that's just what Jim Campbell did for the next 30 years.

Campbell was divorced and childless, truly married to baseball, working with rarely a day off. With World Series wins in '68 as executive VP and general manager, and 16 years later, in '84, as president and CEO, Campbell stands alone in Detroit sports annals as the only leader of a franchise to win championships with two completely different teams in two different eras.

And all of this from a man who admitted he was a poor judge of baseball talent. Campbell thrived by hiring talented people like Lajoie, and before him, Hall of Famer Rick Ferrell, to help him spot the right players. Campbell just turned the profit, grinding players to keep the payroll low and avoiding any and all frills.

As a young sportscaster who began his career in the mid-'70s, I had an acute sense that everything I stood for was anathema to Campbell. I was a rock 'n' roll sportscaster, the first ever on FM radio in Detroit. I was irreverent, as was the young FM audience to which I broadcast. I started on WABX in 1974, an "underground" station, later termed "progressive," and later went to WJZZ. In 1978, I moved more mainstream to WRIF, which still calls itself "The Home of Rock 'n' Roll."

All were FM stations, back when FM was in its infancy. It was fashionable for me to be critical of the icons that the older generation always seemed to kiss up to. On the other hand, WJR, which broadcast the games and was Campbell's "home station," stood for everything I and my audience disliked. Every other word on WJR was "wonderful" or "marvelous," and their sports reporters seemed to kiss up and sugar-coat everything with an "aw shucks" type of nonsense.

Those of us on FM didn't want to or need to play it straight. We weren't beholden to the management of sports teams, and being contrary was a role that nobody else, at least in the broadcast world, seemed to have the desire to play.

What made no sense was that those in the rock 'n' roll youth culture that so reviled Jim Campbell were rabid Tigers fans. Campbell gladly took their money, but never felt inclined to get to know them. I was never sure how much of my radio commentaries he heard or was aware of, but I was certain that Campbell was suspicious of me and my audience. Nonetheless, as a man of propriety, he was respectfully cordial to me.

By 1983, I was becoming pretty well known around Michigan. Besides my ongoing radio association at WRIF and WXYT, I had hosted the new half-hour Tigers pre-game show in '82 and anchored the weekend sportscasts on Channel 4. I wasn't sure what Campbell really thought about me, but in April '83, I got a fairly good indication.

The Tigers opened the season in Minnesota, and the producers of the pre-game show sent me on the road. The second night we were there, our director, Chuck Wasiluk, suggested that since I was just sitting around during the game, I might want to join George Kell and Al Kaline in the booth. I did, offering some fan-style inquisitiveness in my three-inning stint.

But despite my benign comments, Campbell still blew up. He called the powers at Channel 4 and said, "Get him out of there."

All of us, Kaline and Kell included, were taken by surprise. We thought, "What's the big deal?" I had said nothing of consequence and certainly didn't want to alienate the icons, George and Al. Two weeks later, the papers sniffed it out that Campbell had gotten angry, and the headline in the *Free Press* article by Joe Lapointe read, "Zaret gets boot from Tiger booth." *The Detroit News* wrote, "Zaret stirs TV booth rift." Campbell's quote was, "The Tigers want a two-man team on the air, plain and simple. We don't want Eli or anyone else in there."

WDIV's 1984 Tigers broadcast team. Back row: Mike Andro, Toby Tabaczynski, Sue Ganzak, Chuck Wasiluk. Front row: Eli Zaret, Al Kaline, George Kell, Al Ackerman.

Then the station started to panic. They were desperate to retain the broadcast rights, and the contract expired after the '83 season. Channel 2 wanted in on the Tigers cash cow, and Channel 4 General Manager Amy McCombs said that Campbell was within his rights and that there would be no more violations.

George Puscas, of the *Free Press*, printed a Love Letter from a woman in Jackson who wrote, "Jim Campbell has finally made a statement I agree with—keep Eli Zaret out of the broadcast booth during televised Tiger games." I had to take my shot, too. I told Lapointe, "If I was Jim, I wouldn't want me in there either. God only knows that I might say something he doesn't like."

In summary, the whole thing worked perfectly for me. I really had no role in the booth, and nothing of redeeming value to offer above and beyond what George and Al already provided. Yet, I'd tweaked the old boy, gotten two days of publicity out of it and probably got a lot of

Campbell was an enigma—intractable and tight-fisted but with a big heart.

my radio listeners to say, "Way to go, Eli—stick it to that old SOB Campbell!"

Campbell stayed with the Tigers until August 3, 1992, when Monaghan unceremoniously fired him and team president Bo Schembechler before transferring the team to new owner Mike Ilitch. It was Bo's 24th wedding anniversary and his wife, Millie, was dying of cancer. Campbell went out like a soldier, saying in a statement, "I was treated with dignity over 43 years. I don't have anything to be ashamed of. I wish the Tigers well."

As for Mike Ilitch's statement that he had been told by Monaghan that Campbell was going to resign, Campbell said, "I didn't resign. I was dismissed. I want to go out like a gentleman." He did, never returning to the stadium where he had spent most of his adult life. He had been married to baseball, admitting as much after his wife of 15 years divorced him in 1970 because of his unbending devotion to the Tigers. When it happened he said, "She accused me of loving baseball more than her. Damned if she wasn't right."

Campbell had picked up a small piece of the team when Fetzer sold it to Monaghan, banked a few million dollars after the Ilitch sale and then retired to Lakeland. In '93, McLain and I were at spring training and visited Jim at his Lakeland condo. Campbell, despite his stuffiness, had a soft spot for rebels like McLain.

Denny and Jim enjoyed some laughs and nostalgic chit-chat looking at a wall full of pictures in a hallway, including team pictures of McLain's group in its progression from the minor leagues up through the championship in 1968. There was also a framed newspaper cartoon that Campbell took particular joy in showing us. A man wearing a Tigers cap is sitting in a chair. His wife says to a friend, "John lives in dread that Jim Campbell will make some dumb move."

Campbell didn't make too many. Perhaps his greatest stroke as GM was the legendary October 1970 trade of McLain, Don Wert and Elliot Maddox to the Senators for Ed Brinkman, Aurelio Rodriguez and Joe Coleman. That trade helped the Tigers win a division title in '72. Denny knew that Campbell had done the right thing and never faulted him for it.

When Campbell died of a heart attack in late October 1995, Kaline said, "I'll never forget how honest he was. A handshake was all you needed."

McLain said, "He's always been a gentleman. I don't know where you'll ever find another Jim Campbell."

Sparky said, "Working without Jim Campbell will be the most disappointing thing that has happened in my life. He was the nicest, most honest friend I ever had."

Chapter 14

July:
Bean Balls, Boycotts and Slump-Busting

I told him, "I don't know how much money you make...but money don't buy happiness. You can buy the biggest boat and five or six cars, but you're an unhappy person. We got to find a way to make you happy."

> — Pitching coach Roger Craig on Jack Morris after Morris argued with umpires and threw his hat and glove into the dugout on July 18

L et's again play with the numbers a bit. When a team starts out 35-5, it's already 30 games over .500. Were it to play merely .500 ball the rest of the way (61-61), it would finish 96-66, and 96 victories usually wins pennants. The Tigers wound up winning 104, going 69-53 after the record-shattering start. What made the regular season even more compelling was that Toronto wouldn't go away until the Tigers put a dagger through their hearts in a crucial series in early September.

The two wins to end June, including Kirk Gibson's ninth-inning, game-winning, two-run homer off the Twins' Pete Filson, gave way to a very sluggish eight days leading up to the All-Star break. The Tigers would win only two of those eight games.

On July 1, they finished the Twins series with a 9-0 loss to ace Frank Viola. Sparky dismissed it with, "There isn't enough perfume to clean up that one." The 43,484 fans who

JULY 1984

July Record: 16-12

Highlights:
Whitaker, Parrish, Lemon voted All-Star starters;
Morris, Hernandez, Trammell added to All-Star team
11 wins in 12 games after pre–All-Star slump

Stars:

Grubb:	11-25, .440 batting average
Lopez:	13 APP. 1-0, 1.27 ERA, 2 saves
Hernandez:	10 APP. 2-0, 1.31 ERA, 6 saves
Whitaker:	only AL player with more than 1 hit in All-Star Game; hit game-winning inside-the-park homer 7/13

Key Games:
July 13: 5-3 win @ Minn; Whitaker inside-the-park HR in 11th
July 16: 7-1 win vs. Chicago features bean ball war
July 18: 10-6 loss to Chicago; Morris blows up
July 29: 3-0 win vs. Boston; Wilcox 8 shutout innings; 12-game lead

thought that they had paid for more '84 heroics affirmed Sparky's assessment with some fairly lusty booing.

GAMES 78, 79 & 80 @ CHICAGO—The Tigers then traveled to Chicago and dumped all three games. Dave Rozema gave up two-run homers to Harold Baines and Ron Kittle in a 7-1 thumping on July 2.

The next night, Jack Morris got roughed up for the second straight game in a 9-5 loss to Tom Seaver. Sparky, Jack and Roger Craig all insisted that Jack's arm was fine, despite Jack's having allowed 13 earned runs in 10 innings of his back-to-back losses. Morris, at 12-5, along with Lou Whitaker, Lance Parrish and Chet Lemon, were named All-Star starters.

On Wednesday, July 4, Chicago's 8-2 pounding of Milt Wilcox produced the Tigers' first four-game losing streak of the season. Then they went to Texas and took two of three from the Rangers to complete the first half of the season.

GAMES 81, 82, 83 & 84 @ TEXAS—On July 5, they trailed the Rangers, 4-1, in the ninth facing a fifth straight loss. Charlie Hough was working on a five-hitter. With one out, Lemon beat out an infield hit. Larry Herndon singled and Dave Bergman fanned for the second out. John Grubb walked, and Whitaker and Trammell each singled to tie it at four. Then Gibson swatted a three-run homer to win it, 7-4. The amazing Tigers had scored six runs with two out in the ninth.

Juan Berenguer lost, 5-3, to the Rangers on July 6.

In the concluding game of the season's first half, Rozema won, 5-2, and moved his record to 5-1. Willie Hernandez recorded his 16th save and was named to the All-Star pitching staff. Sparky then declared that Willie had been his first-half MVP.

The All-Star break was a welcome respite. Whitaker's wrist was bothering him, and Trammell, although added as an All-Star reserve, would have to miss the game and was put on the disabled list for 10 days with shoulder tendinitis and an inflamed ulnar nerve running the length of his throwing arm. They called up Doug Baker, and Baker and Tom Brookens would cover for Trammell at short.

The pitching was also a legitimate concern. Morris was in a funk that was really just beginning and would alarmingly intensify later in July. Milt Wilcox, who had slipped to 8-6 after a 6-0 start, was hurting again and in need of another cortisone shot, and Berenguer was woefully inconsistent.

There were rumors that the Tigers were looking for pitching and might try to pry Bert Blyleven from Cleveland. Larry Herndon had

Gibson three-run homer, 6 in 9th sink Rangers

just one homer all year and was in the process of losing playing time to Ruppert Jones.

Darrell Evans, 37, though a positive addition to the clubhouse, had just seven homers after hitting 30 in '83 with the Giants. This was legitimately disappointing in light of his three-year, $2.25-million free-agent contract. The Tigers had been just 22-22 since the blazing 35-5 start, so considering the slumps and injuries, the seven-game lead over Toronto was not as imposing as it might have otherwise appeared.

The Tigers may have been muddling on the field, but they remained tremendous box-office and television attractions. Eight of the top 10 shows in Detroit for the week of July 2–8 were either *Tigers '84* pre-game shows, or the games themselves.

The National League won the All-Star game, 3-1, at Candlestick Park in San Francisco. Atlanta's Dale Murphy hit an eighth-inning homer off Hernandez that provided the final run. Whitaker went 2-3, and was the only AL player with more than one hit. Parrish had a sore tongue, of all things, after a collision at home with Padres first baseman Steve Garvey. What hurt more than his tongue was that he dropped the ball, allowing the run to score.

GAMES 85, 86, 87 & 88 @ MINNESOTA—The Tigers came back to start the season's second half and beat the Twins in Minnesota on Friday the 13th. In the 11th inning, Brookens tripled off Rick Lysander and Whitaker followed with an inside-the-park, game-winning homer.

The Tigers won, 6-5, in 12 innings the next night with a classic Kirk Gibson moment. Gibson entered the game in the sixth as a pinch hitter. In the 12th, he stretched a single into a double. Lemon then singled to center, and Gibson charged around third, pumping hard and heading home. The Twins' Dave Engle was blocking the plate, so Gibson blasted him, sending both sprawling in opposite directions. After a few seconds of aftershock, Gibson realized that home plate umpire Vic Voltaggio had not made a call, so he leapt to his feet to tag home, barely eluding Engle's reach. Gibson was then deemed safe on a highly controversial call.

A lengthy argument ensued, but Voltaggio stuck to his decision. Twins Manager Billy Gardner seethed, "I've been in baseball 39 years and when there's a collision at home and the catcher doesn't drop the ball, the runner is out." Replays showed that Engle probably made the tag as he was being taken out by the former football All-American.

The Tigers made it three straight with a 6-2 win on Sunday, July

GAME #86   July 13
Tigers 5, Twins 3

DETROIT	AB	R	H	BI	MINNESOTA	AB	R	H	BI
Whitaker 2b	4	2	2	2	Puckett cf	4	0	1	0
Johnson 3b	5	0	0	0	Brown lf	5	0	2	0
Gibson rf	4	0	0	1	Hrbek 1b	5	1	1	0
Parrish c	4	0	2	1	Engle c	5	0	2	1
Evans 1b	3	0	1	0	Bush dh	3	0	0	0
Bergman pr-1b	0	0	0	0	Hatcher ph	2	0	1	0
Lemon cf	4	0	2	0	Brunansky rf	4	0	0	0
Jones dh	5	0	0	0	Teufel 2b	4	0	0	0
Herndon lf	5	0	0	0	Gaetti 3b	4	1	2	0
Baker ss	2	1	1	0	Jimenez ss	3	1	1	0
Grubb ph	1	1	1	1	Washington ph-ss	1	0	0	0
Brookens ss	2	1	2	0	David ph	1	0	0	0
Totals	39	5	11	5		41	3	10	1

Detroit---------------------- 000 002 010 02 -- 5
Minnesota------------------ 000 020 010 00 -- 3

Game winning RBI -- none, E -- Morris, Baker, DP -- Detroit 1, Minnesota 1, LOB -- Detroit 9, Minnesota 9, 2B -- Gaetti, Whitaker, Parrish, Hrbek, Brookens, 3B -- Brookens, HR -- Grubb, Whitaker, CS -- Lemon, Bergman, SH -- Puckett, Johnson, SF -- Gibson, PB -- Parrish

Detroit	IP	H	R	ER	BB	SO
Morris	7.1	8	3	1	0	4
Hernandez (W)	2.2	1	0	0	2	1
Lopez (S)	1.0	1	0	0	1	1
Minnesota						
Butcher*	7.0	7	3	3	2	4
Whitehouse	0.2	0	0	0	2	0
Lysander (L)	3.1	4	2	2	2	3

* Pitched to 2 batters in 8th

T -- 3:11 A -- 30,050

15. Rozema went his usual 5⅓, with Lopez taking over the last 3⅔. They had been on the road since July 2 and were coming home to host Chicago and Texas. Gibson had claimed that they had their first-half intensity back. The White Sox, '83 AL West champs, were struggling around .500, but still fighting for the lead in the AL West.

GAMES 89, 90 & 91 vs CHICAGO—It was a steamy Monday night in July, and the ballpark was jammed for the Tigers' first home game in over two weeks. If the Tigers had their intensity back, the White Sox were ready to match it. There was a lengthy history of bad blood between these teams.

◆ *Game 89: Bile and Bean Balls*

Where:	Tiger Stadium
Result:	7-1 Tigers
Record:	61-28
WP:	Abbott, 3-2
LP:	Hoyt, 8-10
Standing:	First, 8 ahead
Attendance:	41,935

GAME #89   July 16

Tigers 7, Sox 1

CHICAGO	AB	R	H	BI	DETROIT	AB	R	H	BI
Law R cf	3	0	0	0	Whitaker 2b	4	1	1	1
Fisk c	3	0	0	0	Jones lf	3	1	1	1
Baines rf	4	0	0	0	Kuntz ph-lf	1	0	0	0
Walker 1b	4	0	0	0	Gibson rf	3	2	2	3
Luzinski dh	4	0	2	0	Parrish c	3	1	0	0
Kittle lf	4	1	2	1	Evans dh	4	0	1	1
Law V 3b	2	0	0	0	Lemon cf	4	1	2	0
Hairston ph	1	0	0	0	Bergman 1b	2	0	1	1
Dybzinski 3b	0	0	0	0	Johnson 3b	4	1	1	0
Squires ph	1	0	0	0	Baker ss	3	0	0	0
Fletcher ss	3	0	0	0					
Cruz 2b	3	0	1	0					
Totals	32	1	5	1		31	7	9	7

Chicago	000 000 001	--	1	
Detroit	100 040 02x	--	7	

Game winning RBI -- none, DP -- Chicago 1, LOB -- Chicago 6, Detroit 4, 2B -- Cruz, 3B -- Gibson, HR -- Gibson, Kittle, SB -- Law R, SF -- Bergman, HBP -- by Abbott (Fisk), by Burns (Parrish)

Chicago	IP	H	R	ER	BB	SO
Hoyt (L)	5.1	8	5	5	1	6
Burns*	1.2	0	2	2	1	1
Spillner	1.0	1	0	0	0	0
Detroit						
Abbott (W)	9.0	5	1	1	1	0

* Pitched to 2 batters in 8th

T -- 2:29 A -- 41,935

Chet Lemon remembers:

The Tigers taught me to win, but the White Sox raised me. They drafted me when I was 17, and I made the majors at 20. I played there six years, '75 to '81, when the Tigers traded Steve Kemp for me. Tony LaRussa was our coach when I was there, and eventually became my manager, and [LaMarr] Hoyt was my teammate and had won the Cy Young Award in '83.

In the fifth inning, I hit a roller to Vance Law at third. It was a 1-0 game, and I slid headfirst into first and beat the throw. I had a sore right pinky that had bothered me for a few weeks and I jammed it again on the bag. I also had a sore back, and when I got up, my left hand hurt too. I also had a slight hamstring pull and right behind my knee I had strained ligaments. '84 was crazy that way; every day I had to come in early for treatment.

I stayed in the game. Lou singled me in and Gibby tripled in two more and we led Chicago, 5-0, after five. Then it got a little ugly.

Our starter, Glenn Abbott, had hit [Carlton] Fisk in the top of the sixth, and you know that when that happens the next one is a message or retaliation. But we never threw at anybody. That's just not the way we played the game. Skip wasn't that kind of manager to be throwing at anybody.

I got hit a lot. I wasn't right up on it, but I was close to the plate and sometimes they thought the way to get me out was pitch me in. It don't take a rocket scientist. Pitchers have to protect their teammates and Hoyt was like that. And he was gonna make sure if you throw at my guy, I'm gonna throw at your guy.

None of us would back down when we thought somebody was throwing at us or was pitching us tighter than what's normal. If somebody was trying to do us some bodily harm or retaliate, you wanna protect your players. Jack Morris or Milt or Dan or any of those guys are gonna get on that hill and know if you're throwing at our guys they're gonna bust you in or brush you back, too.

In the bottom half [of the sixth], Hoyt came in on me and umpire Ted Hendry warned him. In the eighth, Britt Burns hit Parrish, and when he took some steps towards Burns, Fisk steered Lance towards first and the benches emptied. Lance and LaRussa got into some heated arguing and Burns was ejected.

I missed the next four games to get over my finger injuries. I'd tape 'em up, but they'd swell. I slid headfirst because I always believed I got there just as fast [as standing up]. On a play where the first baseman gets pulled off the bag, it's almost impossible to tag a guy on a bang-bang play. Everybody will argue that it's slower, that you'll lose time through that bag.

When I'd hurt my hand sliding headfirst a few weeks before that, I was called upstairs by Jim Campbell and he said, "Chet, look, we're in the middle of a pennant race and we can't afford to lose you." He said, "The next time you slide headfirst into first base it's gonna cost you $1,500." It was serious business. I said, "Jim, you know that's just something I do instinctively, it's just the way I play. I play as hard as I can and I don't know how to play any other way." I understood where he was coming from. We didn't want to lose any of our players at that time that could affect our opportunity to finish as strong as we had started.

The very next game, I hit a ground ball to the shortstop in the hole, and lo and behold, there I go headfirst into first base. I got a call the next day in the locker room. It was Jim. He told me, "Chet, I know now that it's not something that you can control because I know you don't want to pay any money. You wouldn't want to give up a dime if you thought somebody wanted to take a dollar from you." We laughed about it. If you watch guys from Pete Rose to all the guys who played the game with an aggressiveness and a vengeance, that's just the way they play.

Chet Lemon

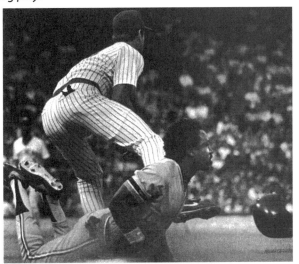

Even the threat of getting fined couldn't cure Lemon's compulsion to slide headfirst into first base.

Parrish was furious after the 7-1 Tigers' victory. Seeing as Abbott had plunked his catcher, Fisk, LaRussa said, "I think it was a case of two guys equally important to his club getting hit with a pitch." That's why Lance was positive that LaRussa wanted to hit him. Parrish countered with, "I know I lost a lot of respect for the manager. In fact, I can say I have no respect for him."

It had been just the latest chapter. In '82, Hoyt had knocked down Trammell three times in a game. Ed Farmer had hit Al Cowens the year before that, and it went all the way back to the early '70s when Tommy John hit Dick McAuliffe.

On Tuesday, July 17, Petry moved to 12-4 by beating the White Sox, 3-2, with a five-hitter for the Tigers' fifth straight win. Darrell Evans' two-run homer in the first made it 3-0 and completed the Tigers' scoring. The night before, Hernandez retired the last four hitters. Petry remarked afterwards that when Sparky came out to see him with two out in the eighth and nobody on, he told Sparky, "I know what you're going to do. Call in Willie." They both knew the reason. Switch-hitting Jerry Hairston was weaker from the right side. Hernandez fanned Hairston and finished it off by striking out Harold Baines and Greg Luzinski in the ninth for his 17th save. Just another night at the office for Willie and the bullpen.

◆*Game 91: Unhappy Jack*

Where:	**Tiger Stadium**
Result:	**10-6 White Sox**
Record:	**62-29**
WP:	**Bannister, 7-6**
LP:	**Morris, 12-6**
Standing:	**First, 8 ahead**
Attendance:	**39,051**

See the picture? That's Jack Morris, playfully winding up and getting ready to deck me during an interview on one of our Channel 4 pre-game shows.

Morris could give an excellent interview, and he could also be surly and standoffish. Kirk Gibson was the same way, but I never took their bad moods or rudeness personally like some other reporters did. As for Jack, many in the media disliked him, and it puzzled me because I felt that they had it backwards. In other words, when Jack was acting like an ass, I looked at it as his problem, because the "good" Jack would inevitably return when his personal conditions changed.

But when Jack was cooperative and passionate, others seemed suspicious, like it was just a respite from the "bad" Jack. Like Kirk, Jack was a fabulous competitor and a deep thinker, and both men could be very hard on themselves. And when Jack did beat himself up, he could take a lot of prisoners, and that's what happened on this day.

This would become a noteworthy loss. Dropping from a nine-game to an eight-game lead wasn't such a big deal. What was a big deal was Jack's continued poor pitching and wildly unprofessional behavior for which he had long been notorious. He lasted only four innings, and gave up seven runs and ten hits and focused his anger on the way home plate umpire Mark Johnson was calling the game. In walking off the mound after an early inning, he threw his cap and glove into the dugout.

Morris had always fought his temper demons. But this was really a bad night and his emotional dam burst. Since his 10-1 start and the elbow flare-up, he was now just 1-3, with a 7.64 ERA.

Sparky and Roger Craig let him stew in his own misery this time, and Jack exited the ballpark before talking to anybody. As a result, he was ordered to come in early the next day to meet separately with both men. While Roger had his private powwow with Jack, Sparky held a closed-door meeting with the rest of the team, later claiming that it had nothing to do with Jack. When Morris returned to the locker room after talking with Roger, he brushed off the waiting reporters. "No interviews today," was his curt reply.

It turned out that there would be no interviews for the next six weeks as Morris not only shut out the press but also withdrew from his teammates. When he opened up again in early September at Sparky's belated insistence, he copped out by explaining that his silence was not his problem but resulted from his growing impatience and disgust with the role of the media. He charged members of the media en masse for misquotes, short quotes that didn't reflect what he was trying to say, for invading his privacy and for having the "power to destroy people."

When asked to be more specific, he teed off on the *Detroit News* beat reporter Tom Gage, of whom he said, "Annoys me to death; knows nothing about the game and should be covering shuffleboard instead." Gage's response was insightful: "Jack's found his scapegoat."

The irony is that in the season of his greatest accomplishment, when he won a championship with teammates he really loved, Jack spent a good portion of the year by himself, in a strange, self-made exile.

GAME #91 July 18

Sox 10, Tigers 6

CHICAGO	AB	R	H	BI	DETROIT	AB	R	H	BI
Law R cf	6	1	1	2	Kuntz cf	3	1	2	1
Hairston lf	5	2	2	2	Garbey 1b	5	0	0	0
Stegman lf	0	0	0	0	Gibson rf	5	1	1	0
Baines rf	2	0	0	0	Parrish dh	3	2	2	1
Luzinski dh	5	1	4	2	Herndon lf	3	0	1	3
Walker 1b	5	1	2	1	Jones ph-lf	1	0	0	0
Squires pr-1b	0	1	0	0	Johnson 3b	4	0	0	0
Law V 3b	5	1	3	0	Brookens 2b	4	0	0	0
Hill c	4	1	1	0	Castillo c	3	1	2	0
Fletcher ss	5	1	3	2	Baker ss	4	1	1	1
Cruz 2b	3	1	0	1					
Totals	40	10	16	10		35	6	9	6

Chicago				130	030	021	-- 10
Detroit				300	200	100	-- 6

Game winning RBI -- none, DP -- Chicago 1, Detroit 2, LOB -- Chicago 9, Detroit 6, 2B -- Fletcher, Castillo, Kuntz, Luzinski, 3B -- Herndon, HR -- Parrish, Hairston, SB -- Luzinski, Law R, Walker, Law V, SF -- Cruz

Chicago	IP	H	R	ER	BB	SO
Bannister (W)	6.2	8	5	5	2	5
Jones*	0.0	1	1	1	0	0
Agosto (S)	2.1	0	0	0	2	1
Detroit						
Morris (L)+	4.0	10	7	7	2	1
Bair	1.0	1	0	0	1	0
Monge	1.0	1	0	0	0	1
Berenguer	1.1	2	2	2	2	1
Lopez	1.2	2	1	1	0	0

* Pitched to 1 batter in 7th
+ Pitched to 3 batters in 5th

T -- 2:59 A -- 39,051

GAMES 92, 93, 94 & 95 vs TEXAS—At the meeting with Roger Craig on July 19, Roger told Morris, "You're an unhappy person. We got to find a way to make you happy." But only Jack could make Jack happy. And by season's end, after he won 19 games and starred in the playoffs and World Series, there was no Tiger any happier than Jack Morris.

Jack's loss on Wednesday would be the only negative during another sterling stretch for the Tigers. They'd won the previous five games and would win the next six. The Rangers were in for four games starting on Thursday, July 19. Wilcox, with seven solid innings, beat Dave Stewart, 9-2, to push his win-loss mark to 9-6.

Roger Craig tried hard to get into Jack's head in '84.

The top of the order was magnificent in this one. Whitaker went 3-5, and Ruppert Jones was 4-4 with a ground-rule double bouncing over the 440 sign in dead center. It was still mid-season but Gibson already reached a personal RBI mark with a two-run homer, his 14th, and Parrish hit his 19th, a three-run shot.

On Friday, July 20, Rozema beat the Rangers and Frank Tanana, 3-1. Rozy, now an outstanding 7-1, had reached his high-water mark for the year.

A huge crowd, 46,219, was on hand as the Tigers beat Texas again, 7-6, on Saturday, July 21. Sid Monge, in relief of a faltering Glenn Abbott, got his one and only Tigers win with four innings of one-run relief. This time it was the bottom of the order coming through; Chet Lemon, Howard Johnson and Dave Bergman—the six-through-eight hitters—each had two hits in an eight-hit attack.

Bergman, who batted eighth on Saturday, was Sparky's leadoff man on Sunday, July 22. He started the game against Charlie Hough with a homer and later scored the other Tigers run as Petry shut out the Rangers, 2-0. Working on a four-hitter with two out in the ninth and a man on first, Sparky went out and pulled Petry. With almost 38,000 fans booing loudly, Sparky was unbowed. He unflinchingly signaled for Hernandez, who popped up Pete O'Brien on one pitch. Game over—nine wins in their last ten games.

GAMES 96, 97 & 98 @ CLEVELAND—On Monday night, July 23, they headed to Cleveland for a mid-week, four-game road trip. Gibson and Parrish hit back-to-back homers off Bert Blyleven in a three-run first to stake Morris. Jack responded by breaking out of his funk with six shutout innings of five-hit ball in a 4-1 win, though he did give the Indians five walks and threw two wild pitches in his six innings of work.

Still, Sparky was thrilled to see Morris get up to 94 miles per hour on the radar gun. Craig, also pleased, said, "He battled the hell out of them." Aurelio Lopez loaded the bases on walks in the eighth but survived. Jack, true to his edict, said nothing afterward to reporters. Wilcox reflected the team's attitude regarding Jack's media boycott by loudly ribbing him, "Hey, Jack, here they come," when the newspaper guys entered. Morris picked up his plate of food and trudged to the trainers' room to eat alone.

Wilcox won his 10th, 9-5, on Tuesday, July 24, making it 11 Tigers wins in their last 12 games. And even though Indians rookie Roy Smith beat them, 4-1, to conclude the series, the lead remained at a season-high 11½ games over Toronto. The Jays were hitting a collective .297 since the break, but designated hitter Cliff Johnson said, "Even Secretariat couldn't catch Detroit this year."

GAMES 99, 100, 101 & 102 vs BOSTON—The Tigers headed home to complete the month against the Red Sox and the Indians. They split a doubleheader with the Red Sox on Friday, July 27, before 49,607, the biggest Tiger Stadium crowd since the season opener. Petry pushed his record to an impressive 14-4 in a 9-1 game-one victory.

Lance Parrish not only hit a two-run homer, he also stole home in the first inning. He made his daring dash while Larry Herndon was caught in a rundown. Nine different Tigers accounted for Detroit's nine hits.

Bob Ojeda three-hit the Tigers in the nightcap, but with Toronto losing again, the Tigers' lead bulged to 12 games.

The game on Saturday night, July 28, drew 49,372. Morris pitched well, but the Tigers lost, 3-2, when third baseman Howard Johnson threw one past first base into the bullpen, allowing the winning run to score in the eighth. HoJo was still the starter, and his six errors in 50 games wasn't outrageous by any means. But they seemed to come at the worst possible times.

The weekend concluded on July 29, with Wilcox pitching eight scoreless innings before Hernandez finished up with his 21st save in a 3-0 shutout over Dennis "Oil Can" Boyd. The Tigers were 70-32, not

GAME #102 July 29								
Tigers 3, Sox 0								
BOSTON					**DETROIT**			
	AB	R	H	BI		AB	R	H	BI
Boggs 3b	4	0	1	0	Whitaker 2b	3	0	0	0
Evans rf	3	0	0	0	Jones lf	4	1	1	0
Rice lf	3	0	0	0	Gibson rf	4	0	0	0
Armas cf	3	0	0	0	Parrish c	3	0	1	1
Easler dh	3	0	0	0	Evans dh	3	1	0	0
Buckner 1b	3	0	0	0	Lemon cf	3	1	1	0
Gedman c	3	0	0	0	Johnson 3b	3	0	0	0
Barrett 2b	3	0	1	0	Bergman 1b	2	0	0	0
Gutierrez ss	2	0	1	0	Baker ss	3	0	1	1
Nichols ph	1	0	0	0					
Totals	28	0	3	0		28	3	4	2

```
Boston------------------ 000  000  000 --  0
Detroit----------------- 020  000  01x --  3
```

Game winning RBI -- none, E -- Boggs, Buckner, DP -- Detroit 2, LOB -- Boston 1, Detroit 5, 3B -- Jones, CS -- Gibson, SF -- Parrish

Boston	IP	H	R	ER	BB	SO
Boyd (L)	8.0	4	3	1	3	10
Detroit						
Wilcox (W)	8.0	3	0	0	0	4
Hernandez (S)	1.0	0	0	0	0	0

T -- 2:09 A -- 42,013

quite equaling the 70-30 Sparky experienced in 1970, his first season with the Reds. The lead was at a season-high 12 games. The Tigers' team ERA was 3.28. "That's almost unheard of in the American League," Sparky calmly noted, referring to the AL's run-pumping designated hitter rule.

GAMES 103 & 104 vs CLEVELAND—The Tigers finished July by splitting a Tuesday evening twinight doubleheader with Cleveland. Berenguer won the opener, 5-1, with six strong innings, but Rozema faltered in the 6-4 loss in the nightcap. Rozy wouldn't win again all season.

After this loss, the first of an eight-loss-in-ten-game stretch, they would raise the ire of the highly demanding, "the hype is over, what have you done for me lately" Tigers fans.

Howard Johnson warms up before playing the Red Sox in July '84. He'd go on to become a two-time All Star with the Mets.

Month by Month

JULY 1984

Cumulative statistics as of the end of the month

BATTING

	AB	R	H	RBI	2B	3B	HR	BB	SO	SB	E	GW RBI	AVG
Jones	100	16	31	20	5	1	6	8	23	1	0	4	.310
Lemon	345	54	107	56	25	5	14	37	52	4	2	4	.310
Trammell	344	57	104	44	22	4	8	38	31	14	7	4	.302
Whitaker	377	61	114	34	17	1	8	42	41	5	13	9	.302
Grubb	105	14	31	13	4	0	5	22	18	1	0	3	.295
Kuntz	94	23	27	17	7	0	2	18	18	1	1	3	.287
Gibson	329	56	91	57	14	6	16	38	70	19	6	13	.277
Garbey	221	31	61	36	11	1	4	10	23	4	7	3	.276
Bergman	171	28	46	30	6	2	5	25	19	3	5	4	.269
Johnson	235	30	62	36	11	0	8	28	48	7	8	5	.264
Parrish	381	51	96	61	12	1	21	21	71	2	2	6	.252
Herndon	286	30	71	25	12	4	1	20	49	3	1	3	.248
Evans	272	39	63	46	9	0	10	53	45	1	1	4	.232
Brookens	160	17	34	16	8	3	1	12	20	4	6	0	.213
Castillo	77	6	15	5	2	0	0	4	16	1	1	0	.195
Baker	50	7	8	5	0	1	0	2	7	0	2	1	.160
DH Hitters	385	59	90	59	14	1	13	51	71	3	0	7	.234
PH Hitters	108	16	36	29	6	0	5	14	19	0	0	2	.333
TOTALS	3597	531	975	506	168	29	110	376	560	71	73	65	.271

KEY: AB–at bats, R–runs, H–hits, RBI–runs batted in, 2B–doubles, 3B–triples, HR–home runs, BB–walks, SO–strike outs, SB–stolen bases, E–errors, GW RBI–game winning runs batted in, AVG–batting average.

AL EAST STANDINGS

	W	L	PCT	GB
DETROIT	71	33	.683	---
Toronto	59	45	.567	12
Baltimore	57	48	.543	14½
Boston	54	49	.524	16½
New York	50	52	.490	20
Milwaukee	47	59	.443	25
Cleveland	44	58	.431	26

PITCHING

	W	L	G	CG	S	IP	H	R	ER	BB	SO	ERA
Hernandez	6	0	50	0	21	91.2	62	20	20	26	81	1.96
Monge	1	0	12	0	0	21	21	9	5	6	11	2.14
Lopez	7	0	45	0	11	93.1	65	31	26	37	62	2.51
Petry	14	4	23	4	0	153	142	54	49	46	90	2.88
Bair	4	2	32	0	4	65	53	23	22	17	45	3.04
Morris	13	7	22	8	0	150.2	138	66	56	51	100	3.18
Rozema	7	3	19	0	0	81.1	81	37	31	16	33	3.43
Wilcox	11	6	22	0	0	130.2	126	65	57	45	71	3.93
Berenguer	5	7	19	1	0	95	94	46	42	43	63	3.97
Abbott	3	3	11	1	0	38	49	30	25	8	6	5.92
TOTALS	71	33	--	14	36	941.1	350	390	342	299	571	3.27

Totals include players no longer with the team and pitchers' errors. KEY: W–wins, L–losses, G–games pitched in, CG–complete games, S–saves, IP–innings pitched, H–hits allowed, R–runs allowed, ER–earned runs allowed, BB–walks allowed, SO–strike outs, ERA–earned run average.

DAY-BY-DAY

Date	Gm #	Vs.	W/L	Score	Winner	Loser	Rec	GA	Att.
7/1	77	Minn	L	0-9	* Viola	Berenguer	55-22	9	43,484
7/2	78	@ Chi	L	1-7	* Bannister	Rozema	55-23	9	32,768
7/3	79	@ Chi	L	5-9	Seaver	Morris	55-24	8	42,094
7/4	80	@ Chi	L	2-8	Dotson	Wilcox	55-25	7	37,665
7/5	81	@ Tex	W	7-4	† Lopez	* Hough	56-25	7	15,265
7/6	82	@ Tex	L	3-5	Mason	Berenguer	56-26	6	22,378
7/7	83	@ Tex	W	5-2	Rozema	Darwin	57-26	7	29,262
7/8	84	@ Tex	L	7-9	Tanana	Bair	56-27	7	16,010
7/12	85	@ Minn	L	2-4	Viola	Petry	57-28	7	29,729
7/13	86	@ Minn	W	5-3 (11)	† Hernandez	† Lysander	58-28	7	30,050
7/14	87	@ Minn	W	6-5 (12)	† Hernandez	† Walters	59-28	7	46,017
7/15	88	@ Minn	W	6-2	Rozema	Schrom	60-28	7	27,965
7/16	89	Chi	W	7-1	* Abbott	Hoyt	61-28	8	41,935
7/17	90	Chi	W	3-2	Petry	* Nelson	62-28	8	34,579
7/18	91	Chi	L	6-10	Bannister	Morris	62-29	8	39,051
7/19	92	Tex	W	9-2	Wilcox	Stewart	63-29	8	26,908
7/20	93	Tex	W	3-1	Rozema	* Tanana	64-29	8	39,484
7/21	94	Tex	W	7-6	† Monge	Noles	65-29	9	46,219
7/22	95	Tex	W	2-0	Petry	* Hough	66-29	9	37,846
7/23	96	@ Cle	W	4-1	Morris	* Blyleven	67-29	10½	16,576
7/24	97	@ Cle	W	9-5	Wilcox	Farr	68-29	11½	15,578
7/25	98	@ Cle	L	1-4	Smith	Rozema	68-30	11½	15,516
7/27	99	Bos	W	9-1	* Petry	Hurst	69-30	12½	
(DH)	100	Bos	L	0-4	* Ojeda	Abbott	69-31	12	49,607
7/28	101	Bos	L	2-3	† Stanley	Morris	69-32	12	49,372
7/29	102	Bos	W	3-0	Wilcox	* Boyd	70-32	12	42,013
7/31	103	Cle	W	5-1	Berenguer	Smith	71-32	12½	
(DH)	104	Cle	L	4-6	Heaton	Rozema	71-33	12	32,158

*Complete game   † Decision in relief

Chapter 15

August: Doubt in the Dog Days

When I had first gotten to the ballpark, Sparky said, "Go get some work in." Sparky tells Bergman, "Jump in there." When I let the ball go…it tailed into his back. Oh, dude—he tightens up in turning away and pulled a muscle in his back. He didn't come back for over a week. I thought, "Nice impression on my frigging teammates now. He'll be on the DL and we haven't even gotten to batting practice yet."

— New Tiger Bill Scherrer on his unfortunate first
day, and first few warm-up pitches as a Tiger

From the All-Star break through the end of July, the Tigers had stretched the lead from seven games to a season-high 12. Regularly playing before crowds of more than 40,000, and with the American League appearing to have been effectively tamed, Tigers followers entered the so-called dog days with the mindset that they would just enjoy the ride.

A Gallup Poll of 1,059 registered Michigan voters asked the question, "Who is the most valuable Tiger?" Lance Parrish edged out Chet Lemon and Willie Hernandez. Parrish called the results "a surprise" and offered Hernandez as his MVP choice. The Tigers experience was there to be savored, and Detroiters were doing a good job of drinking it all in.

If there was to be a bump in the road in the weeks to come, it certainly wasn't something to be concerned about now. The team had all attended Parrish's golf tournament for Cystic Fibrosis on Monday, July 30, and had raised $15,000. At the same time, Lance's wife, Arlyne, pulled in $14,000 more as she

---

AUGUST 1984

August Record: 16–15

Highlights:
Tigers swept 4 at home by Royals (8/3–8/5)
Win 10 of 12 (8/15–8/28)
Lemon struck by fly ball 8/26
Morris implodes in Seattle 8/30

Stars:

Gibson:	.322, 7 HR
Herndon:	.355, 11 RBI
Trammell:	.338, 17 RBI
Lopez:	3-0, 2.96 ERA

Key Games:
Aug 7:   Parrish 11th-inning home run to beat Boston, 7-5
Aug 15: Petry beats Angels to start hot streak
Aug 26   Lemon grand slam, then injured @ California
Aug 28: Bergman injured, HoJo demoted @ Seattle
Aug 30: Morris loses, 2-1, @ Seattle

and her merry band of Tigers wives sold memorabilia at Meadowbrook Mall.

At the ballpark, the bleacher creatures sank to new lows by gleefully chanting obscenities en masse. And in a major surprise, Campbell even allowed the Rolling Stones' "Start Me Up" to accompany Herbie and the grounds crew. Really, could it get much better than this? The Tigers were in the midst of a 12-game home stand, and there were still six more to drink in before they'd head out of town again.

GAMES 105 & 106 vs CLEVELAND—Dan Petry lost, 4-2, to Cleveland on Wednesday, August 1, but Jack Morris came back the next day to beat Blyleven, 2-1. How simple—Lou Whitaker slugged a two-run homer, and Hernandez, pitching the ninth, notched his 22nd save. With just three runs scored in two games, Sparky did express concern that the team batting average had slipped from over .300 to .270 during the past few months. But when asked if it was time to juggle things, he squelched the notion with a sage Sparkyism: "Juggling don't do no good because the guys who aren't hitting still have to go up to the plate." A league-leading ERA of 3.27 was proving to be the best antidote to the hitting woes.

Morris, Tigers squeak by Tribe, 2-1

GAMES 107, 108, 109 & 110 vs KANSAS CITY—The weekend was here, bringing the Royals in for four games, including a double-header on Sunday, August 5. As expected, Tiger Stadium was packed, but fans who had fought for tickets and waited for a chance to join the fun weren't pleased with what transpired. The Royals swept all four. Frank White's grand slam off Milt Wilcox Friday night powered a 9-6 win.

It got worse on Saturday. Sparky's pitching committee of Glenn Abbott, Doug Bair and Sid Monge threw miserably and was booed mercilessly. The crowd even booed Kirk Gibson, who tripled twice but sinned by leaving too many men on base in a 9-5 loss. After getting swept, 5-4 and 4-0, on Sunday, Parrish said in disgust, "I never thought I'd hear fans booing us this year."

Dave Rozema started the first game, the 5-4 loss on Sunday, and although he only gave up three runs in six innings, it was the beginning of the end for him. Willie Hernandez also suffered his first loss of the year in this one when Ruppert Jones just missed Dane Iorg's two-run double in the ninth.

As for Rozema, Sparky thought he had partied too much at Monday's golf outing and demoted him to the bullpen as punishment. Sparky's mandate to starting pitchers was that the two days after you

136

pitch are yours to live as you wish—but the next two are mine. Rozy had crossed the line at the golf outing, and although he would claim to make efforts to live his life in moderation, he kept on screwing up.

Charlie Leibrandt shut them out, 4-0, in the nightcap, and 43,000 disgusted fans seemed to forget about the 35-5 start and all the good stuff that had happened in the interim. Rusty Kuntz, star of the bench in April and May, was temporarily sent to Evansville to make room for pitcher Carl Willis. They just needed arms. The Tigers were off to Boston facing two more doubleheaders in the next two days for a grueling, six-games-in-six-days stretch. Toronto had swept the Orioles while the Royals were doing same in Detroit, and that 12-game Tigers lead was now slashed to eight.

Chet Lemon and John Wathan watch Lemon's pop-up that ends the Tigers' 5-4 first-game loss.

GAMES 111, 112, 113, 114 & 115 @ BOSTON—Fortunately, the Tigers were able to beat nemesis Bob Ojeda, 9-7, in a wild Fenway first game on August 6. Ojeda had shut them out twice earlier in the season, but Chet Lemon's three-run, fifth-inning homer kayoed the Sox lefty. There were 52 hits in the two games, 31 by the Sox.

But the Willis experiment backfired. He was routed in a third of an inning in the 10-2 loss in the nightcap. Tough to blame Willis. He'd left Wichita at 5 a.m., switched planes once, made it to the hotel by 2:30 p.m., and then left for Fenway on the team bus. He had done all that rushing around, only to get shelled hours later. "No excuses. When you get your chances, you got to be ready," said a disappointed Willis.

The Tigers played and split another doubleheader on Tuesday, August 7. Morris was hammered for eight earned runs in 1⅓ innings of an awful, 12-7 first-game loss. It was an extremely poor effort by Morris. Roger Craig was close to exasperation with him, convinced that the criticism of Morris by his teammates was affecting his preparation.

With Jack's vow of silence still in force, everybody else—including Craig—had to talk to the media for him, and by now they really thought it was ridiculous. Lance had to explain Jack's ongoing slump that had seen his 11-2 start fade to 14-8. "He felt that the ump missed a few and he let it bother him. I think he's losing his confidence," Lance dutifully, honestly and laboriously explained afterwards.

Then the Tigers got up and went out for game two.

◆ *Game 114: Green Monster Marathon*

Where:	Fenway Park
Result:	7-5 Tigers in 11 innings
Record:	74-40
WP:	Lopez, 9-0
LP	Gale, 1-3
Standing:	First, 9 ahead
Attendance:	32,120

After Morris was shelled again in game one, the tired Tigers had now lost six of seven, and eight of ten. They were about to play their fourth game in barely over a day, and their sixth in three days. Since the previous afternoon, 47 runs had been scored. These were the dog days, and this was an endurance test. A Tigers loss could put the Jays within seven games again and make it nine Tiger defeats in eleven games.

Lance Parrish led the '84 Tigers with 33 homers, and his two-run, 11th-inning blast in Boston was one of the most important.

The Tigers built a 4-0 lead off Sox starter John Henry Johnson. Larry Herndon homered in the first, just his second homer of the year. Parrish and Gibson homered off Johnson in the third, building a 3-0 lead. They got it to 4-0 in the fifth, when Howard Johnson tripled and scored on a wild pitch. But this was Fenway Park, where offense ruled, and in the seventh, Wilcox buckled. With two out, Dwight Evans cracked a three-run homer over the Green Monster to tie the score, and Jim Rice followed with a solo shot that put the Sox ahead, 5-4.

The Bosox might have stretched it further had not Chet Lemon made a Willie Mays–caliber, over-the-shoulder catch, robbing Mike Easler of extra bases. Later, Lemon also cut down Tony Armas trying to stretch a single with a perfect throw from deep left-center. Lemon would go for 0-6 at the plate but contributed mightily with his glove.

Trailing 5-4 in the ninth, and pinch hitting for Tom Brookens, Dave Bergman led off by doubling off reliever Bob Stanley. He went to third on a ground out and scored when Bill Buckner made an error on Lou Whitaker's grounder, enabling the Tigers to tie it at five. (Think of it: Stanley pitching, Buckner making an error in the World Series two years later, a combination that would hurt the Red Sox in ways they couldn't imagine. But this was now and the game went to extra innings.)

With Lopez throwing 3⅓ innings of hitless relief after taking over for Wilcox in the seventh, the stage was set for a dramatic 11th inning. Trammell singled with one out off Rich Gale. Then, on a perfect hit-and-run single by Lemon, Trammell was tricked by second baseman Marty Barrett into thinking it was a pop-up. Trammell scurried back to first, only to wind up in a force out when Evans cut him down at second.

It was an embarrassing play, and Trammell wouldn't discuss it afterwards. But with Lemon on first and two men out, Parrish rocketed a shot deep into the Boston night for a two-run, game-winning homer. It was his second homer of the game and his third in the doubleheader. "That was a dog fight," said Lemon afterwards.

In two days, they had played 38 innings and been involved in 59 runs, 99 hits and 21 homers.

Of the base-running blunder, Gibson ribbed his buddy, Trammell, the next day, "Hey Tram, you looked like you picked up a football and ran the wrong way." Trammell still wasn't ready to share the humor.

Two decades later, when Lance was asked if he remembered any big, personal moments from the regular season, he thought a moment and said, "I do remember hitting a big home run in Boston in extra innings one night. It was late, we were tired and really needed a win. I'm sorry, but you'll have to fill in the details."

No problem, Lance—and thanks for the memories.

They lost, 8-0, on an "Oil Can" Boyd shutout on Wednesday, August 8, as the pitching staff continued to get battered. The Tigers demoted Carl Willis. What a short, sad trip this had been for him. They called up shortstop Doug Baker to help cover for Trammell, whose sore throwing shoulder had reduced him to DH duties since he returned from the disabled list July 31. And they flew to Kansas City to face the team that had humbled them at Tiger Stadium earlier in the month.

GAMES 116, 117 & 118 @ KANSAS CITY—The Tigers turned the tables and swept the Royals, 5-4, 9-5 and 8-4, on the weekend of August 10–12. Ruppert Jones' eighth-inning pinch homer off Joe Beckwith won it for Lopez on Friday. Lopez was now an eye-opening 10-0. On Saturday, Morris got his split-finger working again and won his 15th, holding the Royals to two runs through eight before getting roughed up in the ninth in the 9-5 win.

They completed the sweep on Sunday with Wilcox winning 8-4. Darrell Evans' two-run triple keyed a four-run first inning. DH Trammell, who hit that dramatic grand slam off Dan Quisenberry back in May, got Quis again, doubling in two runs. They headed home

GAME #114 Aug 7								
Tigers 7, Sox 5								
DETROIT					**BOSTON**			
	AB	R	H	BI		AB	R	H	BI
Whitaker 2b	6	0	1	0	Boggs 3b	5	0	1	1
Trammell dh	5	0	2	0	Evans rf	5	1	1	3
Lemon cf	6	1	0	0	Rice lf	5	1	2	1
Parrish c	5	2	2	3	Armas cf	5	0	1	0
Herndon lf	3	1	1	1	Easler dh	5	0	0	0
Jones ph-lf	3	0	1	0	Buckner 1b	5	0	1	0
Garbey 1b	3	0	2	0	Newman c	4	0	0	0
Evans ph-1b-3b	3	0	1	0	Barrett 2b	4	2	1	0
Gibson rf	4	1	1	1	Gutierrez ss	2	0	2	0
Brookens ss	3	0	0	0	Miller ph	1	1	1	0
Bergman ph-1b	2	1	1	0	Hoffman ss	0	0	0	0
Johnson 3b-ss	5	1	2	0	Gedman ph	1	0	0	0
					Jurak ss	0	0	0	0
Totals	**48**	**7**	**14**	**5**		**42**	**5**	**10**	**5**

Detroit----------------- 010 210 001 02 -- 7
Boston------------------ 000 010 400 00 -- 5

Game winning RBI -- none, E -- Garbey, Buckner, DP -- Detroit 1, LOB -- Detroit 11, Boston 5, 2B -- Rice, Barrett, Boggs, Bergman, Jones, 3B -- Johnson, HR -- Herndon, Parrish 2, Gibson, Evans, Rice, SB -- Whitaker, WP -- Johnson, PB -- Newman

Detroit	IP	H	R	ER	BB	SO
Wilcox	6.2	10	5	5	1	5
Lopez (W)	3.1	0	0	0	0	5
Hernandez (S)	1.0	0	0	0	0	2
Boston						
Johnson	5.0	6	4	4	0	9
Crawford	2.0	3	0	0	0	1
Stanley	1.1	2	1	0	0	2
Clear	0.2	0	0	0	2	2
Gale (L)	2.0	3	2	2	1	1

T -- 3:33 A -- 32,120

Morris gets 15th; Tigers win, 9-5

Wednesday night with a nine-game lead, and a ten-game home stand looming with California, Seattle and Oakland.

After the doubleheader loss to the Royals back on August 5, the Tigers had left town with the resounding boos of 43,000 annoyed fans ringing in their ears.

GAMES 119, 120, 121 & 122 vs CALIFORNIA—They returned to Tiger Stadium on Tuesday, August 14, to play another doubleheader, this time against the Angels. And 38,597 fans came hoping for a better show.

Juan Berenguer and Rozema would pitch for the Tigers. Game one was tied at four in the ninth before Doug DeCinces blooped a Hernandez screwball off the end of his bat for a two-run game-winning single, making it 6-4 Angels and handing Willie just his second loss of the season. The Tigers had men on second and third in the bottom of the ninth, but Gibson bounced back to the mound on a checked swing to end it.

Rozema was pounded for five runs in two innings in the nightcap, and by the middle of the 12-1 loss most had seen enough and went home. It was Rozema's last stand. Sparky demoted him to the bullpen for the rest of the year. Even worse, the Blue Jays swept the Indians and pulled to within 7½ games, the Tigers' smallest gap in a month. It was understandably a somber clubhouse.

"It's still seven and a half [game lead] no matter how you cut it," said a stoic Sparky Anderson. It was time for someone else to step to the forefront and light a spark.

◆Game 121: Brooky's Bash

Where:	Tiger Stadium
Result:	8-3 Tigers
Record:	78-43
WP:	Petry, 15-5
LP	John, 7-10
Standing:	First, 9 ahead
Attendance:	33,940

Tom Brookens remembers:

Tram had that shoulder problem for some time in '84, and it wasn't uncommon that when Tram didn't play short, I did, and then I'd move over into another position later in the game. It had happened in Petry's near

---

GAME #121   Aug 15

Tigers 8, Angels 3

CALIFORNIA	AB	R	H	BI	DETROIT	AB	R	H	BI
Pettis cf	4	0	2	1	Whitaker 2b	5	2	1	1
Wilfong 2b	4	0	1	0	Trammell dh	5	0	1	0
Lynn rf	4	1	1	1	Garbey 1b	3	0	3	0
DeCinces 3b	4	1	1	1	Bergman ph-1b	2	0	2	3
Jackson dh	4	0	1	0	Parrish, c	4	0	0	0
Beniquez lf	4	0	0	0	Herndon lf	3	1	1	0
Sconiers 1b	3	0	1	0	Jones ph-lf	1	0	0	0
Grich ph	1	0	0	0	Lemon cf	4	1	1	0
Narron c	3	0	1	0	Gibson rf	3	3	2	0
Schofield ss	1	1	0	0	Brookens ss-3b	3	0	3	2
Brown ph	1	0	0	0	Johnson 3b	3	1	0	1
Picciolo ss	0	0	0	0	Baker ss	0	0	0	0
Totals	33	3	8	3		36	8	14	7

California	001	100	010	--	3
Detroit	010	201	13x	--	8

Game winning RBI -- none, E -- Wilfong, Sconiers, DP -- California 1, Detroit 2, LOB -- California 4, Detroit 8, 2B -- Pettis, Wilfong, Whitaker, Gibson, 3B -- Pettis, Bergman 2, HR -- DeCinces, Lynn, SB -- Sconiers, Johnson, CS -- Johnson, SH -- Brookens

California	IP	H	R	ER	BB	SO
John (L)	6.0	10	4	3	1	3
Kaufman	0.1	2	1	1	1	1
Curtis	1.0	1	3	1	1	0
Sanchez	0.2	1	0	0	0	0
Detroit						
Petry (W)	8.0	8	3	3	1	5
Hernandez	1.0	0	0	0	0	0

T -- 2:46 A -- 33,940

no-hitter earlier in the season. Every time I switched positions in that game [April 29], it seemed like they'd hit a hard one and it'd somehow find my glove.

I was filling in for Tram again in this game and our rookie shortstop, Doug Baker, came in for me later in the game. I had signed as a shortstop and played my first full season in pro ball at short. They moved me up to Double A the next year and put me at second base. Then I got called up to Triple A my third year and played the full season at third base. So my first three seasons I played all three infield positions, which enhanced my value at the major-league level. I enjoyed moving from one to the other during a game. What's the difference? They hit you the ball, you field it and throw it over there [to first].

Petry was also pitching in this one. He had said that after double-header losses, like the day before, you didn't want it to snowball. We were down 2-1, in the fourth, and I singled Chet in to tie it up off Tommy John. I had struggled at the plate quite a bit early in '84, but I was hitting better by now. I got on again in the sixth. HoJo grounded to short and I nailed Rob Wilfong at second to break up the double play. He threw wild and Gibby scored on the play.

I took a lot of pride in being an excellent base runner. I wasn't a good base stealer but I thought of myself as one of the best base runners on our team. Your responsibility as a base runner is to try to disrupt whoever is gonna turn that thing so they don't even get a chance to throw, or you go in hard and make him think.

They took John out after that inning with the score 4-2 and brought in a righty for the seventh inning. So I went to third for HoJo, and Doug Baker came in to play short. Turns out it was my only three-hit game of the year. But first base was Sparky's best defensive maneuver that night. Garbey went 3-3 and Bergman replaced him and went 2-2 with two triples!

Petry won his 15th and I think it started a nice streak for us. I did an interview on the postgame show on PASS. I walked in the locker room after and there were a million writers in there waiting for me. I said, "Those postgame shows are murder." I hadn't played a heckuva lot all year so it was my way of pokin' a little fun at myself.

But real soon after that [August 19] I blew out a hamstring, and that's the reason why we went into the playoffs with Marty playing third. I re-injured it with about two weeks to go in the season and Sparky kept close tabs on me but I couldn't move real well. So he told me he was going with Marty at third in the postseason, and I couldn't argue. I wasn't 100 percent. That was the biggest disappointment in my pro career; being hurt for the World Series and hardly getting any playing time. But injuries are part of the deal.

Tom Brookens endured a frustrating season in 1984.

From the time he was drafted in '75, Brookens served the Tigers loyally for 15 years, but each spring Sparky always thought he had a better answer at third base. The '84 mess was well documented, as Sparky had thrown Marty Castillo, Barbaro Garbey, Darrell Evans and Howard Johnson in Brookens' face.

"In my 17 years in Detroit, I know I was wrong to Tommy Brookens more than anybody else," Sparky admitted years later. "He shouldda been the lead guy at third every year when we came outta camp. I always took it from him and then I always had to give it back, and Tom Brookens was cheated. If I'd had common sense—and it's easy afterwards to look back—it would have been Tom's job every spring and I wouldn't have worried about it."

When told of what his former manager said, Brookens stayed true to his easygoing persona. "I don't have to forgive him," he said with conviction. "I can honestly say I never felt any resentment against Sparky. People say, 'Cmon, Tom, you gotta be kidding. You didn't feel that you should be starting?'

"I don't feel that Sparky owes me anything. I feel that I owe him a lot to be a part of his ballclub because there were times when I really struggled as a hitter. I never once felt I should waltz in and the job should be handed to me. I felt if I was gonna be the man, I had to earn my way. I feel that to this day."

Garbey sinks Angels in 12th, 8-7

The Tigers reeled off three more wins in a row. In a sweltering afternoon game on Thursday, August 16, they beat the Angels, 8-7, in 12 innings on Barbaro Garbey's pinch double down the left-field line. Howard Johnson scored all the way from first and as he trotted off the field, Garbey's teammates mobbed him while 37,779 roared their approval.

The ending may have been glorious, but Morris had blown a 5-0 lead in another ugly outing. He gave up six straight hits in the third inning and was chased in the fourth on a three-run Brian Downing homer to make it 7-5 Angels. Morris was now an awful 4-6 with a 7.00 ERA since that June 11 elbow twinge. But relievers Bair, Aurelio Lopez and Hernandez held California scoreless for the last eight-plus innings before Garbey's big hit finally decided it. Afterwards, Gibson tore into Jack publicly, saying, "I'm not criticizing his performance, because he didn't intentionally do that. But we came into the clubhouse happy and he was over in the corner pouting. I expected to see him at the front of the (handshake) line."

GAMES 123, 124 & 125 vs SEATTLE—Wilcox beat Seattle, 6-2, on Friday, August 17. Trammell returned to shortstop and although he made an error, he was relieved that his arm felt fine.

Berenguer, back in the rotation due to Rozema's demotion, beat the Mariners 4-3 on Saturday to make it four straight wins.

On Sunday, August 19, Mark Langston beat them, 4-1, on four hits, disappointing 43,277. Lance, who was the DH while Castillo caught, struck out four times and was booed heavily when he ended the game with whiff number four. He "saluted" the crowd by waving his helmet as he returned to the dugout. This game really revealed the mindset of the fans. They pay their money and they want a win. That's expected. But this was a club with a 10-game lead that had done almost everything right all year. Parrish was the team's leading home run and RBI man, and even he wasn't immune from the displeasure of victory-hungry fans.

GAMES 126, 127 & 128 vs OAKLAND—Oakland came to town and got swept before about 110,000 fans Monday through Wednesday, August 20–22. The Tigers clobbered the A's, 14-1, on Monday. Homers by Parrish and Lemon broke the game open in the third. It got so lopsided that former Tiger infielder Mark Wagner came in to pitch the seventh. Morris allowed just three hits over seven innings for his 16th victory but maintained his vow of silence with reporters who figured, incorrectly, that he might be in a good enough mood to talk.

Tigers win a laugher, 14-1

Wilcox won his career-best 14th in Tuesday's 12-6 victory, and they completed the sweep of the A's with Wednesday's 11-4 drubbing in front of 35,335. In the three games with Oakland, the Tigers scored 37 runs on 45 hits and built their lead to a season-high 12½ games. The same fans who booed so lustily just four games earlier were now chanting the players' names and laughing at the inept A's, who made three errors in a clownish performance.

Berenguer was the beneficiary of an 11-hit attack that saw three of the lesser lights, Castillo, Baker and Garbey, get two hits each. Since the doubleheader loss to California that started the home stand on a sour note, the Tigers had won seven of eight to tack five games back on their lead. They headed out west to face the same three teams on enemy turf.

GAMES 129, 130 & 131 @ CALIFORNIA—Petry lost, 5-3, to California's Mike Witt in Anaheim on Friday night, August 24. On Saturday, 51,203 showed up at Anaheim Stadium to see Morris pitch. The last time he had thrown there, he won, 5-1, to push the record to 35-5 with their record-setting 17th straight win on the road. Jack beat 'em, 5-1, again in this one, with ninth-inning help from Hernandez. Evans homered in the fourth, and Ruppert Jones' three-run homer in the sixth off Bruce Kison was the crowning blow. It seemed that all Sparky could justify worrying about now would be to lose a starter to injury.

◆Game 131: Chester's Headache

GAME #131 Aug 26			

Tigers 12, Angels 6

DETROIT	AB	R	H	BI	CALIFORNIA	AB	R	H	BI
Whitaker 2b	4	1	1	0	Pettis cf	4	0	0	0
Trammell ss	5	1	1	0	Brown ph-rf	1	0	0	0
Baker ss	0	0	0	0	Wilfong 2b	5	1	3	1
Gibson dh	4	4	3	2	Lynn rf-cf	5	1	1	0
Parrish c	3	1	1	2	DeCinces 3b	4	1	1	1
Herndon lf	4	1	1	3	Downing lf	4	1	1	1
Garbey 1b	3	0	0	0	Jackson dh	3	0	0	0
Bergman ph-1b	1	0	0	0	Grich 1b	4	1	2	1
Lemon cf	2	1	1	4	Narron c	3	0	1	2
Grubb rf	1	0	0	0	Schofield ss	3	1	0	0
Kuntz rf-cf	5	0	0	0	Beniquez ph	0	0	0	0
Castillo 3b	4	3	3	1	Picciolo ss	0	0	0	0
Totals	**36**	**12**	**11**	**12**		**36**	**6**	**9**	**6**

```
Detroit----------------------------  006  311  001 -- 12
California-------------------------  000  003  120 --  6
```

Game winning RBI -- none, E -- Garbey, Baker, DP -- California 1, LOB -- Detroit 5, California 7, 2B -- Herndon, Wilfong, Lynn, DeCinces, Parrish, 3B -- Grich, HR -- Lemon, Castillo, Gibson 2, SB -- Garbey, SF -- Parrish, DeCinces, Narron, Balk -- Wilcox

Detroit	IP	H	R	ER	BB	SO
Wilcox (W)	6.0	5	3	0	0	5
Bair	1.2	4	3	2	2	1
Lopez	1.1	0	0	0	0	1
California						
John (L)	2.1	2	5	5	6	0
Kaufman	3.2	7	6	6	0	4
Curtis	3.0	2	1	1	1	2

T -- 3:01 A -- 33,008

Where:	Anaheim
Result:	12-6 Tigers
Record:	86-45
WP:	Wilcox, 15-7
LP:	John, 7-12
Standing:	First, 12 ahead
Attendance:	33,008

Chet Lemon remembers:

I'll never forget this one. I'm feeling good and it's a great day for baseball; bright, sunny California day. We were facing Tommy John, who was 40 at the time and was very familiar to us, and it was scoreless in the third when we got to him. He was really wild; walked Gibson and Lance on eight straight pitches to force in the first run. When he walked Herndon on a 3-1 count, [manager John] McNamara pulled him and brought in a rookie right-hander named [Curt] Kaufman. He struck out Garbey to make it two out, still bases loaded.

I worked the count to 3-2. When I hit it the 3-2 pitch I thought it had a chance, but the ball went foul just inside the left field pole and I said, "Dang, that wouldda been nice." I'm saying, "C'mon, you gotta finish this at bat." Next pitch, I hit it real good. I knew it had a shot; I was hoping. I thought it had a chance, and then when it fell on the other side of the fence I was just real excited that we had put four more points on the board. That made it 6-0. It was exciting times for us. You wanted to do whatever you could to make a contribution to the cause and that felt real good. That was big-time. That was the best day because of the grand slam, and then it was a nightmare because of what happened after that.

I think it was the sixth inning when Fred Lynn hit it and the ball got right in the sun. I flipped my sunglasses down and I'm still looking at the sun, and instinctively I went to where the baseball was. I put my glasses back up because I couldn't see the ball and then I flipped 'em back down because I still couldn't pick the ball up. I went twice with the glasses; that's how high it was hit.

Then the ball came down and hit me right between the eyes. I never saw it. The blow was so severe that the glasses split in half and flew all the *way back to the warning track and I was at least 35 or more feet in from the fence. Blood was just gushing from my eye area and then they rushed me out and took me to the hospital and gave me 12 stitches.*

I suffered a mild concussion, and didn't realize until later that I also had what was called vertigo. The force of the blow threw off the part of your ear that keeps your equilibrium. They were gonna leave me there [in Anaheim] but I wanted to go with our team, so I flew to Seattle that night, and flying is probably the worst thing you can do after something like that. Man, that was the most horrible feeling.

I was so sick for the next coupla days that you couldn't imagine. They gave me medication to try and correct the dizziness and stuff I was experiencing. I couldn't even get outta bed. When I stepped, everything was moving. I'd think my foot was hitting the ground and I still had a long way to go.

As for the game, Wilcox won his 15th. Talk about playing hurt. Milt was a veteran. We all understood that after being 35-5, all we could do was lose. In the worst-case scenario we were gonna get around 100 wins even if we played .500 baseball from that point (35-5). So we had to just stay in there and battle. Even though we were relatively young—were all about 25 to 28 years old—but we all had experienced a lot.

Milt was having a great year and he knew what he meant to that ballclub. His shoulder was hurt all year but all our pitchers knew that they had to take the ball when it was their turn and go. Nobody was gonna bail out saying, "I had a hangnail and couldn't go." We had something special and we all wanted it real bad and that's why you saw guys like Milt fight through the hard times. When you think about 162 games—every day—you're gonna have pulled muscles, the travel, and then wake up and play the next day, it's tough. But we were a family.

L–R: Dave Bergman, Pio DiSalvo and Kirk Gibson carry a dazed Lemon off the field in Anaheim.

As it turned out, Lemon would return September 7 for a crucial series in Toronto. But on August 26, with Lemon's status uncertain, they moved up the coast to Seattle, where the 35-5 start had come to an end back in May.

GAMES 132, 133 & 134 @ SEATTLE
◆*Game 132: New Kid in Town*

GAME #132 Aug 28			

Tigers 5, Mariners 4

DETROIT					SEATTLE				
	AB	R	H	BI		AB	R	H	BI
Whitaker 2b	2	0	0	1	Perconte 2b	4	1	1	0
Trammell ss	4	1	1	2	Bradley cf	4	0	1	2
Gibson rf	4	1	1	1	Davis 1b	4	0	1	0
Parrish c	4	0	0	0	Phelps dh	2	0	0	0
Evans dh	4	0	2	0	Presley ph	1	0	0	0
Kuntz pr	0	1	0	0	Cowens rf	4	0	1	1
Grubb lf	4	0	0	0	Henderson lf	2	1	0	0
Castillo 3b	0	0	0	0	Moses lf	1	0	0	0
Jones cf	3	1	2	0	Milbourne 3b	4	1	2	0
Bergman 1b	4	1	1	0	Kearney c	3	0	0	0
Johnson 3b	2	0	1	0	Owen ss	4	1	0	0
Garbey ph-3b-lf	1	0	0	0					
Totals	32	5	8	5		33	4	6	3

Detroit------------------------- 000 100 031 -- 5
Seattle------------------------- 100 000 300 -- 4

Game winning RBI -- none, E -- Johnson, LOB -- Detroit 3, Seattle 6, 2B -- Perconte, Davis, Jones 2, HR -- Gibson, Trammell, CS -- Jones, Kearney, SF -- Whitaker, WP -- Stanton

Detroit	IP	H	R	ER	BB	SO
Berenguer	6.2	5	4	1	4	5
Scherrer	0.1	0	0	0	0	0
Hernandez (W)	2.0	1	0	0	0	1
Seattle						
Moore*	7.0	5	3	3	2	2
Vande Berg	1.0	1	1	1	0	0
Stanton (L)	0.2	1	1	1	0	2
Geisel	0.1	1	0	0	0	1

* Pitched to 2 batters in 8th

T -- 2:51 A -- 8,353

Where: Seattle
Result: 5-4 Tigers
Record: 87-45
WP: Hernandez, 8-2
LP: Stanton, 4-4
Standing: First, 11½ ahead
Attendance: 8,353

Bill Scherrer remembers:

I was with Cincinnati and had pitched over a hundred games for them in '82 and '83. The Tigers traded Carl Willis for me on August 28, and I didn't really know much about the American League. So, when I got there I didn't know a lot of their players. Obviously, I knew they were in first place and had a dynamic team.

I met the team in Seattle that very day, and hours later I pitched. I'd heard that Sparky likes to get you into things quickly. I came in for Berenguer and got a tough lefty, Alvin Davis, to bounce out to Bergman at first to finish the seventh inning. Unfortunately, Juan had just let in three that inning and the Mariners led, 4-1.

Then I saw what this team was all about. We get the three back off Mike Moore in the eighth and tie them; coupla hits, Lou's sac fly brings in one, and then Tram hits a two-run homer. In the ninth, Darrell singles; Kuntz pinch runs and Ruppert Jones doubles him home, 5-4. Willie pitches the last two, scoreless. Just like that. What a formula.

When I had first gotten to the ballpark, Sparky said, "Go warm up, play catch, just to get some work in." Sparky tells Bergie [Bergman], "Jump in there." He did it because I needed a left-handed batter standing there for some frame of reference. After all, my job is to get lefties out. Bergie says, "I'm not jumping in there. I played against him in San Francisco." I dropped down when I threw and lefties didn't like it. Bergie's standing so far away from the plate that even if it was inside it would be outside where he was standing, if you know what I mean.

When I let the ball go, dropping down, dropping my wrist, it tailed into his back. This was like hitting the kid in row 15. Oh, dude—he tightens up trying to get out of the way and pulled a muscle in his back. He fought through it that night and didn't come back for over a week. That's how it happened. I thought, "Nice impression on my frigging teammates now. He'll [Bergman] be on the DL and we haven't even gotten to batting practice yet."

I also remember that the first day in Seattle there was a woman reporter in the locker room. I looked at one of my teammates and said, "Dude, who is this?" This must be an American League thing. I looked at Darrell and said, "My God, when did they let women in the goddamn locker room?"

One thing I'll always treasure—talk about team concept—when I got there in Seattle they [the Tigers] made me feel like a part of it right away. Everybody felt a part of being number one and they wanted me to feel that way too.

When I speak to kids, I tell 'em—it isn't necessarily the greatest players who win championships; you gotta have players, but if you can think that after that year, 15 guys on that team disassembled and went somewhere else, minors or majors, that tells you how dynamic that club was.

The ingredient pieces like Rusty Kuntz, Marty Castillo, Johnny Grubb, Jones and Garbey, Dwight Lowry, even Randy O'Neal. I don't think there were a lotta people that thought the Anaheim Angels were gonna win a World Series in 2002. But they had a team. The Yankees may have big money to get the Giambis and all the rest, but they [teams that have unlimited dollars] are few and far between.

On our road trips, everybody cluttered up with each other at the bars, even if you didn't drink, and that's what makes teams. When you walk into a locker room—were the players that dynamic or were they just the ingredients that made the pieces fit? People don't remember who were the [number] four and five starters in '84. I ask people from Detroit, "Name me three through five in the bullpen that year?" Most people can't.

Lanky Bill Scherrer displays his "drop down" form in spring training '85.

During the Mariners' three-run seventh that night, Howard Johnson let Spike Owen's slow, two-out grounder trickle through his legs, allowing the go-ahead run to score. Phil Bradley then singled in two more unearned runs. With Brookens out with the hamstring problem, Sparky announced that Evans and Castillo would platoon at third the rest of the way.

Johnson, who had appeared to be having a breakout year just a few months previous, would be virtually ignored the rest of the season. Both he and Rozema were in the doghouse—Rozy demoted on August 14, and now HoJo, whose glove Sparky wouldn't trust in the postseason, was joining him. Neither would be back with the ballclub in '85.

Bergman would miss the next eight games as a result of Scherrer's errant practice toss but would return on September 7 to provide one of the biggest moments of the season.

On August 29, Langston beat Petry, 5-1, and on the next day, Morris lost his temper, concentration and the game, 2-1, and brought his unhappiness with himself and his teammates to a head.

GAME 135 @ OAKLAND—In Oakland on August 31, Rozema's wild pitch cost them in the 13th inning. Lopez and Hernandez had combined for over eight innings of one-run relief after Wilcox faltered, and Sparky pitched Rozema for the first time in almost two weeks. Rozy entered the 6-6 game in the 13th, gave up two singles and threw the wild pitch that brought in the winner in the 7-6 loss.

September was about to arrive and the Tigers' bulge was still at 9½ games. But they had lost three straight to end the month.

A's hang on, defeat Tigers in 13th

Month by Month

AUGUST 1984

Cumulative statistics as of the end of the month

AL EAST STANDINGS

	W	L	PCT	GB
DETROIT	87	48	.644	---
Toronto	77	57	.575	9½
Baltimore	72	61	.541	14
New York	71	62	.534	15
Boston	71	63	.530	15½
Cleveland	60	76	.441	27½
Milwaukee	56	79	.415	31

BATTING

	AB	R	H	RBI	2B	3B	HR	BB	SO	SB	E	GW RBI	AVG
Trammell	474	75	148	62	28	5	13	49	52	18	8	4	.312
Whitaker	483	76	142	43	23	1	10	55	54	6	14	11	.294
Gibson	447	83	129	77	20	9	23	55	85	25	11	16	.289
James	171	23	49	32	10	1	11	14	34	1	0	5	.287
Garbey	268	38	77	45	14	1	4	14	31	6	11	4	.287
Lemon	437	68	125	70	27	5	18	45	76	5	2	5	.286
Grubb	137	17	38	13	5	0	5	27	24	1	0	3	.277
Herndon	347	42	93	36	17	5	4	25	55	5	2	4	.268
Bergman	215	32	56	40	7	4	6	29	28	3	5	4	.260
Kuntz	114	26	30	19	8	0	2	20	20	2	1	3	.263
Parrish	487	67	118	83	14	2	29	31	100	2	3	9	.242
Johnson	326	39	79	43	12	1	11	38	63	9	12	7	.242
Evans	340	51	81	58	10	1	13	66	56	1	1	6	.238
Brookens	205	27	48	23	10	4	3	20	29	5	11	0	.234
Castillo	105	12	23	11	3	1	2	7	25	1	4	0	.219
Baker	82	11	13	8	2	1	0	4	11	1	4	1	.159
DH Hitters	509	81	132	76	19	1	19	62	95	7	0	8	.259
PH Hitters	140	20	41	32	7	1	6	18	23	0	0	4	.293
TOTALS	4693	699	1264	667	209	41	155	501	758	92	101	82	.269

KEY: AB-at bats, R-runs, H-hits, RBI-runs batted in, 2B-doubles, 3B-triples, HR-home runs, BB-walks, SO-strike outs, SB-stolen bases, E-errors, GW RBI-game winning runs batted in, AVG-batting average.

PITCHING

	W	L	G	CG	S	IP	H	R	ER	BB	SO	ERA
Scherrer	0	0	1	0	0	.1	0	0	0	0	0	0.00
Hernandez	8	2	66	0	26	119	83	27	27	31	101	2.04
Lopez	10	0	59	0	12	120.2	88	41	35	47	86	2.61
Petry	15	8	30	5	0	201	200	84	76	58	122	3.40
Berenguer	7	8	25	2	0	137.1	126	63	54	58	99	3.54
Morris	17	9	29	8	0	203.1	187	92	80	73	129	3.54
Rozema	7	5	25	0	0	96.2	106	47	41	18	46	3.82
Monge	1	0	17	0	0	34	37	19	15	11	19	3.97
Wilcox	15	7	29	0	0	170.1	165	90	78	57	101	4.12
Bair	4	3	39	0	4	80.1	75	40	37	28	49	4.15
TOTALS	87	48	--	16	42	1223	1155	555	485	394	763	3.57

Totals include players no longer with the team and pitchers' errors. KEY: W-wins, L-losses, G-games pitched in, CG-complete games, S-saves, IP-innings pitched, H-hits allowed, R-runs allowed, ER-earned runs allowed, BB-walks allowed, SO-strike outs, ERA-earned run average.

DAY-BY-DAY

Date	Gm #	Vs.	W/L	Score	Winner	Loser	Rec	GA	Att.
8/1	105	Cle	L	2-4	Farr	Petry	71-34	11	27,271
8/2	106	Cle	W	2-1	Morris	Blyleven	72-34	11½	28,700
8/3	107	KC	L	6-9	† Saberhagen	Wilcox	72-35	10½	39,480
8/4	108	KC	L	5-9	† Beckwith	† Bair	72-36	9½	41,714
8/5	109	KC	L	4-5	† Saberhagen	† Hernandez	72-37	8½	
(DH)	110	KC	L	0-4	Leibrandt	* Berenguer	72-38	8	42,761
8/6	111	@ Bos	W	9-7	† Lopez	Ojeda	73-38	8½	
(DH)	112	@ Bos	L	2-10	Clemens	Willis	73-39	8½	31,055
8/7	113	@ Bos	L	7-12	Hurst	Morris	73-40	8	
(DH)	114	@ Bos	W	7-5 (11)	† Lopez	† Gale	74-40	9	32,120
8/8	115	@ Bos	L	0-8	* Boyd	Abbott	74-41	8	32,563
8/10	116	@ KC	W	5-4	† Lopez	† Beckwith	75-41	8	32,181
8/11	117	@ KC	W	9-5	Morris	Leibrandt	76-41	8	40,501
8/12	118	@ KC	W	8-4	Wilcox	Saberhagen	77-41	9	32,753
8/14	119	Cal	L	4-6	† Aase	† Hernandez	77-42	8½	
(DH)	120	Cal	L	1-12	Kison	Rozema	77-43	7½	38,597
8/15	121	Cal	W	8-3	Petry	John	78-43	9	33,940
8/16	122	Cal	W	8-7 (12)	† Hernandez	† Curtis	79-43	10	37,779
8/17	123	Sea	W	6-2	Wilcox	Moore	80-43	10	36,496
8/18	124	Sea	W	4-3	Berenguer	Geisel	81-43	11	36,719
8/19	125	Sea	L	1-4	Langston	* Petry	81-44	10	43,277
8/20	126	Oak	W	14-1	Morris	Young	82-44	10½	38,431
8/21	127	Oak	W	12-6	Wilcox	Sorensen	83-44	11½	34,065
8/22	128	Oak	W	11-4	Berenguer	Krueger	84-44	12½	35,335
8/24	129	@ Cal	L	3-5	Witt	* Petry	84-45	11	41,459
8/25	130	@ Cal	W	5-1	Morris	Kison	85-45	12	51,203
8/26	131	@ Cal	W	12-6	Wilcox	John	86-45	12	33,008
8/28	132	@ Sea	W	5-4	† Hernandez	† Stanton	87-45	11½	8,356
8/29	133	@ Sea	L	1-5	* Langston	Petry	87-46	11½	10,869
8/30	134	@ Sea	L	1-2	Beattie	* Morris	87-46	10½	9,600
8/31	135	@ Oak	L	6-7 (13)	† Atherton	† Rozema	87-48	9½	15,836

*Complete game † Decision in relief

Chapter 16

Jack

I went to the mound more than once and told him, "If you think you're that good, then you better strike out the next two hitters because any ground ball hit to me, I'm not catching it....you arrogant ass."

— Dave Bergman to a temperamental Jack Morris
during an '84 game

ack Morris pitched a no-hitter the first week of the '84 season to set the tone, and by the time the Tigers came home from the 35-5 start, he had a 10-1 record. Morris was on pace to surpass Denny McLain's 31 wins in 1968 which, perhaps not coincidentally, was the last time the Tigers had run roughshod over the American League.

Through the first two months of the season, reporters scrambling for stories got a lot of material from Morris, who was leading his team's assault on the record book. When he pitched his no-hitter on April 7, in just the fourth game of the year, Morris was gracious enough to visit the press box to assist sportswriters in preparing their stories.

But by mid-July, the ace of the staff had morphed into the ass of the staff, as only the volatile and sensitive Morris could. From mid-July until the end of August, Morris not only refused to talk to reporters but was also estranged from his teammates. In a sport that is defined by its profound ups and downs, Morris spent most of 1984 either in the glow of greatness or in the abyss of confusion and anger. Morris was a perfectionist who couldn't prevent what began as a near-perfect season from crumbling around him.

On May 28, Morris won 6-2 at Oakland, running his record to 10-1. Then, on June 12, he felt a twinge in his pitching elbow after getting battered in Toronto. Over the next six weeks, Morris missed a few starts, and was 1-3 with a 7.64 ERA when he had been able to pitch. And after a particularly poor outing on July 18, he announced that he was done talking to the media for the rest of the year.

Jack maintained his vow of silence until the beginning of September, and finished strongly to reach his final record of 19-11.

The beginning and the spectacular end—with a 3-0 record and just five runs allowed in 25 postseason innings—was Jack Morris at his Hall of Fame–caliber best. But the self-imposed isolation, moodiness and alienation displayed during the middle portion of the season was what made Morris such an enigma.

Jack's emotionalism, volatility and inability to quickly forgive himself and his teammates for their imperfections was an Achilles heel that periodically hobbled him throughout much of his career. Other than that, there wasn't much else to not like about Morris. He was bright, insightful, terrifically talented and totally dedicated to achieving excellence. But when he reached an emotional deficit, you had three choices: ignore him, run for cover or confront his counterproductive behavior.

No '84 Tiger was more loved by his teammates, yet no '84 Tiger frustrated his teammates more than Morris. Dave Bergman didn't play with him until '84, but as a veteran utility man whose success was reliant on emotional control and preparation, Bergman became intolerant when Morris shifted into his childish mode.

"I don't buy the, 'He was a thoroughbred, so he was flighty' theory. That's a crock of shit," Bergman says with a measure of disgust. "I do remember that he went six weeks in '84 without talking to the media, and he went six weeks without talking to us! We said, 'The hell with him.'

"Ruppert Jones joined the team a few months in [June 7]. One game, Ruppert dove for a ball in the outfield and missed it. Jack stares at him; those are the things that we didn't like. And he knew it, and he knew exactly how we felt. I went to the mound more than once and told him, 'If you think you're that good, then you better strike out the next two hitters because any ground ball hit to me, I'm not catching it!' This was our way of telling him to shape up. So he'd punch out the next few hitters and say, 'What do you guys think about that?'

"There was always that emotional shit going on with Jack," Bergman continues. "He was very high-strung, and he'd put his hands on his hips and look at you like, 'How could you not catch that ball.' Our feeling was, 'If you're that damn good, don't let them hit the ball to me; make other pitches, you arrogant ass.' And there were times where he'd say, 'Okay!' and he'd bear down and get 'em out. That's how gifted he was.

"We just didn't need this kind of disturbance during the season, but we were a mature enough club to deal with it. But, I'll be honest. During that period, I didn't care if he showed up or not. We had other pitchers who could've done just as well as him during those six-eight weeks. He was a detriment to the ball club during that period."

Morris' silence and disdain of the media for much of '84 was well documented. But it wasn't until years later that his teammates would fill in the blanks of what happened on the mound and behind closed doors.

Kirk Gibson remains one of Jack's best friends. But as a teammate, Gibson often called him on the carpet. "I said plenty to Jack," Gibson recalls matter-of-factly. "We all did. I can remember standing out in right field and seeing Jack start pouting. You could tell. You could identify it. There were times when I actually thought about running in from right field and scolding him. I came close a few times.

"But Darrell [Evans] was always there before me and Darrell used to just go to the mound and grab the rosin bag, put it in his [Morris's] hand, look Jack in the eye and go, 'Waaaaaa!' [like a baby wailing] and say, 'Throw the fucking ball.' And then Darrell'd go back to first base after giving him the same talking-to we all would have.

"And trust me, we all said plenty to Jack. We'd make fun of it, too, and he realized what he was doing. Jack was extremely competitive. He couldn't separate it. I was much the same. I could relate to Jack more than most. I acted stupid and did plenty of stupid things too."

On July 18, during his pitching and emotional swoon, Jack blew two leads in a 10-6 loss to the White Sox before nearly 40,000 fans at Tiger Stadium. It was the low point in a period of poor performance, and it was the day that Jack went into his shell and shut out the media.

After the '84 season, Roger Craig wrote a book titled *Inside Pitch*. In notes he made that day, Craig wrote, "He (Morris) had a fit over a strike call by (umpire) Mark Johnson. He seems unable to comprehend the serious nature of his frustrations. He ranted and raved. He embarrassed me, himself, Sparky and the front office. He incensed his teammates. Jack has a lot of growing up to do. He's not having fun and he's not a happy person. He has pride and doesn't want to let people down, but then blames others for his failings. He can't channel adversity. He self-destructs. Great pitchers don't let trivial things upset them. Emotional pitchers beat themselves. Now he says he won't discuss baseball with the media. He has become an alien in his clubhouse as players think he is pouting."

Sparky remembers a classic duel with the pitcher he loved like a son: "Jack and me, I don't know how many shouting matches we had. In Toronto, Roger went out to talk to him and he embarrassed Roger out there on the mound, arguing, pacing, stuff like that. I'm watching this and I can't go right back out. The rule says I gotta wait a hitter.

"I wait a hitter and I go out there and get the ball and then when he went up the runway to the clubhouse I followed him right on up. I told him, 'Get your ass in my room,' and, don't forget, this is during the game! And I'm banging things and screaming and going on. I would not try to defend Jack's way of doing things, but we go back to one thing: He cared deeply. And because he cared so deeply, you just accepted that Jack was Jack."

Sparky recalls another time when Jack was struggling to regain his form and emotional grip: "In Milwaukee, we were hitting and Jack was out there at shortstop. He loved to play short during batting practice and before games. We're fooling around and he'd had about three rough outings and he asked me, 'What's the matter with me?' I said, 'I don't know, are you missing on some pitches?' He said, 'No—what's the matter with me?' meaning, why does he behave the way he behaves. I said 'OK, you try and follow me if you're bright enough. You see that thing in the middle—what is that?' He said, 'It's the mound.'

"I said, 'OK. Did you set up in your room on the typewriter and type up your stats or did you climb up on that thing and make 'em happen?' He looked at me and smiled and said, 'I got up there, that's how I got 'em.' I said, 'Then stop telling me about your problems,' and I walked away."

Sparky's point was that Jack was tremendously gifted and already knew everything he needed to know. He just needed to recognize when he was getting in his own way. Morris had all the intelligence, talent and heart he'd ever need. In '91, when Sparky was still man-

Jack Morris, the Tigers' best right-handed pitcher since WWII, about to fire a split-finger fastball.

aging the Tigers and Morris had left for Minnesota, Jack faced John Smoltz and the Braves in Game Seven of the World Series. Sparky played golf with his buddies in California the morning of the game.

"The guys at the golf course said, 'No way, Smoltz versus Morris—Smoltz would win that matchup,'" Sparky says. "So I looked at 'em and said, 'I'll tell you what I'll do, boys. Go get your bank accounts, get 'em up here and put your house up and I'll put up mine that Morris beats Smoltz.' And Jack beat him in 10 innings, 1-0. Jack Morris might be ornery but Jack Morris wants to win. If that makes you bad, give me a whole bunch of Jack Morrises."

From his blowup on July 18 until the end of August, Morris recovered from his elbow soreness and, for the most part, regained his consistency. But on August 30 in Seattle, before fewer than 10,000 fans—and after having won four of his last five decisions—Jack was close to completing a terrific outing when he suddenly lost his temper and the game.

In the eighth inning of a scoreless battle, Morris walked lead-off man Spike Owen on four pitches. The ball-four call was made by his nemesis, Durwood Merrill, the same umpire who had so angered Jack with a ball-four call on Chicago's Greg Luzinski with two out in the ninth inning of his April 7 no-hitter.

This time, Morris responded by asking for a new ball, then fired it toward home plate and wide of catcher Lance Parrish. Parrish refused to go and get it, later saying, "It's like a little soap opera. In the state of mind I was in, I wasn't going to get it." Alan Trammell went to the mound to calm Jack down, and Morris insulted him by turning away and refusing to listen to him. Trammell, talking to Jack's back, said, "Don't be a coward. Don't give up on us."

The next hitter, Jack Perconte, popped a bunt toward the mound in an attempt to sacrifice Owen to second base. Morris charged the ball but fell as it rolled underneath him. Rising to his knees, he threw it 15 feet to the right of first base and it rolled into the right-field corner. In a classic pout, Jack lay motionless on the ground while the game continued on without him.

Gibson retrieved Jack's errant missile and launched a futile heave toward home to try to get Owen. But the ball sailed over Parrish's head, and instead of backing up home as was his responsibility, Jack was mired in his own misery, with his face in the Kingdome carpet. Two runs scored on the play. In the ninth, the Tigers pushed one across and wound up leaving the bases loaded in a 2-1 loss.

Had Jack backed up the play, the result might have been different. Trammell went to the mound again to talk to him and handed him the ball. Morris angrily grabbed it from him. "Embarrassed?" the media later asked him. "Yes, I was," Trammell answered honestly.

Afterward, Parrish said that he was done trying to soothe Jack's feelings. "I don't feel it's my job to reprimand him," Parrish said that night. "It's up to the coaching staff. Let them do it." Parrish was also up to his ears in being the mouthpiece to the media for the silent Morris.

Decades later, Parrish recalls his battles with and for Jack: "Jack, for the better part of his career, was a moody guy along with being one of the greatest athletes I've ever seen, but he didn't know how to control himself on the mound. I used to use analogies and comparisons. I used to tell him, 'Watch Steve Carlton pitch. You can't tell if Steve Carlton is winning 10-0 or losing 10-0. He never changes his expression. Never changes his demeanor.'

"I told Jack, 'Carlton always looks like he's in control.' I said, 'When you pitch and something happens and you throw a fit and lose your mind and kick the ground, the opposition feeds off it. You just light a fire under 'em.' I said, 'Why can't you control yourself, and just worry about pitching?' And he would even admit, 'I know, I know.' And then the next game he'd go out and do it again.

"So we all took turns going out and laying into him," Parrish continues. "One time I went out and said, 'We're sick and tired of playing behind you when you act like this. If you can't get your shit together, something's gonna happen.'

"I thought he was not only hurting himself, but he was hurting us as a team. Number one, it didn't look good; it was an embarrassment to the ballclub to have him act the way he did, and I thought that it had to have an effect on his concentration because he'd self-destruct at times."

Trammell has remained close friends with Jack, and they and Gibson, Dave Rozema and Tom Brookens go on a snowmobiling trip every winter. Time, however, hasn't obscured the memory of the uncomfortable role Trammell had to play as Sparky's so-called captain of the infield.

"Over time," says Alan, "we got to Jack a little bit, but early in his career it was excessive. Sparky used to motion to me, 'Go talk to him.' All I was trying to do was buy some time and get him to step off the mound and regroup. Jack didn't like it. He'd tell me, 'Get the fuck outta here.' I would just stall and try to get him to loosen up and take his mind off it for a few seconds.

"And even though he'd cuss me out or say something stupid, I'd say, 'Jack, are you done?' And somewhere along the line I said, 'You see that little white-haired guy over there? He's telling me to come out here.' And once I told him that, I think he had to take a step back and go, 'Oh. Okay, it's just not Tram coming out here.' I was doing it by order from our manager, otherwise I didn't need to put up with that."

Morris won more games than any pitcher in the '80s. He led the league in wins during the strike-shortened '81 season, when he was 14-7. And had '81 not been abbreviated, he would have won at least 15 games for 10 straight years, starting with his 17-7 in '79, his first full year in the majors.

Jack was one of the great workhorses of his era. He'd start between 34 and 37 games every year and pitch 240-plus innings. He started every Tigers opener from 1980 until 1990, his final year in Detroit. All in all, counting his concluding years in Minnesota and Toronto, he started a major-league-record 14 straight openers. He led the Tigers' staff in wins for 10 straight years. No one else in team history ever led in wins more than three straight years. Sparky loved him for his competitiveness and durability.

That Morris was the dominant Tigers right-hander of the post–World War II era isn't even an issue. By large margins, he leads all other postwar righties in starts, innings, strikeouts, complete games and wins. He won 198 games as a Tiger. The next closest since 1950 is Frank Lary with 123.

As sure as Jack was the Tigers' ace all those years, Dan Petry was right behind him as the number two man. In '81, the season shortened by 53 games, Jack won those 14 games, while Dan won 10. In '82, Jack won 17, Dan won 15. In '83, Jack won 20, Dan won 19. And in '84, Jack won 19, Dan won 18. Petry never questioned his status in the pitching pecking order. He was respectful of Jack and was dedicated to staying with him.

"Although I won't say I was comfortable as number two," Petry emphasizes, "I must say that part of what made me successful was I strived to be as good or better than Jack. He proved he was number one. He was a stud. You want to do well for your teammates and yourself, but I did want to be better than Jack, so I pushed myself. He'd win, so doggonit, I'm gonna win. I gotta stay with him.

"That was a big driving force for me. Now, so many years later, I look back on it, and although Jack and I were never close, I go around town [Detroit] here making a big pitch for him to be in the Hall of Fame. I list all my reasons why. They say, 'Well, if he made the Hall of Fame, he'd have the highest ERA [3.90] of all the starters in the Hall.' So I say, 'So what? Somebody in there already has the highest ERA. Somebody's gotta have it. The guy has four World Series rings and won 254 games, and there may hardly ever be any more 300-game winners.'"

Milt Wilcox was the number three Tigers starter in '84 and had experienced profound career disappointments, including arm trouble in his mid-20s that almost ruined him. Wilcox appreciated Morris' tremendous physical and competitive gifts. As happens with many greats, the attributes tend to be taken for granted, while the flaws draw emphasis.

"That's why Jack was never as great a pitcher as he could have been," Wilcox explains, "because he let too many little things bother him. Jack was always blaming somebody else. He'd look at you and say, 'Well, you got more runs than I got; the team didn't hit for me like they did for you.'

"Jack was a good guy," Wilcox continues, "and a great guy to have on your team. He was always for you; he pulled for everybody, but Jack had this little deal where he'd get upset when he lost a game. So I told him one time, 'When you lose those games, 3-2 and 2-1, the other pitcher is only giving up one less run than you. If you're a good pitcher, those are the games that you win.' I was just trying to tell him, quit bitching. If you lose, 3-2, maybe you should have won that game, 2-1. He was such a competitor that he just wanted to win all the time."

By the end of August '84, and following Morris's blowup in Seattle, Sparky had convinced him to reconnect with the media and repair his relationship with his teammates. Like all good stories, the finish was inspirational. Jack beat the Royals, 8-1, in Game One of the playoffs with seven innings of five-hit ball. And he pitched two complete games in the World Series, beating San Diego, 3-2, in Game One, and 4-2 in Game Four.

If not for Trammell's .450 batting average and the two 2-run homers that supported Jack's win in Game Four, Morris could easily have been Series MVP. Despite missing three starts with the elbow problem in June and a few more with a stiff shoulder in September, Morris was 19-11 in the regular season, 3-0 in the postseason, threw the April no-hitter and pitched two scoreless innings in the All-Star game. And despite all the angst in the middle, no Tiger contributed more to get those rings on their fingers.

Chapter 17

Bless You Boys

Without the Tigers…several industry insiders feel Post-Newsweek would have long since sold WDIV. And there are some who say that sneer-turned-cheer, "Bless You Boys," helped save Al Ackerman's career.

— Bob Talbert of the *Detroit Free Press*
late in the '84 season

On September 4, 1984, before the Tigers hosted the Orioles, Jack Morris was sitting in the Tigers' clubhouse. Morris hadn't talked to the media in the month and a half since his vow of silence following his particularly bad outing on July 18. The Tigers had arrived back in town after a long West Coast trip, and *Detroit News* columnist Jerry Green, who had been on that road trip, walked by Morris's locker.

"I went into the clubhouse as I did before most games when I was doing a column," Green remembers. "Jack said, 'Do you want an interview?' God knows I had tried. I was there every day. There were far fewer media people back then. Ackerman was there, as were a few other print people. Jack had suddenly decided to speak to us again, but as we got started, something set Al and I off. We got into mouthing off at one another and Jack started laughing. It was ridiculous—seeing two guys from the media in a spat."

Morris loved it. "They're showing emotion," he gleefully shouted to his teammates while Green and Ackerman verbally lambasted each other. Morris's excuse for his occasional childish behavior on the mound had been his emotional nature. This seemed perfect vindication for it.

The exchange got vulgar and centered around Ackerman's pet phrase, "Bless You Boys," that had become a rallying cry for the team and its fans. In sports circa 2000, marketing phrases are taken for granted. The Pistons successfully used "Goin' to work" in 2003, and the Red Wings have long created catch phrases and also put them to song.

But in '84, there was a cynical attitude among the competing media that Channel 4, WDIV, was exploiting a marketing phrase, especially a phrase that had started as a put-down but was now being used as a corporate meal ticket. Green thought that exploiting "Bless You Boys" was cheap and uncalled for. Channel 4 had even released a "Bless You

Boys" song and had the foresight (then viewed as audacity) to trade-mark the phrase.

"I didn't approve of those gimmicky things. I'm an old-fashioned newspaper man," Green says today with no regret. "Al had done the same thing with his 'Huckleby for the Heisman' bumper sticker some years before. He knew that Michigan football coach Bo Schembechler refused to hype his players for awards, so he created that to poke fun at Michigan.

"I also don't believe that the media ought to be writing about the media covering the media. I don't believe I'm the story. Al did use 'Bless You Boys' derisively in the beginning. But aside from that, I had extreme respect for Al as a reporter and journalist." The two quickly made up and were seen laughing about the incident later that very evening.

There also were others who didn't approve of Ackerman's exploitation of the phrase. Among his other reasons, Bob Talbert of the *Free Press* hated Ackerman for "Bless You Boys." Ironically, the cheerleading Talbert seemed blind to the fact that he was also shamelessly capitalizing on the team's success. All season long, Talbert had called his column "Tiger Diary," complete with a picture of him wearing a satin Tigers jacket and a Tigers hat. Several days after the Green-Ackerman incident, Talbert wrote the following in one of his columns:

"Channel 4 has to be thankful for having the Tiger telecasts—highest rated in the country and Channel 4's biggest revenue-producer. Good thing. Without the Tigers last year and this remarkable year, several industry insiders feel, Post-Newsweek would have long since sold WDIV. And there are some who say that sneer-turned-cheer, 'Bless You Boys,' helped save Al Ackerman's career."

As we look back, 1984 doesn't seem too long ago, but it was still a very different era with regard to the media. During the Tigers' amazing 35-5 start, only 12 of the 40 games were available on tele-vision. In fact, WDIV, the Tigers' television rights-holder since 1975, had to work on team president Jim Campbell just to get him to agree to televise the home opener vs. Texas on April 10.

After Morris's no-hitter in Chicago on April 7 had drawn a 20.1 rating as the NBC *Game of the Week* telecast, WDIV Program Director Alan Frank quickly negotiated a separate deal with Campbell to televise the opener. The April 8 game, which had been a WDIV-produced telecast, had done an amazing 25.9 rating from Chicago. Campbell hadn't allowed a home opener to be shown on local television since 1972.

It sounds so antiquated in today's climate, but Campbell didn't want to interfere with ticket sales, even though the opener was almost always sold out. But the enormity of these early ratings was just ridiculous. People could not see enough or get enough information about this team, and Channel 4 was ready and eager to meet the demand.

Simply, here's how the ratings numbers work. In 1984, each ratings point represented one percent of the metro Detroit area's 1,600,000 homes, or 16,000 homes. A 25.9 rating translated into 414,400 homes (25.9 x 16,000). The Nielsen ratings service considered each home to have 2.2 viewers, which equates to about 912,000 viewers.

As the season progressed, and the hunger for Tigers baseball increased even more, the people at WDIV became even more wide-eyed over the numbers.

"We were doing 30 ratings for some games," recalls Frank. "We averaged a 27 or 28 rating for the season. Nielsen said that there were 2.2 people per household, but that doesn't count the bars and the groups that gathered. On a typical day in '84, you had 1.4 to 1.5 million people watching every telecast. That's an astounding number."

If you then take the approximately 60 total regular season televised games—45 on WDIV and a dozen or so on NBC's *Game of the Week* and ABC's *Monday Night Baseball*—that's in the neighborhood of 75 million to 100 million viewers. Considering that only 2.7 million went to the games (still a Tigers record by nearly 700,000!), you realize what a major role the media played in 1984.

Today, it's a completely different situation. UPN 50's telecasts of the Tigers average about a 4 rating, with Fox Sports Net getting about a 3. The Red Wings, who became the big sports attraction during the '90s, get about a 7 rating. Different era, completely different beast.

When the Tigers played the Blue Jays on ABC's *Monday Night Baseball* on June 4, 1984, the night that Bergman's homer won it in the 10th inning, the telecast did a 62 share to go along with its 30 rating. That means that by getting 1.5 million-plus to watch, 62 percent of all televisions turned on in Detroit were tuned in to the Tigers.

In July, eight of the top 10 shows in Detroit were Tigers games and Tigers pre-game shows. Considering that there were just four televised games and four televised pre-game shows, each one of them rated in the top 10!

By the time the season was winding down, WDIV was reaping the benefits of a gold mine. There were so many potential sponsors who couldn't buy time on telecasts at any price, the station began creating one-hour Tigers highlight shows. Other stations couldn't do this because as the rights-holder, only WDIV could use the highlights for anything more than brief newscast packages.

Every few days, WDIV director Chuck Wasiluk would find me and say in exasperated tones, "They (the advertising sales department) sold another one." We'd get together with our producer, Toby Tabaczynski, and start cranking out scripts and highlights.

When the season was over and the Tigers won the Series, we thought we'd finally kissed the season goodbye. But Wasiluk sought me out about a week later. I said, "Don't tell me." He smiled and said, "'Tigers '84—the Final Battle.' They promise me that this will be the final extra show."

Mercifully, it was.

The PASS cable service came into being on April 17, 1984. For $11.95 a month you could get most of the Tigers games that Channel 4 wasn't showing. You'd think that people would have clamored to buy it. But not so. There were only a few thousand subscribers.

Alan Frank explains: "People weren't used to paying for things (telecasts). There was cable, but nobody needed cable for Channel 4. It was free. You could still get the 45–50 Tiger games you had gotten all those years, and it was still popular to listen on the radio, so there was the feeling that you didn't really need to pay for more games than you already had. And there was something about going to the ballpark back then that was stronger than it is today."

Many of the Detroit-area bars became PASS signal pirates and would attract full houses to watch Tigers games. By mid-year, most had been identified and forced to pay $300 a month for the rights to offer Tigers telecasts in a public setting.

ESPN didn't go into business until 1979, and by 1984, the 24-hour cable sports network was still in its primitive stages. The reason ESPN even went into business was because satellite signals enabled them to tape events like "Australian Rules Football," and replay that and other "trash sports" ad infinitum. But their baseball highlights were minimal back then because the bulk of baseball games weren't televised locally, let alone nationally.

By 1984, if the Tigers, for example, played a nontelevised game in Minnesota—and if you were willing to pay the fees—a television station in Minneapolis would shoot the first few innings, run it back to the station, and then (you hoped) feed you a play in time for the 11 o'clock news.

In Detroit, you never knew on your late news if Channels 2, 4 or 7 would be able to show you a second-inning RBI single that may or may not have had an impact on an out-of-town Tigers game that night. Generally, the important play happened while the cameraman was scurrying back to the station to send you something that had already been rendered insignificant.

By the mid-'80s, as the use of videotape, the proliferation of cable games and the utility of satellites made comprehensive coverage easier, television sports departments started cutting back. A single anchorman with a good producer and a few tape machines could cover almost all the games.

In 1981, when Jay Mariotti of the *Detroit News* conducted a "Rate the TV sportscasters" poll, each station employed four full-time sportscasters. Local highlights still were hard to find on ESPN, so if you wanted to "see" sports and get local coverage, you needed to watch the local news.

Unlike today, when many stations have just two full-time sports people, the television stations were crawling with sportscasters. In 1981 at Channel 4, we had Ackerman, Don Shane, Jim Brandstatter and me. In '82, we added a fifth, Lions quarterback Gary Danielson.

Channel 7 had Dave Diles, Steve Garagiola, Steve Harms and John Gross, all full-time.

Channel 2 had a sports department called "5 Star Sports." In '81 and '82 they had no fewer than seven sportscasters: Ray Lane, Charlie Neal, Jim Price, Ann Doyle, Stu Klitenic, Lee Valisides and Mark Barasch.

In '84, Channel 4 had successfully used NBC's network success and the popularity of the Tigers to finally battle Channel 7 in the news ratings. Channel 7, with anchorman Bill Bonds, had always hammered the competition. WDIV played the "Tigers card" to perfection by creating vignettes like "Tigers Play of the Week," and, during sweeps (rating periods), attracted big audiences by airing interviews with Sparky Anderson, who was under exclusive contract. In Channel 4's view, it wasn't exploitation, it was merely filling a need.

"It wasn't 'How can we bleed more out of the Tigers,'" says Alan Frank, "as much as it was that the viewers couldn't get enough. So the pressure was on us to do more. 'Give us more Tigers,' the public was saying. 'Is there anything else you can do?'"

And in fact, it was the station, not Ackerman, who initially seized upon "Bless You Boys."

"It was amazing," continues Frank. "Al did start that [slogan] as a cynical putdown the year before. But then we started hearing 'Bless You Boys' parroted back. We recognized a good thing when we heard it. And in the beginning, using it was against Al's wishes. He did not want us to do this, to get people to repeat it. Once we started, he then realized how good it was. I remember we got President [Ronald] Reagan to hold up the shirt and say, 'Bless You

Boys.' The president of the United States saying, 'Bless You Boys.' Al did like that one."

Eventually, Al was all over the idea and did a beautiful job of further ingraining it in the public's mind. And Sparky's book, which hit the streets within days of the Tigers winning the World Series, was appropriately titled *Bless You Boys.*

President Ronald Reagan delivers his special Tigers blessing during a satellite interview with WDIV's Mort Crim.

Chapter 18

September: Finally Taming Toronto

It was awesome. Big win that night. Turned out to be a real big weekend for us; real bad weekend for them.

— Kirk Gibson on Dave Bergman's three-run,
10th inning homer that beat the Blue Jays on
September 7, precipitating a series sweep

The party bubbled on… it looks like we finally have overcome the legend of the '68 Tigers. They had a great year… but the players are tired of the constant reminder. . . we want people to talk about the '84 Tigers.

— Roger Craig in his book *Inside Pitch*, after the
Tigers clinched the AL East on September 18

The final month of the 1984 season began with the Tigers in command of the race but still unable to put it away. August had ended with three straight losses on their West Coast trip, and September began with another defeat. In Oakland, the A's rallied for six first-inning runs off Juan Berenguer to win, 7-5. A Tigers lead that had been 12½ just a little over a week earlier was back to a relatively unsettling 8½. Sparky Anderson said, "We're struggling. We're going through one of those

---

SEPTEMBER 1984

September Record: 17–10

Highlights:
3-game sweep of Toronto, September 7–9
Clinched AL East on September 18
Shattered team attendance record by nearly 700,000 with 2,704,794

Stars:
Petry: 3-0, 2.23 ERA
Scherrer: 1-0, 1.93 ERA, 18 innings, 17 appearances
Simmons: .433, 13-30
Bergman: .327, 18-55

Key Games:
Sept 5: 1-0 Berenguer shutout vs. Baltimore
Sept 7, 8, 9: 3-game sweep @ Toronto
Sept 18: 3-0 division clincher vs. Milwaukee
Sept 29: 11-3 win @ NY: sets team record of 104 wins

periods. No one likes it, but it does happen." Berenguer walked the first two batters, and then Rusty Kuntz, playing center for the injured Chet Lemon, dropped a Dave Kingman fly at the wall. Dwayne Murphy's three-run homer made it an early "case closed."

The Tigers concluded the West Coast trip with a 6-3 win on Sunday, September 2. Sparky called it "One of five or six important wins you absolutely must have." Whether that was an exaggeration or not, a loss would have shaved the lead back to 7½.

Also encouraging in that game was that Dan Petry, who had been 1-4 his last seven starts, improved to 16-8, despite giving up 11 hits and three runs in barely five innings pitched. Marty Castillo, who seemed to be the new third baseman by default, doubled in the first run in a four-run fourth. Lance Parrish, who had been mired in an 0-19 slump, doubled in two more. Aurelio Lopez and Willie Hernandez did it again, combining for the final 3⅔ innings on just one harmless hit.

GAMES 138, 139 & 140 vs BALTIMORE—The Tigers were headed home for three mid-week games with Baltimore prior to the critical showdown in Toronto that would begin on Friday, September 7. They had avoided seeing the lead slashed to 7½ on Sunday, but with losses in the next two games, the lead was cut nonetheless. The schedule-maker was cruel, butting the Orioles series right up against the flight back from Oakland.

Monday, September 3, was not a good night for the Tigers, back home after 10 days out west. With two outs in the eighth inning of a 3-3 tie, Jack Morris walked the bases full of Orioles. Jack would rarely be lifted in that situation, but he'd thrown almost 130 pitches, and Sparky brought in Lopez to face O's rookie Mike Young. The first pitch was a ball and the second pitch was jacked into the upper deck in right-center for a grand slam. The Orioles went on to win, 7-4.

Adding to the alarm, Kirk Gibson left the game after one at bat and was reported to have been admitted to Henry Ford Hospital with a suspected intestinal problem. With Lemon still out after getting conked by Fred Lynn's fly ball in Anaheim, the outfield was looking awfully thin.

Orioles starter Storm Davis was only able to pitch six innings in this one. As he was leaving the dugout for the seventh, he forgot to duck and banged his head on the low dugout roof. He was too dizzy to continue, so Sammy Stewart went the last three, allowing one run. Davis, 6'4", could only be thankful he didn't play in Tiger Stadium 81 games a year.

Jim Campbell was well aware of the problems created by the solid concrete dugout roofs, which were less than six feet high. It was one of Lance Parrish's ongoing pet peeves with Campbell. "I used to beg him," Lance still recalls with an air of frustration, "please fix the dugout. Please raise the roof on the dugout. I would hit my head in that dugout a thousand times and I told him I got a permanent knot on the top of my head because of this dugout. He said, 'I can't do it. I'd have to take some seats out and you ain't worth that!'"

On Tuesday, September 4, with Milt Wilcox missing a turn because of his throbbing shoulder, Dave Rozema got another shot at starting and failed miserably. Sparky pulled Rozema after he gave up three hits to the first four batters. Already, two runs were in and the Tigers went on to lose, 4-1, to the Orioles.

Rozy, a potential free agent at the end of the season, was bleeding dough profusely. He was 0-5, with a 6.66 ERA since being 7-1 back on July 20. Nelson Simmons, an Evansville recall, singled in one and, despite the loss, Bill Scherrer and Roger Mason pitched well against Mike Boddicker.

Juan Berenguer

So, there it was: The Tigers' lead was reduced to 7½ once again after six losses in their last seven games. And, after Wednesday night's series-ender with the Orioles, they'd head to Toronto for one final showdown against the Jays. Out of the blue, Juan Berenguer thrilled 34,065 with 7⅓ innings of two-hit ball in a 1-0 victory over Mike Flanagan. Sparky would later point to this game as another one of the season's key victories.

When Hernandez came in to save him in the eighth, Berenguer ran off, waving his hat to the crowd as the scoreboard flashed, "Juan-derful." It was a moment of baseball romanticism that sent chills up your spine. Berenguer had such a topsy-turvy season, but this was a moment of brilliance for all to savor.

Gibson was due back from the hospital (at least that's where team officials told us he was), and Dave Bergman was slated to return from a strained back that had kept him out for a week. Both would emerge in a major way Friday night against the Jays.

GAME #140   Sept 5

Tigers 1, Orioles 0

BALTIMORE	AB	R	H	BI	DETROIT	AB	R	H	BI
Bumbry cf	2	0	0	0	Whitaker 2b	4	0	1	0
Ayala ph	1	0	0	0	Trammell ss	3	1	2	0
Cruz 3b	0	0	0	0	Garbey dh	4	0	1	0
Young rf	4	0	0	0	Parrish c	2	0	0	0
Ripken ss	4	0	0	0	Herndon lf	3	0	1	0
Murray 1b	3	0	1	0	Evans 1b	3	0	1	0
Lowenstein lf	3	0	0	0	Kuntz rf	3	0	0	0
Rayford c	1	0	0	0	Jones cf	3	0	0	0
Singleton dh	4	0	2	0	Castillo 3b	3	0	0	0
Rodriguez pr	0	0	0	0					
Gross 3b	3	0	0	0					
Sakata 2b	1	0	0	0					
Dauer 2b	1	0	0	0					
Nolan ph	0	0	0	0					
Shelby pr-cf	0	0	0	0					
Dempsey c	2	0	0	0					
Dwyer ph	0	0	0	0					
Roenicke ph-l	0	0	0	0					
Totals	**29**	**0**	**3**	**0**		**28**	**1**	**6**	**0**

Baltimore	000 000 000	--	0
Detroit	100 000 00x	--	1

Game winning RBI -- none, E -- Ripken 2, DP -- Baltimore 2, Detroit 1, LOB -- Baltimore 7, Detroit 5, 2B -- Trammell, Murray, SH -- Trammell, HBP -- by Hernandez (Roenicke), WP -- Hernandez

Baltimore	IP	H	R	ER	BB	SO
Flanagan (L)	8.0	6	1	0	1	4
Detroit						
Berenguer (W)	7.1	2	0	0	3	7
Hernandez (S)	1.2	1	0	0	1	1

T -- 2:30 A -- 34,065

GAMES 141, 142 & 143 @ TORONTO

◆Game 141: The Jays Are Dead, Long Live the Tigers

Where:	**Toronto**
Result:	**7-4 Tigers in 10 innings**
Record:	**90-51**
WP:	**Hernandez, 9-2**
LP:	**Musselman, 0-1**
Standing:	**First, 9½ ahead**
Attendance:	**37,420**

Kirk Gibson remembers:

We'd really cooled off from mid-July through August, and I remember that we still weren't comfortable. We had a vicious rivalry with Toronto for years, and they were very good in '84, and no matter how well we started or how many games we won, they just wouldn't go away. But in truth, we never really got comfortable until I hit the home run off Gossage anyway [in Game Five of the World Series]. Never, not one bit.

We were playing Baltimore a three-game series in early September and I got real sick—really bad flu or whatever. I was taking batting practice before the first game [Tuesday, September 3] and knew I really shouldn't play. I told Sparky I'd go, but I was just too dizzy. I went up for my first at bat and I realized then that I was too sick to play. It hit me really fast and kicked my ass and I missed the whole series against Baltimore.

I didn't go into the hospital, even though the newspaper reports said I had spent two nights in [Henry] Ford Hospital. If I did, then I have no recollection, as strange as that sounds. The team must have put that [information] out for some reason.

We'd played 140 games and I'm real sick, so Sparky was smart enough to know that I needed to recover fully before the big series coming up in Toronto. We lost the first two to the Orioles, and then I flew out with the team to Toronto after Thursday's game when Berenguer beat the Orioles, 1-0, to keep us 8½ up on the Jays.

With the 8½-game lead, Toronto's thinking of sweeping us and then they're only 5½ back. What happens when you start out as good as we started out is that your biggest fear is not finishing it out. You fear somebody getting hurt. If Jack Morris or somebody really vital gets hurt, who knows? So, you can't get comfy.

Back then, we played the Jays at Exhibition Stadium, which was a football field. A football field is crowned and we played baseball across the crown. When you played left or center, you were behind the crown. The crown kicked everything to the wall and the wind always blew off the lake [Lake Ontario]. It was a bitch. It was like a minor-league ballpark between the first and third baselines, and otherwise it was a big football stadium they crammed fans into. The place was really horseshit.

They got a few runs in the third and we eventually fell back, 4-0. I do remember the first two runs they got. Petry was pitching and Jesse Barfield was on. Alfredo Griffin bunted him over, but Lance threw wild past first. The bullpen was down the right-field line with very little distance between the foul line and the stands, and the ball hit the bullpen mound and I remember bobbling it, allowing Barfield to score. And [he said laughing] you know I didn't have the best of hands.

Griffin got to third, and then somebody knocked him in. I ended up playing with Alfredo in LA. Little bastard, he did shit like that; even when I was his teammate he did shit like that. He'd be able to bunt the ball when he needed to, and when the bases were loaded it seemed like he'd always get a double. The guy always put the ball in play, pesky bastard.

We trailed, 4-0, by the eighth, but the thing about our team all that year was that 4-0 meant nothing. We'd get a guy or two on and then anything could happen. Look who could hit homers. Lou could hit one. Tram could hit one. I could hit one. Lance could hit one. Darrell could hit one. Other guys, Barbaro Garbey, Johnny Chaptail [Grubb's nickname], he hit 'em. Herndon, Howard Johnson. We had a ton of power. Bergie off the bench. It was a joke. We never gave up. It didn't matter what the score was, early or late.

Doyle Alexander was pitching for them and had a string of 17 straight scoreless and a 4-0 lead in the eighth. They had a big crowd and they were pumped up. I came up against Doyle with two on and two out. The Jays pitchers would pound us on the inside part of the plate. Fastballs in, sliders in, down and in. We didn't like that. We wanted to get our arms out on something out over the plate and very few teams ever did that to us.

They threw inside so much that they established it in our minds. Alexander, Roy Lee Jackson, Dave Stieb, Luis Leal, they all threw fastball-slider and they'd just pound you in and they got you thinking about it. The goal was that they wanted you to adjust what you're doing at the plate to get you away from your strength. Doyle moved the ball all around, brought it in, sunk it down and away and he pitched some gem games against us.

But I got him this time. Three-run homer. I had some big moments against the Blue Jays in '84 and later. But this was right up there. They

GAME #141 Sept 7

Tigers 7, Jays 4

DETROIT	AB	R	H	BI	TORONTO	AB	R	H	BI
Whitaker 2b	4	1	0	0	Garcia 2b	5	0	1	1
Trammell ss	6	0	1	0	Collins lf	2	0	0	0
Gibson rf	5	1	1	3	Mulliniks 3b	3	0	0	0
Parrish c	4	1	0	0	Iorg 3b	2	0	0	0
Evans dh	3	0	0	0	Upshaw 1b	4	1	1	0
Garbey ph	2	0	1	0	Bell rf	4	0	1	0
Jones lf	3	0	1	0	Aikens dh	3	1	2	2
Herndon ph	0	0	0	0	Johnson ph	1	0	1	0
Castillo 3b	0	0	0	0	Shepherd pr	0	0	0	0
Laga ph	1	0	1	0	Whitt c	3	0	0	0
Brookens pr-3b	0	1	0	0	Webster ph	1	0	0	0
Lemon cf	4	1	2	1	Martinez c	0	0	0	0
Bergman 1b	5	2	4	3	Barfield cf	4	1	1	0
Johnson 3b	2	0	0	0	Griffin ss	3	1	0	0
Grubb ph-lf	1	0	0	0					
Kuntz pr-lf	0	0	0	0					
Totals	40	7	11	7		35	4	7	3

```
Detroit-----------------  000 000 040  3 -- 7
Toronto----------------   002 200 000  0 -- 4
```

Game winning RBI -- none, E -- Parrish, Gibson, DP -- Detroit 1, LOB -- Detroit 10, Toronto 5, 2B -- Bergman, HR -- Aikens, Gibson, Bergman, SB -- Garcia, CS -- Shepherd, SH -- Griffin, Whitaker, HBP -- by Petry (Collins)

Detroit	IP	H	R	ER	BB	SO
Petry	5.1	6	4	2	1	3
Scherrer	0.1	0	0	0	0	1
Bair	1.1	0	0	0	0	1
Hernandez (W)	3.0	1	0	0	1	2
Toronto						
Alexander	7.2	6	4	4	2	5
Key*	0.0	1	0	0	0	0
Jackson+	0.0	0	0	0	2	0
Gott	0.2	1	0	0	1	0
Clark	0.1	0	0	0	0	0
Musselman (L)	1.1	3	3	3	1	0

* Pitched to 1 batter in 8th
+ Pitched to 2 batters in 8th

T -- 3:28 A -- 37,420

brought Jimmy Key in for Doyle and we scratched out another run in the ninth against Key and Roy Lee Jackson, who walked Chet to force in the tying run [4-4].

In the bottom of the ninth, Lance threw out pinch runner Mitch Webster stealing. Roger [Craig] had called a pitchout on the play and the game went into extra innings. Roger really made the other team think. He did stuff like that a lot and he was right a lot. He had a great knack for calling pitchouts and had a great knack of analyzing how pitchers tipped pitches. I learned a lot of those techniques from Roger that I used as a player and use now as a coach.

In the 10th, Dave Bergman hit a three-run homer off Ron Musselman over the right-field wall to win it. It was awesome. Bergie had beaten the Jays with a three-run homer in the 10th back in June. Big win that night. Turned out to be a real big weekend for us; real bad weekend for them.

After the game, Sparky was giddy with the reporters, saying, "Ooooh. Damn. That's what pennant fights are all about." And then he added in perfect Sparky hyperbole, "I wanted this game more than any I've ever managed." Rusty Kuntz, who sat the bench that night, raced into the clubhouse and gushed to any and all, "You are unbelievable. I'd pay to watch you guys play." Musselman, the sixth Jays pitcher and the loser, said, "I got a fastball up in the strike zone to Bergman. He drove it—God!"

It was Bergman's first game back since Scherrer sent him to the bench with the practice pitch to the back on August 26 in Seattle. Bergman went 4-5 that night, even though his back "still hurt like hell."

The Tigers won, 10-4, on Saturday. Morris left with shoulder stiffness in the fifth and the score tied at two. Scherrer pitched 1⅔ innings and got his first and only win of the year. He pitched in all three weekend games and didn't give up a hit. Grubb hit two solo homers and Evans, who started at third base, had one. A disappointed crowd of 41,059 Saturday-afternoon Jays fans saw their final pennant chances all but dissolve. Dave Collins said, "We need a miracle."

Saturday's game had been another NBC *Game of the Week* on NBC. Channel 4 did a local pre-game show, and just prior to the 1:30 p.m. start, I was interviewing the Blue Jays' Rick Leach when Marty Castillo nailed me with a shaving-cream pie. Marty had tipped off my producer, Toby Tabaczynski, who was there to snap the picture. NBC's Tony Kubek later ran the footage during the game to point out how loose the Tigers were despite the pennant race tension. It made

GAME #142   Sept 8

Tigers 10, Jays 4

DETROIT	AB	R	H	BI	TORONTO	AB	R	H	BI
Whitaker 2b	3	2	1	0	Garcia 2b	4	1	1	0
Trammell ss	5	1	3	3	Collins lf	5	0	2	1
Gibson rf	5	0	1	2	Mulliniks 3b	4	0	1	0
Parrish c	5	1	1	0	Upshaw 1b	5	0	2	1
Evans 3b	3	1	1	1	Bell rf	4	2	2	1
Castillo 3b	1	0	0	0	Aikens dh	1	0	0	0
Jones lf	2	0	0	0	Johnson ph	2	0	0	0
Herndon ph-lf	2	0	0	0	Whitt c	2	0	1	1
Grubb dh	4	3	2	2	Webster ph	1	0	0	0
Lemon cf	3	1	0	0	Martinez c	1	0	0	0
Bergman 1b	3	1	1	1	Barfield cf	4	0	0	0
Laga 1b	0	0	0	0	Griffin ss	4	1	1	0
Totals	36	10	10	9		37	4	10	4

Detroit	010	010	260	--	10
Toronto	010	100	002	--	4

Game winning RBI -- none, E -- Griffin, Bell, LOB -- Detroit 6, Toronto 10, 2B -- Mulliniks, Bell, Trammell, Upshaw, 3B -- Bergman, HR -- Evans, Bell, Grubb 2, SB -- Collins, CS -- Whitaker, SH -- Castillo, HBP -- by Lopez (Garcia), WP -- Leal

Detroit	IP	H	R	ER	BB	SO
Morris	4.1	5	2	2	1	2
Scherrer (W)	1.2	0	0	0	1	3
Lopez (S)	3.0	5	2	2	1	2
Toronto						
Leal (L)	6.2	7	4	4	3	9
Clark	0.2	1	1	1	0	0
Lamp	0.2	2	5	0	3	0
Acker	1.0	0	0	0	0	0

T -- 3:06 A -- 41,059

me feel a part of things—for a moment I was one of the boys, not just one of the boys who reported on them.

The Tigers won, 7-2, on Sunday to move 11½ ahead. It was also their 92nd win, which tied their total from '83. Gibson had eight RBIs in the three-game sweep. In the seventh, the Tigers led, 4-2, and had two on and two out. Bobby Cox brought lefty reliever Bryan Clark in to pitch to Kirk, who hit the first pitch over the right-field fence for a three-run homer, and the sweep was complete. As the ball sailed out, Lemon said from the bench, "Well, that's it, Toronto." Kirk's quote in the papers was, "It came at a good time and nailed the coffin shut, so to speak. I was drained before I got sick. The rest replenished me."

GAMES 144, 145 & 146 @ BALTIMORE—There were 19 games left, with nothing left to accomplish but to pare down the magic number, make it official and prepare for the postseason. They went to Baltimore for three, September 10–12, and won just one of them when Petry got his 17th.

GAMES 147, 148 & 149 vs TORONTO—The Tigers came home to face those recently ravaged Jays and took two out of three September 14–16. Even though winning the division was a lock, the crowds were still huge—nearly 140,000 for three games. The smallest crowd was the 44,349 on Saturday afternoon, September 15, for a 2-1 Tigers win.

Wilcox allowed just one hit through seven, but Ruppert Jones thrilled the crowd on a chilly day. His fourth-inning homer broke a

GAME #143	Sept 9

Tigers 7, Jays 2

DETROIT	AB	R	H	BI	TORONTO	AB	R	H	BI
Whitaker 2b	5	1	1	0	Garcia 2b	4	0	1	0
Trammell ss	5	2	2	1	Collins lf	4	2	2	0
Gibson rf	5	1	3	3	Mulliniks 3b	2	0	1	1
Parrish c	5	0	2	2	Iorg ph-3b	1	0	0	0
Evans 3b	2	0	1	0	Upshaw 1b	4	0	2	1
Castillo pr-3b	1	0	0	0	Bell rf	4	0	0	0
Jones lf	3	0	1	0	Aikens dh	3	0	0	0
Herndon ph-lf	0	0	0	0	Manrique ph	1	0	0	0
Grubb dh	3	1	1	0	Whitt c	2	0	0	0
Lemon cf	4	0	0	0	Martinez ph-c	1	0	0	0
Bergman 1b	4	2	2	0	Shepherd pr	0	0	0	0
					Barfield cf	4	0	1	0
					Fernandez ss	3	0	1	0
Totals	**37**	**7**	**13**	**7**		**33**	**2**	**8**	**2**

Detroit	002	001	400	--	7
Toronto	100	001	000	--	2

Game winning RBI -- none, E -- Barfield, Trammell, DP -- Detroit 1, Toronto 1, LOB -- Detroit 7, Toronto 6, 2B -- Upshaw 2, Mulliniks, Gibson, Parrish, 3B -- Collins, HR -- Grubb, Gibson, SB -- Gibson, CS -- Parrish, SH -- Herndon, SF -- Mulliniks, HBP -- by Hernandez (Martinez), Balk -- Wilcox

Detroit	IP	H	R	ER	BB	SO
Wilcox (W)	6.0	8	2	2	0	5
Scherrer	1.0	0	0	0	0	0
Hernandez	2.0	0	0	0	0	1
Toronto						
Clancy (L)*	6.0	11	6	5	2	2
Clark+	0.0	2	1	1	1	0
Gott	3.0	0	0	0	0	1

* Pitched to 3 batters in 7th
+ Pitched to 3 batters in 7th
T -- 2:39 A -- 37,392

The Tigers' class clown, Marty Castillo, pies me on live TV before the Tigers beat Toronto 10-4 on September 8.

Lou Whitaker's grand slam off Jack Lazorko beats the Brewers on September 17, but the Tigers couldn't clinch.

1-1 tie, and in the eighth, with Hernandez in, Jones leapt to snare a Cliff Johnson drive before it could fall over the nine-foot left-field fence to tie the score. The crowd roared, "Rupe, Rupe," when he came off the field. After an 8-3 win on Sunday, the magic number was down to four.

GAMES 150, 151 & 152 vs MILWAUKEE—On Monday, September 17, with extra police on hand to quell any celebrations run amok, the Tigers beat the Brewers, 7-3, for Roger Mason's first career win. Whitaker slugged a grand slam in a six-run sixth. But in Boston, the Jays rallied in the ninth to beat the Red Sox, 5-4, on Garth Iorg's two-run single off of Bill Buckner's glove, and the celebration was put off for a day.

◆ *Game 151: The Clincher*

Where:	Tiger Stadium
Result:	3-0 Tigers
Record:	97-54
WP:	O'Neal, 1-0
LP:	McClure, 4-8
Standing:	First, 13 ahead
Attendance:	48,810

Randy O'Neal remembers:

They called me up from Evansville on September 5. I thought that my manager, Gordie McKenzie, was kidding when he told me I was called up. I said, "To where?" I drove up to Detroit that night, and then I flew with the team to Toronto. They got me up and sat me down in the pen a few times during that great sweep we had there to lock up the race.

Then we went to Baltimore. Same thing. I'm up, I'm down, never getting in the game. Finally, in Baltimore on September 12, they said, "You're in." I run in, take my eight warm-up pitches, and then look in to the plate and go, "Holy shit. That's Cal Ripken!" And on deck is Eddie Murray. What a start to a career—facing two Hall-of-Famers.

You think about the big leagues all your life and finally you're there. You can't fathom it. I threw a fastball by Ripken for strike one; then a slider on the corner for strike two; a forkball that he fouled off his foot.

Then I tried to get cute and go away from him, but a slider goes right down the middle and he parted my hair with it. I was like, "Wow, welcome to the big leagues." Turns out I went three innings and that was the only hit they got off me.

That was Wednesday, September 12. A few days later, Roger [Craig] told me I was scheduled to start next Tuesday, the 18th. Sparky was trying to set up the rotation for the playoffs, and it just happened to be my night. We could have clinched on the 17th when Roger Mason, who was called up with me, had his turn. We won that game, but the Blue Jays beat Boston to keep our magic number at one. I say "thanks" to Sparky, because he could've started the other guys. Petry, Morris, Wilcox, all asked him if they could go. I knew that they wanted to pitch that game, but he kept me slotted in.

I was living at the Book Cadillac [Hotel in downtown Detroit], and I don't remember which mall it was, but I was so nervous that I went to the mall during the day and walked for about three hours. Once I got to the park I was fine. It was during the day that the waiting killed me. When I'm driving to the mall, I'll never forget listening to the radio and they're going, "Who is this guy starting tonight, Randy who? Where's Morris, where's Petry?" And that kinda fired me up, made me aggravated and I wanted to give 'em something to remember. And I did, I hope.

The first guy was [Robin] Yount and he struck out on a fastball that was up. He kinda helped me out on that pitch, and it settled me in and helped me move forward. They had Yount, [Paul] Molitor, Cecil Cooper, [Jim] Gantner, a good-hitting team.

We got a run in the first, and I got in a little trouble with the bases loaded in the third, but got out of that. In the bottom of the seventh, Brookens hit a homer to make it 3-0.

I had a shutout through seven on four hits and definitely wanted to stay in, but I knew that Sparky wanted Willie out there. It was the guy's Cy Young year. I do remember the ninth because of all the [police] horses that they had brought in for crowd control. And the crowd was nuts, like nothing I'd ever seen before.

Willie mowed 'em down and when it ended, I followed the team pouring out of the dugout, and I was dog-pilin' with everybody else. A fan came up and tried to grab my hat and I stuffed it down my jacket and then he tried to grab my jacket. It was crazy. I'm pretty sure it was Gibby who forearm-shivered a guy like he did at Michigan State and just launched this guy.

One of the biggest thrills happened the day after. You do your sprints to the foul poles with the pitchers, and my second time over I hear the crowd chanting my name, "O-Neal; O-Neal." Had to be 20,000 there for batting practice! I'll never forget it because it would echo in that stadium. It's a shame. I loved that old stadium. The new one [Comerica Park] doesn't

Randy O'Neal

GAME #151   Sept 18

Tigers 3, Brewers 0

MILWAUKEE	AB	R	H	BI	DETROIT	AB	R	H	BI
Yount dh	4	0	2	0	Whitaker 2b	3	1	0	0
Gantner 2b	4	0	0	0	Trammell ss	4	1	2	0
Cooper 1b	3	0	1	0	Gibson rf	3	0	0	0
Loman lf	4	0	0	0	Parrish c	3	0	1	2
Clark rf	4	0	1	0	Herndon lf	4	0	1	0
James cf	3	0	1	0	Garbey dh	2	0	0	0
Brouhard ph	1	0	0	0	Grubb ph	1	0	0	0
Sundberg c	4	0	0	0	Lemon cf	3	0	0	0
Romero ss	3	0	1	0	Evans 1b	2	0	0	0
Lozado 3b	3	0	0	0	Brookens 3b	3	1	1	1
					Castillo 3b	0	0	0	0
Totals	**33**	**0**	**6**	**0**		**28**	**3**	**5**	**3**

Milwaukee			000	000	000	--	0
Detroit			100	001	10x	--	3

Game winning RBI -- none, DP -- Milwaukee 1, LOB -- Milwaukee 7, Detroit 6, 2B -- Trammell 2, HR -- Brookens, CS -- Parrish, WP -- Tellmann

Milwaukee	IP	H	R	ER	BB	SO
McClure (L)*	5.0	4	2	2	4	3
Tellmann	0.2	0	0	0	1	1
Caldwell	1.1	1	1	1	0	1
Kern	1.0	0	0	0	0	2
Detroit						
O'Neal (W)	7.0	4	0	0	1	6
Hernandez (S)	2.0	2	0	0	0	2

* Pitched to 3 batters in 6th

T -- 2:26 A -- 48,810

Willie Hernandez leaps for joy as the Tigers clinch the division.

have the ambiance and feel of Tiger Stadium. One thing I forgot to mention: I was born in Ashland, Kentucky, and my dad used to take the train as a young boy to Detroit and see games at Briggs Stadium [later named Tiger Stadium]. Back then at 14-15 years old you could go anywhere [safely]. He told me it was a great city, and he was happy I was drafted by the Tigers.

After the clincher, I'd pitched a total of 10 innings and hadn't allowed a run. I just remember that I wanted to keep things as low-keel as possible 'cause I wanted a chance at the World Series, and I wanted to be here the following year and make the club.

I was happy to play seven years in the big leagues. I had health problems after I left Detroit; blew my shoulder out with San Francisco and had total reconstruction afterwards. I did the best I could with what I had [17-19 career record[and I probably should have had my shoulder taken care of earlier. It didn't pan out the way I wanted it to, put it that way.

The Tigers tried to activate me for the playoffs—Baker hurt his knee—but they [Major League Baseball] said you had to replace a shortstop with another shortstop. I threw batting practice before one game, but that's as close as I got to the postseason.

But I don't have to tell you how much of a thrill it was to clinch the division in my first major-league start and to be on a champion in your first year in the majors.

After beating the Brewers again, 4-2, on Wednesday, September 19, there were 10 games to go. The Jays led the third-place Yankees by only two games, and with the Yanks coming to town Sparky said he was going to use his main guys and play hard because he "owed it to Toronto" in the Jays' desire to finish second and make a few extra bucks.

GAMES 153, 154 & 155 vs NEW YORK—The Yanks beat Wilcox, 5-3, on Friday, September 21. Petry, who'd been rested with a tired arm the last 10 days, shut out the Yanks on four hits and nine strike-outs on Saturday to push his record to 18-8. Morris won his 19th, 4-1, on Sunday to close out the home season. For three games that didn't matter, the Tigers drew an average of well over 40,000 a game.

GAMES 156, 157 & 158 @ MILWAUKEE—For the last six games, all on the road, Sparky gave substantial playing time to the rookies. Scotty Earl and Doug Baker filled in for Whitaker and Trammell, and Nelson Simmons and Dwight Lowry got opportunities as well. Simmons went 9-21 at the plate in his first six games and got some respectable ink for it. There really wasn't much else to write about or accomplish. O'Neal beat the patsy Brewers again, 9-1, on September 25, for win No. 102.

GAMES 159, 160, 161 & 162 @ NEW YORK—They finished with four in New York, and Sparky said he wanted to win two of them to surpass the '68 Tigers record of 103 wins. Morris, with Hernandez in relief, lost a 2-1 duel to Bob Shirley in game No. 159. Doug Bair won game No. 160, 4-2 on Whitaker's two-run, 12th-inning homer. But in that game, Lemon bumped umpire Al Clark and there was talk that he might be suspended for the playoffs. Turned out that the league didn't pull the trigger on Lemon. And Berenguer beat Ron Guidry as the Tigers exploded for 11 runs to win No. 104 on the next-to-last day of the season.

They lost a "who cares" finale, 9-2, on September 30, and that was it. The final mark was 104-58. Sparky said it was a record that would last for a long time.

Now it was on to some pressing business: taking out the Kansas City Royals.

Month by Month

SEPTEMBER 1984 (FINAL)

Cumulative statistics as of the end of the month

BATTING

	AB	R	H	RBI	2B	3B	HR	BB	SO	SB	E	GW RBI	AVG
Laga	11	1	6	1	0	0	0	1	2	0	0	0	.545
Simmons	30	4	13	3	2	0	0	2	5	7	0	0	.433
Trammell	555	85	174	69	34	5	14	60	63	19	10	5	.314
Whitaker	558	90	161	56	25	1	13	62	63	6	15	12	.289
Garbey	327	45	94	52	17	1	5	17	35	6	12	4	.287
Lemon	509	77	146	76	34	6	20	51	83	5	2	5	.287
Kuntz	140	32	40	22	12	0	2	25	28	2	1	4	.286
Jones	215	26	61	37	12	1	12	21	47	2	0	6	.284
Gibson	531	92	150	91	23	10	22	63	103	29	12	12	.282
Herndon	407	57	114	43	18	5	7	32	62	6	3	4	.280
Bergman	271	42	74	44	8	5	7	33	40	3	8	5	.273
Grubb	176	25	47	17	5	0	8	36	36	1	0	5	.267
Johnson	355	43	88	50	14	1	12	40	67	10	14	8	.248
Brookens	224	32	55	26	11	4	5	19	33	6	12	0	.246
Lowry	45	8	11	7	2	0	2	3	11	0	0	1	.244
Parrish	578	75	137	98	16	2	33	41	120	2	7	12	.237
Castillo	141	16	33	12	5	2	4	10	33	1	2	1	.234
Evans	401	60	93	63	11	1	16	77	70	2	2	7	.232
Baker	108	15	20	11	4	1	0	7	22	3	5	1	.185
Earl	35	3	4	1	0	1	0	0	9	1	2	0	.114
DH Hitters	616	98	162	87	24	1	27	75	123	7	0	9	.263
PH Hitters	186	26	58	42	11	2	6	26	31	0	0	5	.312
TOTALS	5644	829	1529	787	754	46	187	602	941	106	127	97	.271

KEY: AB-at bats, R-runs, H-hits, RBI-runs batted in, 2B-doubles, 3B-triples, HR-home runs, BB-walks, SO-strike outs, SB-stolen bases, E-errors, GW RBI-game winning runs batted in, AVG-batting average.

AL EAST STANDINGS

	W	L	PCT	GB
DETROIT	104	58	.642	---
Toronto	89	73	.549	15
New York	87	75	.537	17
Boston	86	76	.531	18
Baltimore	85	77	.525	19
Cleveland	75	87	.463	29
Milwaukee	67	94	.416	36½

PITCHING

	W	L	G	CG	S	IP	H	R	ER	BB	SO	ERA
Scherrer	1	0	18	0	0	19	14	4	4	8	16	1.89
Hernandez	9	3	80	0	32	140.1	96	30	30	36	112	1.92
Lopez	10	1	71	0	14	137.2	109	51	45	52	94	2.94
Petry	18	8	35	7	0	233.1	231	94	84	66	144	3.24
O'Neal	2	1	4	0	0	18.2	16	7	7	6	12	3.38
Berenguer	11	10	31	2	0	168.1	146	75	65	79	118	3.48
Morris	19	11	36	9	0	241.1	224	110	98	87	149	3.65
Rozema	7	6	79	0	0	101	110	49	42	18	48	3.74
Bair	5	3	47	0	4	93.2	82	42	39	36	57	3.75
Wilcox	17	8	33	0	0	193.2	183	99	86	66	119	4.00
Monge	1	0	19	0	0	36	40	21	17	12	19	4.25
Mason	1	1	4	0	1	21	20	9	9	10	14	3.86
TOTALS	104	58	--	19	51	1464	1358	643	568	489	914	3.49

Totals include players no longer with the team and pitchers' errors. KEY: W-wins, L-losses, G-games pitched in, CG-complete games, S-saves, IP-innings pitched, H-hits allowed, R-runs allowed, ER-earned runs allowed, BB-walks allowed, SO-strike outs, ERA-earned run averages.

DAY-BY-DAY

Date	Gm #	Vs.	W/L	Score	Winner	Loser	Rec	GA	Att.
9/1	136	@ Oak	L	5-7	Young	Berenguer	87-49	8½	25,021
9/2	137	@ Oak	W	6-3	Petry	Conroy	88-49	8½	20,393
9/3	138	Bal	L	4-7	† Stewart	Morris	88-50	8½	36,797
9/4	139	Bal	L	1-4	Boddicker	Rozema	88-51	7½	27,767
9/5	140	Bal	W	1-0	Berenguer	* Flanagan	89-51	8½	34,065
9/7	141	@ Tor	W	7-4 (10)	† Hernandez	† Musselman	90-51	9½	37,420
9/8	142	@ Tor	W	10-4	† Scherrer	Leal	91-51	10½	41,059
9/9	143	@ Tor	W	7-2	Wilcox	Clancy	92-51	11½	37,392
9/10	144	@ Bal	L	1-3	* Flanagan	Berenguer	92-52	11½	27,440
9/11	145	@ Bal	W	9-2	Petry	Swaggerty	93-52	11½	25,193
9/12	146	@ Bal	L	1-3	* Martinez	Mason	93-53	10½	24,561
9/14	147	Tor	L	2-7	Clancy	Morris	93-54	10	46,040
9/15	148	Tor	W	2-1	Wilcox	* Stieb	94-54	11	44,349
9/16	148	Tor	W	8-3	Berenguer	Clark	95-54	12	45,488
9/17	150	Mil	W	7-3	Mason	Waits	96-54	12	34,091
9/18	151	Mil	W	3-0	O'Neal	McClure	97-54	13	48,810
9/19	152	Mil	W	4-2	Morris	Candiotti	98-54	14	23,056
9/21	153	NY	L	3-5	Montefusco	Wilcox	98-55	14	42,238
9/22	154	NY	W	6-0	* Petry	Christiansen	99-55	13½	38,897
9/23	155	NY	W	4-1	Morris	Fontenot	100-55	14½	39,198
9/24	156	@ Mil	W	7-3	Berenguer	Hartzeil	101-55	14½	9,506
9/25	157	@ Mil	W	9-1	O'Neal	Gibson	102-55	15½	8,804
9/26	158	@ Mil	L	5-7	† Searge	† Lopez	102-56	14½	8,853
9/27	159	@ NY	L	1-2	Shirley	† Hernandez	102-57	14	16,732
9/28	160	@ NY	W	4-2 (12)	† Bair	† Cowley	103-57	15	19,422
9/29	161	@ NY	W	11-3	Berenguer	Guidry	104-57	15	35,685
9/30	162	@ NY	L	2-9	Rassmussen	O'Neal	104-58	15	30,602

*Complete game   † Decision in relief

Chapter 19

Gibby

Kirk Gibson will be the next Mickey Mantle.

— Sparky Anderson talking about Kirk Gibson, 1980

Straighten up, or I'll send you home to your mama, cryin'.

— Sparky Anderson to Kirk Gibson, 1983

Kirk Gibson was miserable. The 1983 season was his worst as a Tiger, and probably his worst year as a human being. People become their own worst enemies, and until they finally recognize it, they stew in their own bile, feel sorry for themselves and blame everybody except the jerk in the mirror.

In '83, with deliberate and forceful intent, Sparky Anderson backed Gibson into a corner. He threatened him with his livelihood if Gibson didn't redirect his entire approach and relationship with the game. Reluctantly at first, and then with the intensity and determination that was true to his nature, Gibson turned the finger that he had pointed at many others back toward himself.

The 1981 season had been a revelation for him. After wrist problems the previous June had aborted his 1980 season—which was effectively Gibson's rookie year—he had broken out in the second half of the strike season of '81 by hitting .375 for an overall .328 batting average. Just one year after Sparky had tabbed him as the next Mickey Mantle, Gibson was looking quite capable of approaching those lofty expectations.

But it didn't last, and 1982 proved to be a major disappointment. Injuries were largely and legitimately responsible for that: a sore left knee, a strained left calf, a stomach ailment and a badly sprained left wrist, which had also plagued him in '80. He was hitting a respectable .278 with eight homers and 35 RBIs when he went on the disabled list July 15. Doctors put Gibson's ailing wrist in a cast and his season was declared over.

In the spring of '83, Sparky zeroed in on Gibson. Sparky had read the gossip columns, had also been observing on his own and had listened to what others told him. The picture that came into view was one that Anderson would not tolerate, not from the "next Mickey Mantle," let alone any player who would be a part of his team.

In Sparky's view, a 25-year-old raw talent like Kirk Gibson still needed to display a burning passion to improve his professional approach and demeanor or simply become another "my way or the highway" casualty of Sparky's tight code of ethics and behavior.

Sparky wouldn't stand for arrogance and was thoroughly disgusted by the stories he'd heard about Gibson's carousing as well as his disrespect for other people. Sparky realized that Gibson no longer seemed appreciative of the level of dedication required for the continued improvement necessary to play a very demanding sport.

Sparky can smile about it years later because his logic and his approach worked. "I said, here's a kid that in high school was everything. He went to college and he didn't play baseball his first two years, and he was a great football player, an All-American."

His voice rises, as if mimicking the passion of Gibson. "Then he plays baseball one year in college and he's an All-American in that sport, too. And I'm thinking and watching and I'm saying to myself, 'This young man has everything there is.' But if he isn't being the professional he should be, what else could I do?"

After injury-plagued seasons in '82 and '83, Kirk Gibson had a breakout year in '84.

Alan Trammell was a year younger than Kirk but had been a baseball player all his life and was much further ahead in his development. By 1980, at the age of 22, Trammell had already hit .300 in only his third year in the majors.

"Gibby was a football player, let's be honest," Trammell says to soften what is to follow. "He was very raw. No doubt. I compare him to Bo Jackson, who came along a few years later. Very raw. But it takes time. He didn't play much baseball from Little League to college, and it hurt him. He had catching up to do. He was headstrong, he didn't listen and he wasn't a good outfielder. He was erratic and didn't hit the cutoff man.

"Sparky couldn't let him continue on that way. He sat him down in '83 and embarrassed him. He said to Kirk, 'I'm gonna teach you, and you're either gonna get tough and get it or I'll send you home to your mom.' He put him in against tough pitchers and didn't play him against the softies and he hit .227. Sparky made him grow up."

After coming off the injury-shortened '82 season, Sparky's suspicions were affirmed in the spring of '83. After observing Gibson in Lakeland, Sparky ambushed him on the eve of the opener.

"We opened the year in Minnesota," Gibson clearly recalls. "We flew up there, had our workout, and he (Sparky) called me into his office and said, 'You're not starting. I'm gonna platoon you with John Wockenfuss as designated hitter.'

"The opening-day pitcher for the Twins was a lefty, Brad Havens. He (Sparky) said, 'You'll hit against righties only.' I went ballistic. It crushed me. He kicked me in the ass and he made it really tough on me. He didn't give me any credit, he didn't cut me any slack, and I spent most of the year fightin' him. And because I was fightin' him, how was I supposed to fight the other team?"

Since the story had a happy ending, Sparky still enjoys telling it: "He (Gibson) has great character about him. He'll stand up to me. I have the utmost respect for a player if he'll set down in my room and look me dead in the eye and just nail me to the cross.

"He did it that day. He got so angry he closed the door. As I told him what his role would be, he even backed me into a corner and he was never afraid to do that. So, he's storming long enough and I said to him, 'Are you done yet, are you done?' And he said, 'Yeah,' and I said, 'Would you please rise, open the door and get your ass outta here?'"

The "next Mickey Mantle" had become a misguided mess. As the season was about to open, Gibson seethed over his mistreatment, still lacking the wherewithal to recognize that Sparky's method was to remind him that his fate was still in his own hands, if he chose to swallow hard, quit blaming others and just pursue it.

Gibson readily admits today what eluded him then: "I was signed as a number one draft pick in my hometown and pretty much was overwhelmed with my situation. I lost my focus. I wasn't a good player. I had poor work habits. I was a bad person too, mistreating others, and it showed. I was pampered coming up, and then it came time for me to produce and I didn't produce.

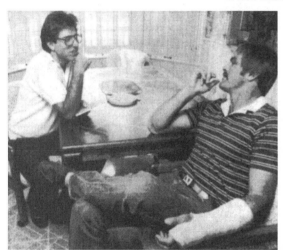

"I was hardheaded. I had a good second half in '81 but I had hurt my wrist in '80, hurt it again in '82, and by '83, Sparky was just tired of waiting for me, that's all. He brought me to my knees in '83. He'd platoon me at DH and put me in against the toughest guys. I hit .227 and it took a big September (.319) just to bring me there."

It was painfully obvious to Sparky that Gibson was arrogant, confused and ill-equipped to handle the responsibilities that accompanied his status as a ballplayer and a public figure. His baseball soul mate and future brother-in-law, Dave Rozema, was there alongside him, and the two acted like a pair of idiots.

Visiting Kirk at home in '82 while he recovers from wrist problems.

But Kirk was in a league of his own as a hometown sports hero. When he screwed up, it was news. When he stiffed a kid looking for an autograph, it had ramifications. He had some gaping holes in his ability to project a positive public persona, and he wasn't aware enough to know how to cover it up. He seemed to think that if he signed a few autographs, it entitled him to be rude at other times; if he did an interview once, he could tell the reporter to get out of his face the next time. So instead of constructing himself into an icon who represented his team and the city of his birth, he remained arrogant and underproductive.

Sparky was very perceptive when it came to understanding athletes, but it didn't take Freud to see that Kirk Gibson was the master of his own personal and professional morass. In his blatant denial of how he treated people and what he needed to do to succeed as a professional, he became surly and withdrawn. For years, he had routinely abused people who merely wanted just a moment of attention or needed to talk to him as part of their job.

Our Tigers television director, Chuck Wasiluk, remembers, "When I asked him (Gibson) to appear on the pre-game show, I'd never know if he'd say, 'OK,' or tell me to 'get lost.'"

Joe Lapointe, then a writer for the *Detroit Free Press*, offers his analysis of what it was like to deal with the Tigers' principal characters.

"Anderson was glib and more than willing to talk," recalls Lapointe. "Some of the players were quite nice and mature towards the media—Dan Petry, Lance Parrish, Chet Lemon, Trammell, Rozema and a few others. And some of the guys were crude and vicious and immature.

"Gibson was the worst, although he had plenty of media groupies to excuse and explain away his hostile and menacing treatment of male and female reporters. He was, quite simply, an unpleasant bully... smart, too. Smart and cunning."

Gibson's abandonment of the social graces was embarrassing, uncalled for and, for someone bright enough to know better, inexcusable. Someone with the world at his feet, like Kirk Gibson, needed to get slapped around, grow up and decide to just get the hell out of his own way.

The stench of 1983 wouldn't go away either. In Gibson's mind, it was not supposed to have happened to someone like him. He was not supposed to be a utility man who barely hit his weight, and at age 26 he was going backward as a player. Thankfully, by the end of '83— and at the brink of exasperation—he had begun to grasp that his downward spiral toward personal and baseball oblivion had come by his own hand.

The Tigers were a good team in '83, finishing 92-70 in second place behind Baltimore. The outfield of Larry Herndon in left, Lemon in center and Glenn Wilson in right had performed well. Wilson had 500 at bats and hit .268 with some power, and was a much better fielder than Gibson. He also had a far more powerful, accurate arm and, not lost to those who controlled his fate, a far better attitude.

Wilson was thrilled to be in the major leagues and was accommodating to everyone he encountered. Additionally in his favor, he was a year younger than Gibson and had also been a number one pick in 1980, two years after Kirk was taken in the first round. When '83 ended, Kirk couldn't deny the significant reality that Wilson was emerging with star potential and that the Tigers were doing just fine without Kirk Gibson.

"He (Sparky) broke me by the end of '83," Kirk recalls. "It took all year, but he hadn't known how long it would take. Obviously, I didn't like what was going on either. Sometimes in life, you think you're going north, but you look at your compass and discover that you're going straight south.

"That was me in every aspect in '83. Sparky was saying, 'Lookit, you either straighten up or you're out of the game. You can bounce around or I'll send you home to your mama cryin'. I was already cryin' inside and knew that I wasn't the person my wonderful mama had raised me to be."

By season's end, Kirk had gotten the message that Sparky had always tried to impress upon all his players: The world goes on without you. The game, the team, is much bigger than you. As Sparky loved to say, "Babe Ruth is in his grave, and the game goes on."

On the advice of his Seattle-based agent, Doug Baldwin, Kirk visited the Pacific Institute in Seattle. The Pacific Institute partially describes its philosophy: "That individuals have a virtually unlimited capacity for growth, change and creativity, and can readily adapt to the tremendous changes taking place in the world."

To the outside world, Gibson was supposed to be able to handle everything. He was the blond-haired, All-American boy, with talent spilling out of his pores. But reality was that baseball was a difficult game, and he was still relatively new to it. He wasn't a talented fielder or thrower and had failed as a center fielder. The only reason he'd been put in center in 1981 was because Sparky didn't think he was good enough to handle right field.

"The Pacific Institute changed my attitude around," Gibson says thoughtfully. "I re-motivated myself and really worked myself into good shape. When I came to spring training in '84, Roger Craig put me under his wing. He was the pitching coach, but Roger cared and felt responsible about every player. Every day, as soon as batting practice started, we'd go out behind center field and he'd hit me fungoes. And you know how positive Roger was; he'd hit me fungoes and he'd build me up. He'd talk to me all the time and helped me with the process of forgetting the player I was in '83 and becoming a guy who believed in himself again and was focused on the game.

"In the spring of '84, Roger really went to bat for me to Sparky. He told him, 'You better leave that guy out there; you gotta leave him out there. You gotta let him play whether it's (against) a lefty or a righty.' And that was the first year Sparky gave me the chance to do so. There'd be some tough lefties and they'd sit me down, but for the most part they played me every day. But Roger worked with me, because he felt he could make a difference, and he did."

Gibson, despite his bluster, anger and associated rough edges, is a very bright man. Once he "got it," he got it. He had been jolted into seeing his blind spots. And when the Pacific Institute made him understand that people can write their own scripts once they learn how to do it, the clouds parted and he again became driven in positive ways.

It was a stunning turnaround in spring training '84. Gibson quit drinking and other activities that could affect his health or be used as an excuse for failure. His instructors had taught him to visualize his success and turn those vivid images into reality. He had fully bought in to a self-help package that made sense to him and equipped him for the challenges he faced.

A month into spring training, through Craig's urging and the changes in him that Sparky could see, the Tigers traded the promising Wilson and gambled on the "new" Kirk Gibson. He started 1984 batting fifth and floated from there to seventh.

But, by the beginning of May, Sparky announced, "Kirk Gibson will bat third against righties for the rest of his career." His team was 20-4, writers were flocking for quotes and Kirk was producing admirably in the slot behind Whitaker and Trammell, and in front of Parrish. But compared to his ill-fated "Mantle" quote from years back, Sparky was making no more bold pronouncements about Gibson. At least not yet.

Like most straight shooters on the team, Parrish had had his moments of skepticism about Gibson. It took the '84 season for Lance to believe that Kirk was capable of changing.

"I used to think, this guy is so big and strong, but he played the game so hard that he was always hurt," Lance says. "I'm not trying to knock him, but here you have a big, tough strong guy and every time you turn around something happened. But I never questioned his ability. I thought he had unbelievable ability. I just hoped that sooner or later he would get a grip on what it took to develop into what we had all expected he would become.

"He sure picked the right year for it to all come together. I never really thought about who would play right to start the season. Would it be Glenn or would it be Kirk? I just assumed they'd both be on the team. I was real disappointed when Glenn got traded. I liked Glenn; he was probably my best friend on the team. We shared a lot of interests and I thought he was an up-and-coming star. And they just shipped him out. Boom. Just like that. But it worked out, so what do I know?"

Gibson learned to accept his shortcomings and channel them productively. In football, there was always somebody to hit on the next play as a release of frustration. And as a record-setting Michigan State receiver, he experienced none of the anguish and alienation that goes with a 3-30 batting slump. In baseball, not only can't you hit somebody after you strike out, but you also have to make the lonely trek back to the dugout, listen to the catcalls and realize that it may be an hour or a day before you have a chance to atone.

"I was a football player and was satisfied to remain a football player," Kirk explains. "My dad used to say, 'Why don't you give baseball a try?' and I'd say 'no.' After my junior year at State, it looked like I was going to be a pretty high draft choice in the NFL, and that's when Darryl Rogers (MSU football coach) told me to play baseball. He didn't want me at spring practice, and he wanted me to have better leverage with the NFL.

"So I played baseball and struggled miserably. The failure aspect of the game was brutal. Striking out and having nowhere to release your frustration. In fact, I was going to quit right in the beginning of the season. But Danny Litwhiler (MSU baseball coach) encouraged me to stay. I mean it. I was gonna quit. Period. I think the very next day I hit a coupla homers and went on to have a ridiculously good season.

"At the end of the school year, the scouts were everywhere," Gibson continues. "Just everywhere. And then I had some talks with the Tigers. They had the eleventh or twelfth pick and all these other teams were calling me, too. Bob Sullivan set it up, a scout from Grand Rapids. I was invited to Tiger Stadium, and Dick Tracewski threw me batting practice and I just crushed the ball. You can ask Bruce Fields. He was there, too, because they were also looking at him. I remember [that] Lance, who was my age but in his second year in the majors, told Trixie to throw me a curve.

"I hadn't met Lance, but I just stared him down with a 'Shut up, asshole,' kinda look. But that's the day it hit me, at Tiger Stadium. I'd been there so many times as a kid, but I'd never been in the locker room and it was like, 'Holy shit.' And then I started cranking 'em in the upper deck and said to myself, 'This is cool.' It was the first time. That was the day that I became real excited about playing baseball."

With the 1978 June draft looming in a few weeks, Fields had also been invited down from Lansing for a look. Fields played at Lansing Everett, Magic Johnson's high school.

"It was a pre-draft, closed tryout at Tiger Stadium on a Saturday morning before a Saturday afternoon game," remembers Fields, Tigers' batting coach in 2003. "I was 17 and my mom, brother and high school coach came with me. I got there before Gibby, and Tracewski threw batting practice to me. I ran a few 60s [60-yard dashes], threw from center and took about 20 minutes of BP. The Tiger coaches were there; Bill Lajoie was off to the side and so were Houk [Tigers manager Ralph] and Les Moss, who was a minor-league manager.

"I was done and they said, 'Stick around, we have somebody else coming out,' and in walks Gibby. They didn't ask him to run or throw—all he did was take BP. I'd seen him play football at Michigan State, but I didn't know much about him playing baseball.

"They told me to shag for him in right. He's hitting the ball hard. I'm standing there under the overhang and he hits a few balls into the upper deck. They had the old wooden seats and he hit a few so hard that they broke the seats. The wood chips are all but falling on my head and I'm thinking, 'Oh my God, this guy can rake.' He hit for 15-20 minutes. I had hit one ball out and I was happy about that."

It didn't turn out that badly for Fields. "They signed both of us. He was first round and I was seventh. I went to Bristol (Virginia) and he went to Lakeland. In '84 I was in Double A at Birmingham. I was still trying to find my way in the minors and two years later, I finally got to Detroit."

But it was just a cameo for Fields. A few years later he got a brief look in Seattle with the Mariners. Fields played 14 years of pro ball and got a grand total of 113 major-league at bats, hitting .274.

But Kirk was fast and powerful, and his exploits at MSU made him a sizzling-hot commodity. "The Yankees were real interested also," says Gibson. "I hit .391 at State; I was fast, stole bases, had power, the kind of things they look for. Their [Yankees] scout, Birdie Tebbetts, flew out and took me out to dinner with my mom and dad and said, 'George Steinbrenner told me I can't go home unless you agree to sign with the Yankees if we draft you.'

"Believe it or not, Jerry Krause, who was the Bulls GM during the [Michael] Jordan years, was the Mariners GM. He came and met me. Danny Kaye was part owner. But I told all the teams drafting in front of the Tigers that I was coming back to play football my senior year at State no matter what, so they shouldn't draft me. It was a little tricky. The Tigers were ready to give me the right to play football as a senior if I signed. I'd play 50 or so games in Lakeland that summer and then go back and play football."

Dave Bergman had played his entire career in the National League and met Kirk in Lakeland in March '84.

"My first impression was that this guy can flat run," Bergman says. "I've never heard anybody run like he did. People say, 'Whaddya mean, never heard.' Well, when he ran, you could hear his feet pounding the ground. He was so heavy with his feet, so powerful."

Kirk had suffered a lot of foot problems early in his career because of the way he ran. And his speed was notorious. Gil Brandt, who spent 29 years with the Dallas Cowboys as their personnel director, and scouted and timed thousands of football players, said that Gibson's 4.2 in the 40-yard dash was the fastest he had ever seen. Bergman noticed not just the speed, but the intensity.

"Blond hair blowing in wind, and every time he hit the ball his helmet would get knocked off and he'd run like a madman," Bergman recalls. "I didn't know what the heck was going on. I'd also heard about him and Rozy and their off-field antics and energetic personalities, but in baseball, there's always stuff like that. I enjoyed both of them early on. I was on the quiet side, but I liked the action that seemed to follow them."

Despite his struggles leading up to '84, and how disappointed Sparky was in the person Gibson had become, Sparky, like others, remained intrigued by the way Gibson embraced key situations.

"He was the kind of player who wanted to be up in the bottom of the ninth with two outs," says Milt Wilcox. "His attitude was, 'I wanna be at bat. I want the chance to win this game.' You don't get a lot of guys who want to do that, but Kirk always wanted to be there. He made a lotta outs but he's also gonna hit those big ones for you. And Gibby really didn't have to worry about much in playing right field. He didn't have a strong enough arm to play center, but Lemon ran everything down and made Kirk a better player and took some pressure off him, too."

Although the World Series home run off Goose Gossage was the most memorable, Gibson produced a long list of dramatic, final-inning hits in '84. He homered in the ninth off Steve McCatty to beat the A's, 2-1, on May 30. On June 29, he hit a two-run homer in the ninth off Twins lefty Pete Filson to win, 7-5, before 46,000 at Tiger Stadium. On July 5, in Texas, with the Tigers mired in a four-game losing streak and staggering toward the All-Star break, he hit a two-out, three-run, ninth-inning shot off Charlie Hough to win, 7-4. In a key September series with Toronto, with the Tigers trailing 4-0 in the eighth, he hit a three-run shot off Doyle Alexander, which enabled Dave Bergman to later win it with a homer in the 10th.

The title of Gibson's autobiography, *Bottom of the 9th,* was chosen to reflect the relative strengths and weaknesses that made his career unique. When you add it all up, he was an average player. He was a below-average fielder with a weak arm and he didn't hit for average—just .268 for his career.

But Gibson had extraordinary speed, and after his mental makeover at the Pacific Institute, developed the mental toughness to visualize and then realize success in pressure situations. That's one of the main reasons that Sparky didn't deep-six him when the temptation existed to do so.

"I try to explain him to people," Sparky says. "He knew how to make things happen. And I'd say to people, 'Wait a minute, do you want somebody that doesn't care?' I'll tell you this, around that clubhouse I watch and judge, and when you win and Kirk Gibson goes 0-for-four, he's as happy as a lark with people. He'd be joshing with Tram and Parrish and everybody. He'd go three-for-four and you'd lose, there'd be no joshing. That's the difference of what people think a good person is."

As for hitting clutch home runs, like the ones off of Gossage in '84, and off Dennis Eckersley in '88 for the Dodgers, Gibson forgoes standard modesty to say what he is most proud of in regard to his mental makeup and self-belief.

"I had a knack for it," he says. "When things got tense like that, I just wanted to be up there. Lefty or righty. They bring a lefty in, it's a dead-face challenge. They're saying, 'We're bringing a lefty in because we don't think you can hit this guy.' For whatever reasons, I performed pretty well in those situations. I believed in my ability to deliver, and really, without Roger Craig in the spring of '84, I probably wouldn't have gotten the opportunity."

Back in the good graces of his manager, visualizing and producing success as he had been taught that winter, and juiced by the team's amazing start in '84, Gibson was experiencing another rapid career rise. But he still wasn't playing against all the tough lefties.

Bergman recalls a story that best describes the rebuilt respect and respective personalities of Gibson and his manager: "I could tell that Sparky and he had a relationship that was very special," Bergman begins. "Sparky went into the platoon mode a month or so into the '84 season and there were some left-handers that Kirk wouldn't play against. So when you didn't play, you were expected to run with the pitchers. Sparky was out there in the outfield with everybody, and he was pretending that he was a defensive back. You'd throw the ball to Roger Craig and then you'd kinda go out for a pass. That's how you'd get your running in.

"And here's Sparky talking all kinds of garbage to Gibby about 'I'm gonna knock you on your ass,' and Gibby kept on telling him, 'Listen, you better get outta my way because I'll run you over. If I zig and you zag, I'm knocking you on your ass.' And I'll be a son of a gun, Gibby zigged, Sparky zagged and Kirk gave him a forearm shiver and knocked him down and rolled him over a few times.

"We're watching with our jaws on the ground. A few seconds go by and Sparky staggers up. His eyes are watering because he got knocked for a loop. You could tell that Gibby was real concerned that he had hurt him. Anyway, Sparky goes over to Gibby and said, 'I've been stung by a bee harder than that.'"

Gibson hit .282 with 27 homers and 91 RBIs in '84. At that point, the home runs and RBIs were career highs by a wide margin. He also completed his journey from Sparky's doghouse—and the personal and professional hell he'd created for himself—to World Series Champion and hometown hero, all culminating when he hit the Game

Five home run off Gossage that clinched the title.

But statistics were never the measure of Gibson's value. He was a clutch hitter extraordinaire and because of that, on the club's centennial celebration, fans voted him onto the all-time Tigers team.

Gibson sustained his 1984 level for the next three years, but after the '87 season, he left as a free agent to play for the Dodgers. Although the owners were in collusion, the Tigers still took the cheap route, offering him $2.3 million for two years, while the Dodgers offered him $4.5 million for three years. He was left with no choice. The Tigers had forced him to leave, as they had Parrish the year before. Tigers owner Tom Monaghan, in one of the most idiotic, ill-informed and naive statements in Tigers history, called Gibson "a disgrace to the Tigers uniform" because of his unshaven appearance.

Gibson went on to shove it up Monaghan's and Jim Campbell's respective rear ends by earning the National League MVP Award in '88 and then, hobbling from a variety of leg injuries, hit the pinch home run off Eckersley that was later voted as one of the top 10 moments in baseball history.

Some years later, Monaghan left Gibson a message that he would like to have lunch and set the record straight. Kirk thought it over, and never returned the call.

Chapter 20

Sweet Lou and Tram

I don't think I ever looked at Lou and Tram as being near great-ness. I don't think you do that until it's all said and done and you see some of the things they accomplished. I used to say to people that maybe the reason I stayed around as long as I did at third was because we had Lou and Tram. That allowed me to [hit] less and still be an important part of the team.

— Tom Brookens on Lou Whitaker and Alan Trammell

They were two kids of opposite color from opposite coasts with opposing upbringings. Their pairing was a function of scouting wizardry, a general manager with a vision and the meshing of their individual brilliance. As the record shows, they outlasted all of their coaches and teammates. For two decades, they were a constant and a rarity in sports: Two players who played two decades, side by side, for the same team and, in the end, achieved eerily similar statistics and equally outstanding legacies.

Lou Whitaker was drafted by the Tigers in 1975 just after he turned 18. He was immediately dispatched to Bristol, Virginia, in the Appalachian Rookie League, and played 42 games at third base.

Alan Trammell, nine months younger than Lou, was drafted in 1976. Like Lou, he was also sent to Bristol and made the All-Star team, hitting .271. Lou wasn't there to play with him, however, having been moved up the chain to Class A Lakeland in the Florida State League in his second year with the organization. But Tram's progress was so rapid in the rookie league that the Tigers bumped him two steps up the ladder to Double A Montgomery, Alabama, to finish the '76 season.

Lou hit .297 at third base in Lakeland in '76 and was named league MVP. His team-mates were taken by his grace and agility that year and nicknamed him "Sweet Lou." Lou liked it, and it stuck with him for the rest of his career.

Lou was then kicked up the ladder to Double A Montgomery and joined Tram there for the '77 season. As Bill Lajoie recalls, that's when Jim Campbell's vision took hold. "Campbell told farm director Hoot Evers, 'I want you to move Lou to second because Trammell is the shortstop of the future and I want him to have a partner.'"

"But Hoot liked Lou at third and didn't want to move him, and Jim said, 'Hoot, if you don't move him to second base, you can go home to Texas and I'll give you another job.' No shit. And then Lou was moved." Lajoie smiles and says, "And that's one of the few times Jim ever said 'You do this or that, or else.' He let the guys under him do their jobs, and moving Lou [to second] after Lakeland was one of the very few times that Jim ever demanded something."

At age 19, Trammell was named the 1977 Southern League MVP, hitting .291 with a remarkable 19 triples. Lou was performing at an equal level with Tram, hitting .280 with 38 steals. Things were moving quickly. The dynamic infield pair led Montgomery to the Southern League pennant, and both bypassed Triple A Evansville altogether when they were summoned north to Detroit in the September call-ups.

On September 9, 1977, in the second game of a doubleheader in Boston, Whitaker and Trammell made their major-league debuts. In an 8-6 loss to the Red Sox that night, both singled in their first at bat, and Whitaker rapped out three hits on the night. Lou played 11 games in September, making no errors; Tram played 19 games and made only two errors.

The future had arrived, as manager Ralph Houk had touted to the Detroit media all summer, and as the youngsters settled in, the days of infielders Chuck Scrivener, Tom Veryzer, Mark Wagner, Steve Dillard and Tito Fuentes were nearing the end. Only Dillard and Wagner survived as Tigers backups in '78.

Under Houk, the youth movement that he'd promised Tigers fans began to blossom in '78. After four straight sub-.500 seasons, the Tigers went 86-76. Lou and Tram each played in 139 games. Tram hit .268, while Lou hit .285 and was named AL Rookie of the Year. Keyed by the young pair, the Tigers led the league with 177 double plays.

Houk's job was to usher in the youth that Lajoie had been gathering under the Campbell edict of 1973. Jason Thompson, who'd been drafted the same year as Lou, hit 26 homers in '78. Steve Kemp, drafted in '76, hit 15 homers, played with passion and displayed star potential. Lance Parrish, who had also been called up at the end of '77, hit 14 homers in just 85 games. Jack Morris, Dave Rozema, Steve Baker, Mark Fidrych, Dave Tobik and Pat Underwood—all Lajoie draftees—were making progress and getting Tigers fans to begin believing again.

"Lou and I only played for Ralph a year and a month," Trammell says of his first major-league manager. "The end of '77 and all of '78. He let us just go and play. Ralph was perfect for us at that point of our careers. He was behind us, he encouraged us and he wasn't real hard on us. Sparky came on in June '79, and he was hard on us as far as enforcing things. But the first year, Ralph was more laid back and allowed us to make some mistakes. I didn't feel overwhelmed with him, like everything I did had to be perfect. He let us grow at a good pace."

The Tigers' best player at the time was center fielder Ron LeFlore, who could steal 100 bases and hit for average. Incredible as it seems 25 years later, aside from the rookie Whitaker, LeFlore was also the only black player on the club. Even though it was a different day and age, the Tigers had long aroused suspicions of racist tendencies because so few blacks had played for the organization. Campbell had rescued LeFlore from Jackson (Michigan) State Prison after then-Tigers Manager Billy Martin had been tipped off by a guard who coached the prison baseball team. LeFlore was the Tigers' best player, but was otherwise conniving and selfish, and not the kind of baseball citizen they wanted. But the Tigers needed him until they could come up with something better.

Tram and Lou in their prime.

In the spring of '78, since Whitaker and LeFlore were the only black players on the team, it wasn't unreasonable to assume that they might gravitate to each other. To LeFlore, Whitaker wasn't so much black or white, but just more fresh, young meat to shock and influence for his own rebellious pleasure.

LeFlore was personable, incredibly street-smart and utterly fearless, and many of the younger players found him intriguing. What was even more compelling about him was that he was completely unintimidated by authority figures. To management, he had become a necessary evil that, at some point, would have to be jettisoned.

At the Tigers' annual spring barbecue in Lakeland in '78, before Lou's first full season, LeFlore was entertaining a group of five or six of us, including the rookie, Whitaker. I could see that Jim Campbell was observing our group from nearby. I imagined his mind racing: 'Do I nip this in the bud now or wait for another time?' Obviously, the last guy Campbell wanted influencing an innocent like Whitaker was a verified shady character like LeFlore.

Campbell slid over to the edge of the group and listened to find out what the devious LeFlore was cooking up. Of course, with Campbell now lured into his realm, LeFlore started to pick up his game, trying to cajole Lou to do some things with him and tempting Campbell to jump in. Predictably, after LeFlore offered an off-color remark to tweak Campbell's well-established sense of propriety, the

Tigers boss could resist no longer.

Campbell leaned in and said in a joking manner, but with what I observed as decidedly serious undertones, "Lou, that's why I don't want you hanging around this guy." LeFlore had his opening, glanced at all of us and shot back, "Hey, why don't you just get lost, baldy."

While we all stood in shock, LeFlore giggled gleefully as Campbell recoiled and turned red. As a few seconds uncomfortably ticked away, I could sense Campbell quickly deciding whether to go on the attack or to gracefully exit. After a pause, he smiled and said, "Hey,

Jim Campbell switched Lou from third to second base and he became the best in all of baseball.

I'll see you fellas later." To LeFlore, disrespecting and humiliating an authority figure in front a stunned crowd was as good as it got. But it was really just another sad commentary on how LeFlore's dysfunctional youth greatly undermined him and cut short his career.

As it turned out, Lou's strong survival skills and sense of right and wrong steered him away from LeFlore. Sparky arrived in '79 and, as Kirk Gibson likes to recall, one of Sparky's sayings was "You must always pick the weeds out of the garden." LeFlore was one of the first to go, plucked from Sparky's garden and thrown out after the '79 season.

The '79 through '82 seasons were big growth years for Lou, Tram and the young cast of Tigers. The team finished fifth twice and fourth twice, but over .500 in each of those years in the very tough American League East Division. And all the while, Sparky was weeding. He wanted good players who were good people who would take his direction. He also weeded out young players, like Kemp and Thompson, to the surprise and dismay of many, including those he kept.

Before the '78 season, Trammell married his high school sweetheart, Barbara Leverett. Until the Tigers drafted him, he had never been out of Southern California, and being shipped to Bristol fresh out of high school two years earlier had provided a powerful jolt of homesickness. Barbara was game to leave the comforts of home, but marriage was a must, and they wed on Alan's 20th birthday, February 21, 1978.

Lou met Crystal McCreary in Detroit during his rookie season of '78 and got married the next year. Lou and Tram were continuing to grow as teammates and fellow major-leaguers, while building strong family foundations in their personal lives.

I don't think that the fans or the media really got to know either player, but they certainly got more coherent answers out of Alan than they did from Lou. Tram was friendly, cooperative and gave the media the basic stuff it needed, but he either refused, or simply wasn't able, to provide much depth or personal insight.

We knew that there was more to Tram because of all the things his teammates would tell us, but he established that he would only go so far with us, and that was fine. In Trammell's 20 years in the Tigers uniform, I don't recall either a single inflammatory nor a deeply insightful comment from him. But he was always receptive and likable.

During his early years in Detroit, Lou tried to cooperate with the press but had trouble formulating concise answers. He would veer so far off the subject that it was virtually impossible to conduct a timed broadcast interview with him. And when he joined Chet Lemon in becoming a Jehovah's Witness in the early '80s, Lou retreated even more deeply under Lemon's wing and became that much more remote from the outside world.

Lance Parrish's career followed a similar track with Alan and Lou, and he recalls, "I had a good relationship with Lou. He, Tram and I played together in instructional ball, and that's where I really got to know him. Lou was probably a little more outgoing early in his career but as he progressed into the majors, he became a very private person. He probably made all of you feel he was different or had something against you, but he just didn't feel comfortable talking about anything. If you put a microphone in front of him he got nervous, and he definitely wasn't comfortable in front of a TV camera. That was his personality. I appreciated that. Everybody misread him.

"Later in his career, he got a little deep into his religion. When he and Chet both became Jehovah's Witnesses, we had to stop going onto the field when they played the national anthem, and that bothered some of us because it was against their [Lou's and Chet's] religion to honor the American flag." [This was not disrespect for the flag or country. Jehovah's Witnesses believe that saluting the flag violates the Biblical command against worshipping graven images.] "Whenever they played the anthem, they [Lou and Chet] tried to find a hole to jump in. I disagreed with that, but that's what they believed.

"When we played in the All-Star game in '84 in San Francisco, there was no dugout deep enough or clubhouse close enough for them to go to hide in when the anthem came on. All they had was a little closet for a bathroom in the dugout and they both ran in there and closed the door. I thought, 'You've got to be kidding!'"

"Lou was uncomfortable," says Trammell. "A lotta times he ducked the media because he was shy. But Lou learned from Sparky that when he had a bad game he wouldn't hide. It was when he had a good game that he might hide to avoid talking about himself. Sparky taught us the same things: How to be professional, how to go about your business, how to play the game, and even though Lou didn't express those things, he understood it all. We were similar because we both paid attention to Sparky."

Trammell had one of his best seasons in '84 despite battling elbow and shoulder problems all year.

"I have an old saying," Sparky muses with the wisdom of 50 years in baseball. 'It's not the players' job to know me, it's my job to know my players. Can't we be different and all be shooting at the same star?'"

As for Lou, Sparky recalls with a twinkle in his eye, "He always called me Daddy. He was raised by his grandma. Before games, I used to love to walk in the outfield and shag and do that stuff because I could talk to guys. And when Lou was really playing good, I never had conversations with him. I'd just walk by and hit him and I'd say, 'Little man, ooh are you playing good.' And I'd just keep on walking and I'd hear him say, 'Thank you, skipper.'

"That's all Lou needed. You didn't have to give Lou adulation and all that. He didn't want that because, in his way, if you started giving him all that, he'd think you were bribing him. He didn't want that. And that's why in managing, it's your job to know them, not the other way around."

Although Lou would relax and relate well with his teammates, Trammell was more gregarious than most of the Tigers. And no matter how many players came and went, he remained the Tigers' most serious sports fan. Tram would recite statistics and endlessly offer opinions on all sports. When he was particularly animated and relentless, Gibson would yell at the top of his lungs, "Tram—shut up!!" Tram scoured all the sports pages and wasn't ashamed to admit that, one-dimensional or not, he was a sports guy, and that's all he ever wanted or needed to be.

Sparky also speaks of Trammell with the same degree of affection. "He'd agitate everybody. I'd be in the shower and see him agitating Parrish, and I'm thinking, 'My God, he's going to get killed.' He'd agitate Gibby, agitate Jack. He had a way of doing that and yet they loved him.

"I told him, 'You love to stir the pot.' 'Oh yea,' he'd say, 'I like that.' That's why they did what they did as players. I'll be long gone, but they'll look back and realize how fortunate they were. That was a great group of people. They were very talented, but they were a great group of people that made good things happen."

While Tram loved "stirring the pot" and was always sticking his nose in the middle of clubhouse activities, Lou retreated with Lemon. Ironically, considering Campbell's concern over how LeFlore might influence Whitaker, Lemon came from Chicago in '81 to essentially replace LeFlore. Lemon was a few years older than Lou and much more worldly. While Lou was raised in rural Martinsville, Virginia, Lemon was a big-city kid and went to Fremont High in Los Angeles, which had produced a remarkable number of future major-leaguers, including Bobby Tolan, George Hendrick, Bob Watson and "Disco" Dan Ford.

Lou may have struggled to express himself concisely, but Chet was a quick and capable communicator. When it came to their careers, Chet and Lou were equally serious, but Chet was more sophisticated in dealing with people. The two soon became a powerfully positive influence on each other.

Lemon, who nearly died a few years ago from a rare blood disorder but has fought back to health and has a very important job overseeing nearly 25,000 kids in Florida youth sports programs, explains their friendship.

"Lou was like my little brother," Chet says. "We talked about the more serious things outside the game and could relate to each other because we had the same religious beliefs. I was a Witness before I came to Detroit and had the privilege of introducing 'the truth' to Lou. We served as a protection for each other. It's a tough thing being a major-league athlete. A lotta people don't understand that when you reach that level it's a whole different game and it's so easy to get distracted. We needed to stay focused on what we were doing all the time, and we were a source of encouragement for each other.

"Lou went out there every day and worked at his craft," Lemon continues. "Just like Herndon, he was great with his teammates, but he never had a lot to say. He never said anything bad about anybody, he just played his game every day. That's what you look for, guys who are willing to gird up their loins—having a great day or having a bad day, whatever it is—go between the lines and give it your best. And that's what it was with us. We'd go out on the road and eat and spend time doing things and talking about things."

A baseball clubhouse is a complex melting pot of 25 strong-minded individuals from different backgrounds and different parts of the world. Sparky's realization of that enabled him to maintain harmony under the umbrella of certain basic behaviors and understandings. Chet and Lou forged a tight union to the exclusion of others, but the beauty of it was that it still merged seamlessly with the goals of the group.

"Lou is a serious individual," says Lemon. "He wasn't much of a kidder. I wasn't much of one either or a practical joker or anything like that. Our joy came from doing our craft and doing it well and that's the inner joy and peace you had knowing you were doing your job. If you look at the players we had, that's how most of 'em were. But you had to have guys like Dave Rozema, who kept it loose and kept the clubhouse alive. Like Darrell Evans, who was a leader on our ball club. Jack Morris, Gibby, Tram, those guys were on each other all the time, endlessly."

Lou and Tram played an American League record 1,915 games as teammates and produced more double plays than any pair in history. Between them, they made eleven All-Star teams (Tram six, Lou five) and won eight Gold Gloves (Tram five, Lou three). Both have statistics equal and superior to many in the Baseball Hall of Fame, which may or may not eventually invite them in.

Whitaker and Joe Morgan are the only second basemen in history with 2,000 hits and 200 homers. Trammell hit 185 homers and batted over .300 seven times. Both were great fielders, though Lou was more of a magician, with remarkable range and a rocket arm.

Dave Bergman came along in '84 to play first base. "Both Lou and Tram should be in the Hall of Fame," says Bergman emphatically. "For their talent, stats and what they did for a ballclub. Lou would come in before a game and say, 'I'm gonna get four hits,' and he would.

"I know that some people felt that Lou didn't appear to give all he had. Some perceived his style as coasting. He could have been a superstar among superstars. Sparky would say, 'I'll take 50 percent of Lou over 100 percent of anybody else.' Lou might say, 'I gave 100 percent all the time.' I'll tell you this—he's the only second baseman I played with who could go behind second base, throw over his shoulder, and still handcuff you!"

Sweet Lou and Tram—for 20 years, two smooth and solid pieces, right in the center of the puzzle.

Chapter 21

October: Wire to Wire

Thank you for the thrill of my life.

> — Ruppert Jones to Sparky Anderson after Game Five
> of the World Series (Sparky had brought Jones back
> to the major leagues after Pittsburgh released him in
> the spring)

*There is nothing like this. Absolutely nothing. There's no weight
on my feet.*

> — Dave Bergman, also after Game Five

After the final game in New York Sunday afternoon, September 30, Tigers players and coaches said goodbye to the rookies who wouldn't be on the postseason roster and then flew to Kansas City. The playoffs were to begin on Tuesday, a mere 48 hours after the conclusion of the regular season. Many Tigers wives flew in at their own expense to see the two games at Kauffman Stadium, because the Tigers' policy was to pay for the wives' airfare only for the World Series.

The Tigers held a 90-minute workout in Kansas City Monday afternoon, October 1, as the players displayed varying degrees of nervousness and excitement. Jack Morris, who would pitch Game One, said, "If you make this bigger than life, you're in trouble. It's the biggest game of my career, yet [I have to treat it] as if it's just another game."

The Royals won the West with an 84-78 record, fully 20 wins fewer than the Tigers. Except for George Brett's superiority over Marty Castillo at third, the Tigers looked to be equal or better at every other position.

The Royals starting staff went four deep with Bud Black and 20-year-old rookie Bret Saberhagen—

OCTOBER 1984

October Record: 8–1

Stars:

Alan Trammell:	.364, (4-11) ALCS; .450, 9-20, 2 HRs World Series (MVP)
Kirk Gibson:	417, (5-12) ALCS (MVP); .333, 6-18, 2 HRs World Series
Willie Hernandez:	Appeared in 7 of 8 postseason games; allowed 2 earned runs in 9.1 innings pitched
Jack Morris:	3-0, 2 complete games; 5 earned runs in 25 innings pitched

---

who'd beaten the Tigers three times during the season—plus Mark Gubicza and Charlie Leibrandt. But Morris and Dan Petry were better than any of their four, and with Willie Hernandez in the bullpen, even the great Dan Quisenberry didn't give the Royals an edge in that department.

A legitimate postseason controversy was an umpires' strike on the eve of the playoffs. In the contract signed with the union in 1982, Major League Baseball had allowed the umpires to renegotiate salaries and the selection procedure of umps to be used in postseason play.

The umps who were deemed worthy to work the postseason were scheduled to receive $10,000 each for the playoffs and $15,000 for the World Series. They wanted a total package of $500,000 so they could also disburse money to those who weren't assigned postseason work. Baseball's answer was to use college umps, and those who worked the Tigers-Royals series were joined by former big-league umpire Bill Deegan, who was called out of a five-year retirement to work home plate.

There were no discernable umpiring gaffes when the Tigers bombed the Royals, 8-1, in Game One. Alan Trammell, who had hit .420 against the Royals on the year—including the dramatic grand slam off Quisenberry—singled, tripled, homered and walked twice.

As discussed earlier in this book, the first inning alone was breathtaking evidence of how the '84 Tigers put people away. Lou Whitaker singled off Bud Black to start the game, Tram hit one over Darryl Motley's head and off the left-field wall to score him, and Lance Parrish brought Trammell in with a sacrifice fly. Motley should have caught Trammell's triple, but the two runs enabled Morris to calm down. He spun a five-hitter for seven innings before leaving with a blister on his middle finger.

In the third, the Royals worked the bases full, but Kirk Gibson made a somewhat stumbling, but nonetheless critical, grab of Brett's sinking liner to end the threat. Afterward, Sparky threw a backhanded compliment at Gibson, joking that if it had been 1983, Brett "would have been running for a while."

Larry Herndon homered off Black in the third. Trammell homered in the fourth to make it 4-0 and also singled in Whitaker in the fifth for his third hit and third RBI. Hernandez

Oct 2   Game #1   ALCS

Tigers 8, Royals 1

DETROIT	AB	R	H	BI	KANSAS CITY	AB	R	H	BI
Whitaker 2b	5	2	1	0	Wilson cf	4	0	1	0
Brookens 2b	0	0	0	0	Sheridan rf	2	0	0	0
Trammell ss	3	2	3	3	Jones ph-rf	1	0	0	0
Baker ss	0	0	0	0	Brett 3b	4	0	0	0
Gibson rf	5	0	2	0	Orta dh	4	1	1	0
Parrish c	4	1	1	2	Motley lf	4	0	0	1
Herndon lf	3	1	1	1	Balboni 1b	4	0	0	0
Jones ph-lf	1	0	0	0	White 2b	3	0	1	0
Kuntz ph-lf	1	0	0	0	Slaught c	3	0	2	0
Garbey dh	5	1	2	0	Concepcion ss	3	0	0	0
Lemon cf	5	0	0	0					
Evans 1b	4	0	2	1					
Bergman pr-1b	0	1	0	0					
Castillo 3b	4	0	2	1					
Totals	40	8	14	8		32	1	5	1

Detroit	200	110	121	--	8
Kansas City	000	000	100	--	1

Game winning RBI -- Trammell, E -- Sheridan, DP -- Kansas City 1, LOB -- Detroit 8, Kansas City 5, 2B -- Evans, 3B -- Trammell, Orta, HR -- Herndon, Trammell, Parrish, SF -- Parrish, WP -- Huismann

Detroit	IP	H	R	ER	BB	SO
Morris (W)	7.0	5	1	1	1	4
Hernandez	2.0	0	0	0	0	2
Kansas City						
Black (L)	5.0	7	4	4	1	3
Huismann	2.2	6	3	2	1	2
Jones	1.1	1	1	1	0	0

T -- 2:42 A -- 41,973

pitched two hitless innings to finish it up, and the Tigers rolled to an easy victory. It was to be their last easy victory of the playoffs or the World Series.

◆ *Game 2 of ALCS: Bye Bye Balboni—Almost*

Where:	**Kansas City**
Result:	**5-3 Tigers in 11 innings**
Record:	**Tigers 2-0; Royals 0-2**
WP:	**Lopez, 1-0**
LP:	**Quisenberry, 0-1**
Attendance:	**42,019**

Lance Parrish remembers:

I was extremely confident that year, and also had a tremendous amount of confidence in our ballclub. We had won Game One the night before, but still, the thing I remember thinking was, it would be an absolute shame to come this far and end up losing the playoffs when we'd had such a great year and accomplished so much. And when we beat the Royals, I felt the same way about the World Series. That was always in the back of my mind, though I can't say that I really dwelled on it.

Like we did so often in '84 (including the night before), we scored right away. Kirk doubled to right off Bret Saberhagen, knocking in Lou, who'd reached on an error by their shortstop, and then I hit a double to right-center knocking Kirk in. Kirk had a great series. He won the MVP of the playoffs and he homered in the third, so we led 'em, 3-0. They got a few [runs] off Petry, who pitched pretty well that night. Willie came in in the eighth and gave up the tying run [3-3]. Hal McRae hit a pinch double and Willie shouldn't have pitched. At least that's what Sparky said in the papers—that he had strep throat. But Aurelio came on in the ninth and did the job.

With two out in the ninth, Aurelio walked Willie Wilson. I considered situations like that to be part of the game that I looked forward to. It was a huge challenge to me every time a Willie Wilson or a Rickey Henderson [another top base stealer] got on base. That's where I had an opportunity to shine, so I was hoping that he [Wilson] would go. My arm felt great the whole year, and I knew that if I had an opportunity, I had a real good shot at throwing him out.

Roger Craig was uncanny at calling pitchouts at the right time. I don't know how he picked it out and knew when the runners would go, but very seldom would he call a pitchout and the runner wouldn't go. I used to look in the dugout after he'd do it and I'd just laugh because it was amazing to

Oct 3   Game #2   ALCS

Tigers 5, Royals 3

DETROIT	AB	R	H	BI	KANSAS CITY	AB	R	H	BI
Whitaker 2b	5	1	1	0	Wilson cf	5	0	1	0
Trammell ss	5	0	1	0	Sheridan rf	2	1	0	0
Gibson rf	4	2	2	2	Jones ph-rf	3	1	1	0
Parrish c	5	0	2	1	Brett 3b	5	0	2	0
Evans 3b-1b	4	1	0	0	Pryor pr-3b	0	0	0	0
Jones lf	4	1	0	0	Orta dh	3	0	0	1
Grubb dh	4	0	1	2	McRae ph	1	0	1	1
Lemon cf	5	0	0	0	Wathan pr	1	0	0	0
Bergman 1b	1	0	1	0	Motley lf	4	0	2	0
Brookens 3b	2	0	0	0	Balboni 1b	5	0	1	0
Garbey ph	1	0	0	0	White 2b	5	1	0	0
Castillo 3b	1	0	0	0	Slaught c	5	0	1	0
					Concepcion ss	2	0	0	0
					Iorg ph	1	0	1	1
					Biancalana ss	1	0	0	0
					Washington ph	1	0	0	0
Totals	**41**	**5**	**8**	**5**		**44**	**3**	**10**	**3**

Detroit	201 000 000	02	--	5
Kansas City	000 100 110	00	--	3

Game winning RBI -- Grubb, E -- Concepcion, Saberhagen, Brookens, Slaught, LOB -- Detroit 7, Kansas City 11, 2B -- Gibson, Parrish, McRae, Grubb, HR -- Gibson, SB -- Bergman, CS -- Wilson, SH -- Grubb, Evans

Detroit	IP	H	R	ER	BB	SO
Petry	7.0	4	2	2	1	4
Hernandez	1.0	2	1	1	1	1
Lopez (W)	3.0	4	0	0	1	2
Kansas City						
Saberhagen	8.0	6	3	2	1	5
Quisenberry (L)	3.0	2	2	1	1	1

T -- 3:37 A -- 42,019

me that almost every time he'd call a pitchout it would work. Anyway, it made my job easy. He called it, Wilson went, and we got him [at second] to send it to extra innings.

I felt confident with everybody who came out to pitch for us. That was one of the great things about our ballclub. It seemed like everybody who came in did the job. Lopey, to me, was just as good as Willie was, it was just that Willie got all the accolades because of the season that he had. But Aurelio did a heckuva job the entire year setting him up.

Aurelio could throw five or six pitches, but his number one pitch most all the time was his fastball. He loved to throw his fastball and he had a good one that night. In the 10th, George Brett and Darryl Motley singled off Aurelio, and Steve Balboni came up with two out in what would become a memorable at bat.

John Grubb watches his game-winning two-run, 11th-inning double in Game Two of the ALCS.

We kept on coming after him with fastballs, and he fouled six of 'em off in a ten-pitch at bat. Aurelio kept wanting to throw fastballs, and we kept on trying to go up the ladder a little bit, moving it off the plate a little bit, and he just kept on getting a piece of it. And finally Lopey threw one that Balboni got a hold of. But the Kansas City park played big then, and when he hit it, everybody probably took a deep breath. But I felt like he didn't get all of it and Chet ran it down at the wall. It's one of those things; when somebody wants to come after somebody, go ahead! Aurelio did and it was exciting.

I led off the 11th, and I think I hit a ground ball between short and third. I was retired on a fielder's choice, but there were two on against Quisenberry, who had relieved Saberhagen in the ninth. With one out, Johnny Grubb hit a line drive to right-center between Lynn Jones and Wilson, who had been shading Grubb to left-center. The ball short-hopped off the wall and Evans and Ruppert Jones scored to make it 5-3.

Man, everybody was so excited. Every game was like the seventh game of the World Series and everybody was pumped up. When we took the lead and they had only one more at bat, we had a real good chance of winning.

Lopez retired the side in the 11th and we're up two games to none, and I remember knowing then that we'd finish it. I didn't know if it would be *one, two or three more games, but I was confident we'd get the job done. I felt that [we would] even though they had a good ballclub and they had played very well against us in Detroit that year.*

My wife, Arlyne, was due to deliver our daughter any day. We had an off day Thursday after the second game, and I'll never forget because a buddy of mine came to the airport when we flew back [to Detroit] after Game Two. He insisted that they let him through to where we exited the airplane, which was unheard of because the crowds were huge and they were keeping everybody back.

We didn't get in until the middle of the night, and he told them that my wife was in labor and he needed to take me to the hospital. That wasn't necessarily true. Actually, it wasn't true, but he just figured he'd get in there and help me get out. We had an off day the next day, so we went to the hospital that day.

I had been on call the whole time in Kansas City. I kept on running up to the clubhouse and calling, "Is everything OK?" I was totally into the game, but I was also totally into my wife being this close to giving birth. I slept maybe a few hours the night we got back, and at six that next morning we went to the hospital.

I knew that if we didn't have the baby that day that there was a good chance I wasn't going to be around for the birth. We had induced labor for [sons] David and Matt, so what the hell? She had gone full-term. They induced labor so I could go to the World Series with the baby already delivered. We went to the hospital on the off day and even though she was dilating, she was stuck. So they induced labor and she gave birth to Ashley Lyne between games Two and Three.

It really took a burden off and was wonderful timing. I was in another world actually. But I went home and finally got a good night's sleep, and we beat the Royals Friday night.

Turns out, Arlyne begged the doctor to let her take the baby to San Diego for the Series. So they came with us in the team charter!

Grubb, 36, was another role-player extraordinaire in '84. He only batted 176 times during the season and was used mostly as a pinch hitter and occasional DH. Game Two was his only playoff exposure, and his game-winning double off Quisenberry was his only hit.

"He's been a good player, teammate and cheerleader for us from the beginning," praised Trammell. Grubb had a Clark Kent look with black glasses and an unassuming manner.

"I've never been the guy in the spotlight like this," Grubb said. He had come up with men on first and second and one out, and thought Quisenberry might have walked the bases full to pitch to the right-handed Lemon. Instead, he offered Grubb a fastball up on a one-and-two pitch and the quiet man delivered.

One scene after this game stands out as much as anything that happened that season. After Grubb's double gave the Tigers the extra-inning lead, and Lopez retired the Royals in the 11th, I took the elevator from the fourth floor of the press box down to the locker room.

When the door opened on the third floor, Jim Campbell and Bill Lajoie rushed on. I had never seen Campbell so completely out of character. The stoic old baseball man was giggling like a schoolkid, giddy and loud. I asked Lajoie about that some time later, and he said that when Balboni hit the ball off Lopez in the 10th, Campbell had assumed it would end the game and had stood up in disgust and said, "Let's go." When Lemon flagged it at the wall, Campbell was stunned and pleased. Then, when the Tigers won it so dramatically, he was overjoyed. It was a revelation to see him in such high spirits and to not mind allowing a reporter to glimpse past his rough exterior.

The Royals would now have to win three straight at Tiger Stadium to survive. They had swept that four-game series there in early August, so they had a sliver of a chance.

◆ *Game 3 of ALCS: The Little Things*

Darrell Evans

Where:	**Tiger Stadium**
Result:	**1-0 Tigers**
Record:	**Tigers 3-0; Royals 0-3**
WP:	**Wilcox, 1-0**
LP:	**Leibrandt, 0-1**
Attendance:	**52,168**

Darrell Evans remembers:

Sparky said after this one, "No one would have dreamed that one run would hold up in this ballpark." And there were only six hits in the game—three for each team. But that's what's so great about baseball: It can come down to a one-pitch game—one pitch for [the] whole season, the whole time you've been together, six-seven months. I tried to emphasize that to the guys from the start; it actually comes down to that—we're in the play-offs and the games are tough. One pitch, one play, two inches can make the difference. That's why baseball is the great game it is, and why this game was a classic.

In the eighth, I wouldn't have made that play under different conditions. There were two out and Dane Iorg was on first with Willie Wilson batting. I was thinking, "Willie's not gonna hit the ball down the line." Normally, with two outs and a man on first, I might not try to get off the base that much and instead try to protect the line.

But with Willie up, I knew he wasn't normally going to pull the ball, so I tried to get off holding the runner on as quick as I could. If I wouldn't have been thinking about all that, it might not have happened the way it did, so you get satisfaction out of plays that people don't necessarily appreciate; you appreciate it by doing it yourself, and then it happens in an important situation like that.

Lou's playing Willie up the middle and in a little bit—so I'm cheating to get off as far as I can. Milt throws, I move off as far as I can, and Willie rips it into the hole. I dive and caught it backhand. I look up and Milt's not quite there and Willie's running—all these things go through your mind in a split second and I'm saying, "Oh, I gotta get up and beat him to the bag."

So I slid into the bag—and you don't want to slide head-first because the guy's running, and Milt's right there and you can't run across the bag because you'll run into guys, so I beat Willie to the bag to end the inning. You run across the field and this energy—this magic—is coming from the stands. You're three outs away from going to the World Series—heck, you can't buy that stuff.

Marty Castillo made a backhand stab on Motley in the seventh, and looking back you remember all those plays. When you're in those games and your whole life dream is there; how many opportunities will you ever get to be in this situation? So much goes through your mind. You have to trust everybody else. Looking around, you hope the other eight guys are feeling this and, obviously, they were. It was so great to have guys like that. Marty not only made that play, but he hit a home run in the World Series! How many people hit a home run in a World Series?

The other thing was that one run. Only run the whole night comes in the second inning. Garbey gets an infield single; Chet forces him and I line a single to center, sending Chet to third. Marty's up, double-play situation. We got so much joy out of doing the little things, like breaking up double plays and running the bases right. We got just as much from those things as we did about home runs and that stuff; it was very much appreciated on our ballclub.

When you're standing on first in that situation, you go, "Okay, if he hits a ground ball I gotta do something." So you get a little better lead, a little better jump. The ball wasn't hit particularly hard and Sparky had the grass six inches high, so that helped. Also, you're playing against Frank White, who knows who's gonna break up double plays and who's not, so psychologically you plant that seed.

Back at that time you could pretty much do anything to break up

Milt Wilcox blew away the Royals with a brilliant two-hit playoff-clinching performance.

Oct 5	Game #3	ALCS

Tigers 1, Royals 0

KANSAS CITY	AB	R	H	BI	DETROIT	AB	R	H	BI
Wilson cf	4	0	0	0	Whitaker 2b	4	0	0	0
Sheridan, rf	2	0	0	0	Trammell ss	3	0	0	0
Jones ph	1	0	0	0	Gibson rf	3	0	1	0
Brett 3b	4	0	1	0	Parrish c	3	0	0	0
Orta dh	3	0	0	0	Herndon lf	2	0	0	0
McRae ph	1	0	1	0	Garbey dh	3	0	1	0
Washington pr	0	0	0	0	Lemon cf	3	1	0	0
Motley lf	4	0	0	0	Evans 1b	2	0	1	0
Balboni 1b	2	0	0	0	Castillo 3b	3	0	0	1
White 2b	3	0	0	0					
Slaught c	3	0	1	0					
Concepcion ss	2	0	0	0					
Iorg ph	1	0	0	0					
Biancalana ss	0	0	0	0					
Totals	**30**	**0**	**3**	**0**		**26**	**1**	**3**	**1**

Kansas City	000 000 000	--	0
Detroit	010 000 00x	--	1

Game winning RBI - Castillo, E -- Slaught 2, Balboni, DP -- Kansas City 1, LOB -- Kansas City 5, Detroit 5, SB -- Castillo, Gibson, Evans

Kansas City	IP	H	R	ER	BB	SO
Leibrandt (L)	8.0	3	1	1	4	6
Detroit						
Wilcox (W)	8.0	2	0	0	2	8
Hernandez (S)	1.0	1	0	0	0	0

T -- 2:39 A -- 52,168

double plays as long as you didn't go out of the baseline, roll block—all that stuff. Marty grounds to Onix Concepcion at short, and I remember the slide. I wound up halfway into left field trying to get White, and Marty hustling—I can see him right now barely beating the play. Chet scores, and rather than an inning-ending double play, you look back and see how an innocent kind of play scores the one run that puts us into the World Series.

Of course, if Wilcox doesn't pitch the game of his life—eight innings with just two hits and eight K's—none of the other stuff matters. He's one of those guys you kid about—how can he get away with that stuff? He was a great power pitcher in the National League, and then overcoming arm problems and learning how to finesse is such a tribute.

He was the third guy and different from the two power guys, Jack and Dan. Then Milt comes in and throws all his changing speeds. He knew when to walk a guy, when to challenge a guy, and then you get him in a big-game situation like that one and he pitches as good a game as has ever been pitched, probably. He went through so much for us and never complained. Only complaint we had was that smell from the DMSO [the horse liniment Wilcox used on his shoulder to reduce pain] all the time. I didn't make as many trips to the mound because of that!

But you look back—everybody is hurt during the season. There was often a question whether Milt was able to pitch on a given night—but he always went out there. We weren't aware of what he was going through at the time. The guy's a warrior, and you have to have enough of these guys and that's why it's so hard to win. You appreciate that part more than the talent.

Supposedly, the highest-paid players and the most talented teams win, but that doesn't always happen. We had more leaders on that club than any team I ever played on, and that's what this is all about—being a leader.

Celebration number two: Trammell, Hernandez and Evans after sweeping the Royals.

Gibson was named American League Championship Series MVP, going 5-12 for a .417 average with two RBIs, a homer and a stolen base. He also made the running catch on Brett's bases-loaded liner in Game One that was deemed the defensive play of the playoff. Trammell, at 4-11, .364, was a candidate, as was Wilcox, with an eight-inning two-hitter in the clincher.

Ironically, Wilcox had set a record: As a 20-year-old, he had also won the pennant-clincher in relief back in 1970 for Sparky when the Reds swept Pittsburgh. Wilcox thus became the first player to win clinchers in both leagues. But Gibson's MVP selection typified his progress in '84. It wasn't until two months into the season that

Sparky stopped platooning him with Rusty Kuntz, and the decision continued to reap dividends.

The Tigers popped 36 cases of champagne and celebrated in the locker room for the second time in 15 days. Fans who hadn't been able to watch the game from inside tried to force their way into the ballpark. But they were unable to break through the wire-screened barrier on Michigan Avenue, and eventually dispersed, incident-free.

The replacement umpires had done a respectable job, and with the strike still unsettled, were prepared to call the World Series as well.

The AL champs rested Saturday, and were half-surprised, half-peeved that Sparky called them in on a rainy Sunday for some stretching and batting practice. They took the charter to San Diego Sunday night, where they would commence the final leg of their journey Tuesday in Game One of the World Series.

As the Tigers were taking infield practice in San Diego before they cleared the field, a plane flying over the stadium toward right field was trailing a banner. Don't forget, this was 1984, and the banner read, "Stroh's Says, Go Padres!" I looked at it in disbelief. Wasn't Stroh's Detroit's beer? Wasn't the damn factory right there on I-75? What kind of turncoat nonsense was this?

Stroh's had gone national in 1982 and was now being sold in California. The brewer had every right to advertise as it saw fit, but I still thought it was a bush-league thing to do.

Larry Herndon's two-run homer would provide Morris with the winning margin in the Tigers' 3-2 win in Game One. Jack went the distance on nine hits and allowed no runs after Terry Kennedy's two-run double in the first erased a 1-0 Tigers lead. When the game ended, Herndon was nowhere to be seen, having dashed to the hotel where a clubhouse boy later brought him his clothes. Herndon was extremely modest and shy, and it wasn't until the next day, when it was too late, that he even agreed to briefly touch upon his big hit.

Twenty years later—now that's another story.

◆Game 1 of World Series: The Quiet Man Delivers

Where:	**San Diego**
Result:	**3-2 Tigers**
Record:	**Tigers 1-0; Padres 0-1**
WP:	**Morris, 1-0**
LP:	**Thurmond, 0-1**
Attendance:	**57,908**

Oct 9   Game #1   World Series
Tigers 3, Padres 2

DETROIT	AB	R	H	BI	SAN DIEGO	AB	R	H	BI
Whitaker 2b	4	1	1	0	Wiggins 2b	4	0	1	0
Trammell ss	5	0	2	1	Gwynn rf	2	0	1	0
Gibson rf	4	0	0	0	Garvey 1b	4	1	1	0
Parrish c	3	1	2	0	Nettles 3b	2	1	2	0
Herndon lf	3	1	2	2	Salazar pr-3b	1	0	0	0
Garbey dh	4	0	0	0	Kennedy c	4	0	2	2
Lemon cf	4	0	1	0	Brown cf	4	0	0	0
Evans 1b	3	0	0	0	Martinez lf	4	0	0	0
Bergman pr-1b	0	0	0	0	Templeton ss	4	0	0	0
Castillo 3b	2	0	0	0	Bevacqua dh	3	0	1	0
Grubb ph	0	0	0	0					
Brookens ph-3b	1	0	0	0					
Totals	**33**	**3**	**8**	**3**		**32**	**2**	**8**	**2**

Detroit	100 020 000 --	3
San Diego	200 000 000 --	2

Game winning RBI -- Herndon, E -- Martinez, DP -- Detroit 1, San Diego 1, LOB -- Detroit 9, San Diego 6, 2B -- Whitaker, Kennedy, Parrish, Bevacqua, HR -- Herndon, SB -- Trammell, Gwynn, CS -- Trammell, Gibson, Gwynn

Detroit	IP	H	R	ER	BB	SO
Morris (W)	9.0	8	2	2	3	9
San Diego						
Thurmond (L)	5.0	7	3	3	3	2
Hawkins	2.2	1	0	0	3	0
Dravecky	1.1	0	0	0	0	1

T -- 3:18 A -- 57,908

Larry Herndon remembers:

I just wanted to do my part. Sparky always stressed taking care of your job, and it had bothered me that I started poorly in '84. I wasn't doing what I could do to affect the team positively. At that time [the start of the World Series], I was a platooned left fielder with Ruppert Jones. I was just a small piece in that puzzle.

That's how I viewed it. I kinda felt that as the year went on, I took up my role of helping out against left-handers. I took it as the ups and downs of baseball because we were winning. Early on, I said to myself, these guys are going good now, and I'm just gonna have to pick it up at some point and do my part because everybody won't stay this hot all year.

That's what was amazing about playing in Detroit with the guys I was playing with. Guys never really cared about numbers. They cared about winning ball games. After every win I was happy, no matter what. I steadily worked so I could pick up my part.

We got a run in the first. Lou led off with a double off Mark Thurmond, and Tram singled him in. Then they got two in the bottom of the first. I slipped in left on a double by Terry Kennedy [Steve Garvey and Graig Nettles had singled]. I didn't get to it as quickly as I could. If I didn't catch it I would've at least cut it down. It wouldn't have been a two-run double, I don't think. But it didn't faze me. I figured we'd win the game anyway.

It was still 2-1 Padres in the fifth. With two out, Parrish doubled. Lance was at second and I knew it was time to do something. I said to myself, "You're up against a left-hander. You don't want to put this on anybody else. Take care of this and get Lance home… you gotta get him in."

A home run was the last thing on my mind. Enos [Cabell, his former Tigers roommate] had faced Thurmond in the National League and told me, "This guy's gonna keep everything away from you. He's gonna go away." I was locked in on the outside part of the plate. I saw a straight fastball on the outside part of the plate, and I went through it and the ball went out of the ballpark and we got two runs. It was a pure line drive over the fence in right. It gave Jack a 3-2 lead. Nettles and Kennedy singled to open the sixth, but Jack then struck out the side.

I played with Jack, hung out with Jack. You just saw that soldier, and

Lance Parrish greets Larry Herndon after Larry's two-run fifth-inning homer.

he'd get that look, "That's all I need, boys." You'd see that look on his face going into the dugout after the inning and you knew you just had to play good defense for him.

In the seventh inning, [Kurt] Bevaqua led off with a double down the right-field line. I'm in left backing up on this play, running towards third, and I'm looking at Gibby coming up with the ball in the right-field corner and I'm thinking, "Gibby will make a good throw to the cutoff man—he's gonna do this."

Lou and Tram—give them the ball in the right spot and they'll make a strong throw. I could see the whole thing unfolding. I was running so I didn't see when Bevaqua slipped between second and third, but I remember thinking, "We're gonna have him no matter what." Lou's relay to Castillo was perfect. It was the prettiest thing watching it from left field as I'm going to back up third—to see these guys line up and make a perfect play. That was the first out in the seventh, and Jack got everybody else out the rest of the way and we won, 3-2.

Along with Herndon, the bullpen pitchers have a great view of Gibson's seventh-inning relay to Whitaker.

You want to know why I wouldn't talk that night? I didn't look at it as a big deal. I got a hit. That's all. I got a hit. Jack pitched like nobody's business that day so I didn't want the attention—I didn't need the attention. All of that should've gone to Jack. I was just happy to get out of there with a win.

What I tried to do was play every game the same. It was the World Series, but it was still another game. I didn't put that much emphasis on things and that made it easier for me. That's how I prepared myself. It sounds corny, but that's how I tried to deal with it. When I needed to talk, I could say what I needed to say, but I was just a part of things. I'm not an ego guy; I just try to get my job done. To keep things toned down, the best thing is not to say anything unless you really had something to say.

[The] good thing about this team is I felt at home with all of them. Me and Jack would go eat and shop. Me and Danny Petry would go shop and hang out. Chet and Lou, Lance and Gibby. I wouldn't have a problem going anywhere with any of 'em. I felt at home, and I still feel the same way about them all. I made some good friends up there. Guys were from different parts of the country and had different interests, but when it came to walking into that clubhouse and going between the lines, we were as much of a family as you could get.

It didn't hit me—the magnitude of the media—the number of people who were covering the World Series. Now it does, because we won a World Series. At the time you don't know. You think you might win it four-five years in a row. We won one, and I'm very proud to be a part of that team and the people I played with there.

Oct 10 Game #2 World Series

Padres 5, Tigers 3

DETROIT	AB	R	H	BI	SAN DIEGO	AB	R	H	BI
Whitaker 2b	4	1	1	0	Wiggins 2b	5	1	3	0
Trammell ss	4	1	2	0	Gwynn rf	3	0	1	0
Gibson rf	4	1	2	1	Garvey 1b	3	0	0	0
Parrish c	3	0	0	1	Nettles 3b	1	1	0	1
Evans 3b-1b	4	0	1	1	Kennedy c	4	1	1	0
Jones lf	2	0	0	0	Bevacqua dh	4	2	3	3
Herndon ph-lf	2	0	0	0	Martinez lf	3	0	0	0
Grubb dh	2	0	1	0	Templeton ss	4	0	3	0
Kuntz ph	1	0	0	0	Brown cf	3	0	0	1
Lemon cf	3	0	0	0	Salazar cf	1	0	0	0
Bergman 1b	2	0	0	0					
Brookens ph-3b	1	0	0	0					
Totals	**32**	**3**	**7**	**3**		**31**	**5**	**11**	**5**

Detroit	300	000	000	--	3
San Diego	100	130	00x	--	5

Game winning RBI -- Bevacqua, E -- Trammell, Gibson, Herndon, DP
-- Detroit 1, San Diego 1, LOB -- Detroit 3, San Diego 8, HR --
Bevacqua, SB -- Gibson, CS -- Wiggins, Gwynn, Bevacqua, SH --
Garvey, SF -- Parrish, Nettles, Balk -- Petry

Detroit	IP	H	R	ER	BB	SO
Petry (L)	4.1	8	5	5	3	2
Lopez	0.2	1	0	0	1	0
Scherrer	1.1	2	0	0	0	0
Bair	0.2	0	0	0	0	1
Hernandez	1.0	0	0	0	0	0
San Diego						
Whitson	0.2	5	3	3	0	0
Hawkins (W)	5.1	1	0	0	0	3
Lefferts (S)	3.0	1	0	0	0	5

T -- 2:44 A -- 57,911

The Padres won Game Two, 5-3, erasing a three-run Tigers lead. The Tigers got all three in the first off Ed Whitson. Whitaker, Trammell and Gibson each singled on the first pitch. Whitson's fourth pitch was a ball and Gibson stole second on it. Andy Hawkins relieved Whitson after two were out, and held the Tigers to one hit over the next 5⅓ innings to get the win.

Sparky later admitted that he probably kept Petry in too long. Kurt Bevacqua, the 37-year-old journeyman—and goat of the Game One loss when he stumbled attempting that seventh-inning triple— cracked a three-run homer off a Petry slider in the fifth to put the Padres ahead, 5-3.

As he approached home, Bevacqua blew kisses to his wife in the stands. Petry gave up eight hits and three walks, and struggled throughout. Craig Lefferts shut down the Tigers in the final three innings. Aurelio Lopez, Bill Scherrer, Doug Bair and Hernandez similarly shut down San Diego, but the 5-3 margin remained the final score. The Series was now even at one heading to Detroit for games Three through Five.

Thursday was the customary travel day, with the Series set to resume in Detroit Friday night. The Padres, only in existence since 1969, came from their bland home at Jack Murphy Stadium and arrived in their unspeakably ugly, yellow and brown "taco" road jerseys to play in historic Tiger Stadium. Ugliest of all, their pitchers allowed 11 walks in the pivotal third game.

◆ Game 3 of World Series: Marty and Chet—The Homer, the Catch

Where:	**Tiger Stadium**
Result:	**5-2 Tigers**
Record:	**Tigers 2-1; Padres 1-2**
WP:	**Wilcox, 1-0**
LP:	**Lollar, 0-1**
Attendance:	**51,970**

Milt Wilcox

Milt Wilcox remembers:

It was a strange game. I was having shoulder problems during that game, that's why I didn't have my best control, but I can't tell you why the Padres pitchers were wild. The Pods walked 11, and when that happens it seems like the ump's strike zone got smaller and smaller, and it was small for me because he was calling it that way for those guys, so he had to call it the same for both teams. That made that game drag on.

Actually, we really weren't expecting to play the Padres—we were kinda geared towards Chicago and we didn't really know that much about 'em [the Padres]. The Cubs had been the dominant National League team the last month and a half, and it was like the Padres were there by default because the Cubs [who led the NLCS, 2-0] didn't finish 'em off.

Marty Castillo hit a two-run homer in the second inning, when we got four runs. Marty had also knocked in the only run in the playoff clincher on that fielder's choice. Marty was put in because of his defense. His main position was catching, and he had good, soft hands, and Sparky put him at third and you never worried about bad throws

Oct 12	Game #3	World Series

Tigers 5, Padres 2

SAN DIEGO					DETROIT				
	AB	R	H	BI		AB	R	H	BI
Wiggins 2b	5	1	2	0	Whitaker 2b	3	1	0	0
Gwynn rf	5	1	2	0	Trammell ss	3	1	2	1
Garvey 1b	5	0	1	1	Gibson rf	2	0	0	1
Nettles 3b	2	0	0	1	Parrish c	3	0	1	0
Kennedy c	3	0	0	0	Herndon lf	4	0	1	1
Bevacqua dh	4	0	1	0	Garbey dh	5	0	0	0
Martinez lf	4	0	1	0	Lemon cf	5	1	2	0
Templeton ss	4	0	2	0	Evans 1b	2	1	0	0
Brown cf	3	0	0	0	Bergman 1b	0	0	0	0
Salazar ph	1	0	1	0	Castillo 3b	4	1	1	2
Totals	36	2	10	2		31	5	7	5

San Diego	001	000	100	--	2
Detroit	041	000	00x	--	5

Game winning RBI -- Castillo, LOB -- San Diego 10, Detroit 14, 2B -- Wiggins, Trammell, Garvey, HR -- Castillo, SB -- Gibson, SF -- Nettles, HBP -- by Harris (Gibson), WP -- Lollar

San Diego	IP	H	R	ER	BB	SO
Lollar (L)	1.2	4	4	4	4	0
Booker	1.0	0	1	1	4	0
Harris	5.1	3	0	0	3	5
Detroit						
Wilcox (W)	6.0	7	1	1	2	4
Scherrer	0.2	2	1	1	0	0
Hernandez (S)	2.1	1	0	0	0	0

T -- 3:11 A -- 51,970

Marty Castillo with the biggest hit of his career, a two-run second-inning homer off Tim Lollar as the Tigers take a 2-games-to-1 lead.

because he had a gun and was accurate too. Any offense from him was a plus, and I think he was probably more shocked than anybody that he hit the home run. He's the kinda guy you could kid around and tell him that the game made his career and he kinda downplayed it, but Marty was a great guy to have on the team, and those are the extra guys you gotta have to win championships.

That was the whole thing to our team all year, how our bench came through and got big hits and carried us—Kuntz, Garbey, Castillo, etcetera—coming through all the time for us. Whenever Sparky would push a button it worked, and that's how the whole season went for us.

I went six innings and gave up seven hits and two walks. As I said, I was having shoulder problems because those cortisone shots only work for a short period of time, especially when I had so many and I could feel the pain coming back there.

Most games, after I'd get taken out, I'd go in the clubhouse and ice down, but these are games you dream about since you're six-seven years old, and I remember Chet going back and catching that ball in the seventh. [Bill Scherrer started the seventh and left with one run in and a man on. Terry Kennedy hit a shot off Willie Hernandez that Lemon pirouetted on and flagged down over his shoulder to kill the rally.]

Chet made great plays, and he was probably one of the most unsung players on that team—you put him out in center field and it's like a wind-up toy—he just does everything for you.

Willie Hernandez throws the final pitch of Game Three.

Then Willie blew 'em away in the eighth and ninth. I told Willie if it wasn't for me he wouldn't have won the Cy Young Award—he owed me a lot, and I told him I wanted part of that new contract [the one that he signed the following winter], but it never worked out!

The media room [at Tiger Stadium] was under the stands in center field, and so what they did is load you on a golf cart and had it swing around so you could get close to the people in the stands and they'd cheer for ya. My son, Brian, eight at the time, got to ride out there with me and that was a big thrill for him.

I knew I probably had pitched myself out in '84. I waited and waited in my career to keep from cutting [operating] on my shoulder, 'cause once you cut on it you never know how it's gonna come out. And back in those days it was at the beginning of rotator cuff and AC joint surgery, so it was a 50-50 proposition if I'd ever be able to pitch again. Nowadays, if I'd had the operation, they would give me a year off and some time to rehab me back on a slow agenda.

If it [the Series] had gone six games, I'd have pitched the sixth game. We only had a three-man rotation in the playoffs. Danny pitched Game Five and Jack would have been up for Game Seven.

The 11 walks tied a Series record and the 5-2 win put the Tigers in position to end it in Detroit with wins in the next two games. Morris was set to pitch on Saturday afternoon, in a game that would again feature starring roles by Morris and Trammell, and all but ensure that the Tigers would complete what they had begun, and finally emerge from the shadow of the '68 team.

◆ Game 4 of World Series: America Meets the MVP

Where:	**Tiger Stadium**
Result:	**4-2 Tigers**
Record:	**Tigers 3-1; Padres 1-3**
WP:	**Morris, 2-0**
LP:	**Show, 0-1**
Attendance:	**52,130**

Alan Trammell remembers:

This was the greatest game of my career, no doubt about it. To be on the World Series stage and hit two homers in your home ballpark—that's pretty nice.

They were both off Eric Show and both with Lou on. In the first inning Lou gets on. I'd never faced Show before but I was swinging well and was very confident. It got to 2-0 and he threw me a little slider that didn't do anything and my eyes lit up and boom! I took a good swing and it went out.

And the same thing happened the next time I got up. Third inning; Lou gets on base again, like he always seemed to do, and it got to 2-0 again and boom—another home run and we've got the four runs. I didn't hit long high ones. I had to really get it [to hit a homer]. My swing and the way I hit 'em, they were both line drives. The first went a couple of rows back, and the second hit the facing of the upper deck, more of a line drive.

Next time up, fifth inning, Lou was on second with a double, and with nobody out I hit a bullet to left field, and because there was nobody out, Alex Grammas, our third-base coach, stopped him. So we had first and third with nobody out and we didn't score. That could have been a five RBI game. I had three-for-three right out of the chute. Didn't matter. Jack held 'em down and we won, 4-2.

What my feeling was after this game was that we didn't want to go back to San Diego. We had clinched the division at home. We had beaten the Royals for the pennant at home and we wanted to celebrate the World Series at home. Not that you can't celebrate in the road city, but we felt

Oct 13   Game #4   World Series

Tigers 4, Padres 2

SAN DIEGO	AB	R	H	BI	DETROIT	AB	R	H	BI
Wiggins 2b	3	0	0	0	Whitaker 2b	4	2	2	0
Summers ph	1	0	0	0	Trammell ss	4	2	3	4
Roenicke lf	0	0	0	0	Gibson rf	4	0	1	0
Gwynn rf	4	0	1	0	Parrish c	4	0	0	0
Garvey 1b	4	1	1	0	Evans 3b	2	0	0	0
Nettles 3b	4	0	0	0	Brookens 3b	1	0	0	0
Kennedy c	4	1	1	1	Grubb dh	1	0	0	0
Bevacqua dh	3	0	1	0	Garbey ph	2	0	0	0
Martinez lf	2	0	0	0	Jones lf	1	0	0	0
Flannery ph-2b	1	0	1	0	Herndon ph-lf	2	0	1	0
Templeton ss	3	0	0	0	Lemon cf	2	0	0	0
Brown cf	3	0	0	0	Bergman 1b	3	0	0	0
Totals	**32**	**2**	**5**	**1**		**30**	**4**	**7**	**4**

```
San Diego ----------------- 010 000 001 -- 2
Detroit   ----------------- 202 000 00x -- 4
```

Game winning RBI -- Trammell, E -- Wiggins, Gwynn, DP -- San Diego 2, LOB -- San Diego 3, Detroit 4, 2B -- Bevacqua, Whitaker, Garvey, HR -- Trammell 2, Kennedy, SB -- Gibson, Lemon, CS -- Lemon, WP -- Morris 2

San Diego	IP	H	R	ER	BB	SO
Show (L)	2.2	4	4	3	1	2
Dravecky	3.1	3	0	0	1	4
Lefferts	1.0	0	0	0	0	0
Gossage	1.0	0	0	0	0	1
Detroit						
Morris (W)	9.0	5	2	2	0	4

T -- 2:20 A -- 52,130

**Alan Trammell hits his
second two-run homer
off Eric Show to put the
Tigers ahead 4-1 in
Game Four.**

*that we didn't want to fly all the way back to San Diego. We wanted to
take care of business at home and we ended up doing that.
The Padres had a veteran team with Dick Williams at the helm. Garvey,
Gossage, Graig Nettles and Tony Gwynn, early in his career. And Gary
Templeton, Terry Kennedy—they had a nice little ballclub.*

*We respected them, but we feared no one—no matter who we played,
we felt we were gonna win. We were very confident inside, but until Gibby
hit that second home run on Sunday [in Game Five]—that was the first
time that I realized that we had won. Hell, we're up three games to one so
you feel you're in good shape but you never want to take anything for
granted and put your guard down and get complacent. Next thing you
know, the momentum's changed.*

When this one was over—a tight, five-hit, no-walk gem by Morris
that took a little more than two hours—the Padres looked nothing
like a team capable of coming back. They had certainly rallied
before, winning the last three against the Cubs in the NLCS. Reality
was that it had happened four times previously in the World Series—
'25 Pirates, '58 Yankees, '68 Tigers and '79 Pirates.

But the caution the Tigers expressed about a Padres comeback
seemed hollow. The Padres' starting pitching had been exposed

throughout the postseason as substandard. Show alone had given up seven homers in 7⅓ innings against both the Cubs and Tigers. Combined, the four Padres starters had yielded 13 runs to the Tigers in just 10 innings. Morris already had two complete game wins and was available again for a possible Game Seven, so the Padres were as done as done could be, despite all the "It ain't over…" Yogi-isms being tossed around.

Sparky was using his stage that Saturday afternoon to promote his players to the national media. Of Trammell, he said, "Can you tell me why that man doesn't get more recognition? He is the best shortstop in the game, but nobody outside of Detroit knows it." And if that didn't get their attention, he added, "He's the best shortstop I've ever seen."

With his Reggie Jackson–type performance, Trammell moved ahead of Morris as the top Series MVP candidate. He had nine hits in 16 at bats by now and had become just the fourth player to knock in all of his team's runs in a Series win. He patiently dealt with dozens of reporters, explaining that his improved hitting had resulted from a change in his stance in '83, when he started keeping his left shoulder in a little longer on the pitch.

At one point, a Hall of Fame representative came by to see him and requested, and received, the bat Trammell used to hit the two 2-run homers. Trammell then both defused and justified Sparky's effusive praise:

"He talks a lot," Alan, then 26, patiently explained, "but mostly he speaks from his heart. I appreciate what he's saying, especially since he's seen some great shortstops, like Dave Concepcion. He said he was going to build us up around the country. I understand that and don't let it affect me. When I go on the field, the last thing I think about is what Sparky Anderson is saying about Alan Trammell."

Winning Sunday and not going back to San Diego—now that was something to think about.

◆ Game 5 of World Series: Gibby Gets the Goose

Where:	**Tiger Stadium**
Result:	**8-4 Tigers**
Record:	**Tigers 4-1; Padres 1-4**
WP:	**Lopez, 1-0**
LP:	**Hawkins, 1-1**
Attendance:	**51,901**

Oct 14   Game #5   World Series

Tigers 8, Padres 4

SAN DIEGO	AB	R	H	BI	DETROIT	AB	R	H	BI
Wiggins 2b	5	0	2	1	Whitaker 2b	3	1	1	0
Gwynn rf	5	0	0	0	Trammell ss	4	1	0	0
Garvey 1b	4	0	1	1	Gibson rf	4	3	3	5
Nettles 3b	3	0	1	0	Parrish c	5	2	2	1
Kennedy c	4	0	0	0	Herndon lf	4	0	1	0
Bevacqua dh	3	2	1	1	Lemon cf	3	0	2	1
Martinez lf	4	0	2	0	Garbey dh	1	0	0	0
Salazar pr-cf	0	0	0	0	Grubb ph	0	0	0	1
Templeton ss	4	1	1	0	Kuntz ph	0	0	0	1
Brown cf-lf	2	1	1	1	Johnson ph	1	0	0	0
Bochy ph	1	0	1	0	Evans 1b	4	0	0	0
Roenicke pr	0	0	0	0	Bergman 1b	0	0	0	0
					Castillo 3b	3	1	2	0
Totals	**35**	**4**	**10**	**4**		**32**	**8**	**11**	**8**

San Diego ----------------------- 001 200 010 -- 4
Detroit ------------------------- 300 010 13x -- 8

Game winning RBI -- Kuntz, E -- Parrish, Wiggins, DP -- San Diego 1, LOB -- San Diego 7, Detroit 9, 2B -- Templeton, HR -- Gibson 2, Parrish, Bevacqua, SB -- Wiggins, Parrish, Lemon, CS -- Herndon, Salazar, SH -- Whitaker, Trammell, SF -- Brown, Kuntz, HBP -- by Hawkins (Grubb), WP -- Hawkins

San Diego	IP	H	R	ER	BB	SO
Thurmond	0.1	5	3	3	0	0
Hawkins (L)	4.0	2	1	1	3	1
Lefferts	2.0	1	0	0	1	2
Gossage	1.2	3	4	4	1	2
Detroit						
Petry	3.2	6	3	3	2	2
Scherrer	1.0	1	0	0	0	0
Lopez (W)	2.1	0	0	0	0	4
Hernandez (S)	2.0	3	1	1	0	0

T -- 2:55 A -- 51,901

Gibson hitting the first of his two homers in Game Five—a two-run shot that staked the Tigers to an early lead.

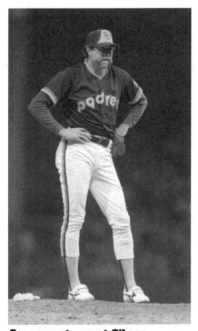

Gossage stares at Gibson moments before throwing the pitch that all but ended the World Series.

Kirk Gibson remembers:

I want to set a few things straight about our focus and motivation. Sparky did a real good job of making sure that we set our goals. The biggest thing that he did was back in '81, the strike year, when we went into Milwaukee for the last series of the season, and we had to at least win two out of three to win the second half of the season.

With two games left, we trailed the Brewers by a game and a half. Jack lost a tough one, 2-1, when Rollie Fingers blew us away in the ninth. They beat us and we were going home, and Sparky said, "Everybody sit here on the bench and watch." When we were going back later on the plane he said, "How did you like watchin' that celebration? Go home and think about that—that should be you." That had a huge impact on us.

So there we were. One game away. We jumped everybody out of the gate in '84 and we played well against Kansas City. We were still scared to death because we knew we'd be a failure if we didn't finish it out.

In the first inning, Tram or Lou was on. [Lou singled; Tram grounded into a fielder's choice.] I can still see that pitch clear as day. Mark Thurmond threw me a breaking ball, and I hit it into the lower deck in right. We got Thurmond out of there before the inning ended and led 3-0.

They came back to tie it off of Petry with a few runs in the fourth.

We loaded 'em in the fifth. I think I led off with a single. There were a few walks. [Andy Hawkins walked Herndon, and reliever Craig Lefferts walked Lemon.] I was on third and Rusty pinch hit for Grubb and hit a fly ball to short right that Gwynn shouldda caught. But Alan Wiggins was playing second and Wiggins caught it for whichever reason and I just went on my own. It was my own read. Terry Kennedy was the catcher and I was gonna run his ass over if I needed to. I was gonna just pound him. But Wiggins never got a good throw.

It was still 4-3 in the seventh. I fanned to start the inning. Gossage came in to pitch to Lance, and Lance hit a bullet over the left-field wall. They got one back [Bevaqua's home run off Hernandez in the top of the eighth to make it 5-4, Detroit].

When I came up in the eighth, there was one out and two on. Marty was one of 'em I remember. Tram or Whitaker was the other. [Tram sacrificed Whitaker, who had beaten out an attempted sacrifice bunt. Castillo, who had walked, went to third.]

So it was second and third, one out. [Padres manager] Dick Williams told him to walk me, but Gossage had owned me—had K'd me on my first big-league at bat—and he thought he could strike me out. When a guy's told to walk you and he doesn't walk you, it's a challenge. "Oh, OK. I accept that." I knew where he was coming from but I couldn't think about the failures I'd had against him. I had to say, "OK, you've had your time, you've pushed it too far and this is gonna be my time."

The Mary Schroeder Detroit Free Press front page picture that captures the euphoria of winning the World Series.

I saw Williams hold up four fingers, and I saw Gossage say "No." He'd already told Gossage to walk me from the bench, and when Gossage said "No," he had to come out and that's when Gossage told him, "No, I can strike him out." I looked at Sparky and Sparky says, "He's gonna walk you," and I said "No. Uh unh." That's when I said, "I'll bet you ten bucks. If he pitches to me I'll crank him."

First pitch was a cutter down and in, ball one. So it was 1-0 and I was sitting on the fastball; I told myself to keep my hands high and my stroke short. The ball got outta there quick. It was 8-4.

Soon as I hit it was the first time I knew we were world champions. That's the first time we could let our guard down and we all knew that. They weren't coming back on us now. That was a crusher right there. We had Willie (Hernandez) and there was no fucking way. Tiger Stadium was packed, and I'll just never forget the whole scene. The sound. The sights. I remember seeing my mom and dad after I crossed home plate. Joanne (Gibson's wife) was with them in my seats behind the on-deck circle. It was awesome. They were like everybody else, standing and cheering wildly. And in reflection, [compared] to where I was the previous year, in '83— that's the game of baseball in a nutshell right there. As low as you are today, you'll be that high tomorrow if you stick with it.

Chapter 22

Series Postscript

I regret that I missed Gibby's historic blow off Gossage. I was already heading down to the clubhouse, anticipating a long line, and I needed to get in there quickly for postgame interviews. Kirk's timing was great. Mine wasn't. I would estimate, however, that I showed that homer on the television highlights probably a hundred times in the years to come.

I remember going down Michigan Avenue to the station a few hours later, drenched in champagne and beer, and then going on the air looking like a guy who'd been thrown in the pool with his clothes on. I'd missed all the mayhem and violence in the streets—the man shot dead, the burning of four cars, and the presence of the riot police.

Detroit's finest hour had turned so ugly that it would further brand the city as a war zone. The photo of young Bubba Helms—his gut hanging out—with a burning car on his left and a Tigers pennant in his hands still haunts Detroit's image.

Trammell would be named World Series MVP for his .450 batting average and Game Four home-run heroics. And he received a "Tiger Blue" Pontiac Trans-Am as his prize. A season that had begun with a bizarre injury the previous Halloween was now complete.

"I was wearing a Halloween costume, a Frankenstein," Tram remembers, "and it was my brother-in-law's costume. He had army boots and he put wood blocks on the bottom of them to make it seven feet tall. I borrowed it the next night to go to a party with my wife and we had the boots in the trunk and we were getting ready to leave and she said, 'C'mon, let's show the neighbors.' So I put the darn things on and as I was walking next door, one of the wood blocks fell off, so I lost my balance and since the boots go up over my ankle, I couldn't get out of 'em, so I fell. My knee got tweaked as I went down and I tore cartilage. I had surgery right after Halloween and I had to rehab it and it was never quite right because I had to get another knee surgery after the season. I had my shoulder and my knee done at the same time five days after the World Series. But we did win best costume! I was standing in the corner that whole night against a wall thinking, 'This is killing me.'"

Clearly, Trammell's greatest year wasn't pain-free. He also missed 43 games at shortstop in '84 with elbow nerve and tendinitis problems.

Tram drove the Trans-Am for three or four years after 1984 and put 30,000 miles on it. In '98, when he left to work for the Padres as a coach, he donated the Trans-Am to CATCH, Sparky's children's charity.

Police can't contain the flood of Tigers fans in their mad dash onto the field.

Epilogue

Paying the Price

On August 21, 1984, Milt Wilcox won his career-high 14th game. He'd finish at 17-8, and considering what he put his pitching shoulder through all year, Wilcox's performance in '84 may stand apart from all others.

Curiously, the Tigers hadn't even wanted him in '84. Wilcox became a free agent after '83 and had been rated in the top 10 percent of American League pitchers. This classified him as a Class A free agent. The rules of the time dictated that up to six teams could draft him, and six did. The Tigers didn't want to give a pitcher with his history of shoulder problems anything longer than a one-year contract.

As it was, Wilcox had been in Evansville rehabbing his shoulder as late as August '83. The Tigers had been pursuing Walt Terrell of the Mets over the winter, and only when they failed to pull off a deal for Terrell did they come back to Wilcox and reluctantly offer him the same two-year deal that the Padres had been willing to give him.

"I put it all behind me," Wilcox reflects. "It's a business. I'd been there seven or eight years, and you just let things go. I knew we had a good team, and when we jumped off to the great start, I said, 'I'm not missing a start this year. I don't care what it does to me in the long run, I don't want us going into any losing streaks and have it be my fault.' I didn't miss more than a few starts all year."

Wilcox had taken cortisone shots in the past and had spent his share of time on the disabled list but vowed that there would be none of that in '84. Sparky and Roger Craig wanted him to go six or seven innings at the most, and then give it over to the bullpen. As it turned out, he made 33 regular-season and two postseason starts in '84 and completed none. And it took seven cortisone shots to get him to the finish line.

Only three of those shots were reported by either the medical team or Wilcox. "They wanted to keep the numbers down because it wouldn't look good. I went to see Dr. (Robert) Tietge seven times that year. He wasn't the team surgeon anymore but was treating me on the side. I had problems in my AC joint, the joint right on top of the shoulder, not the rotator cuff, but the AC joint referred pain to the rotator cuff area.

"We'd inject the joint with Xylocaine, which deadens the pain, and then follow it with the cortisone to quiet the inflammation. It started in May and went through the end of season. I'd go through withdrawal from the cortisone. I'd get hot flashes, sweat and my heart would start beating real fast. I kept a lot of the symptoms away from the trainers because I didn't want them to refuse me from getting it any more."

After winning his 17 games, Wilcox was slated to pitch Game Three of the playoffs against the Royals. They played the first two in Kansas City on Tuesday and Wednesday, October 2 and 3.

"We were in Kansas City, and I told Sparky and Roger that I needed another cortisone shot. Problem was, I'd taken one just two weeks before. With cortisone, the more you use it, the less effect it has. First time it lasts six weeks, then five, then maybe four or three. So now it's only two weeks since my last shot. I asked if I could go see Dr. Tietge, who was at a resort in Chicago.

"They got me a private plane and nobody knew. So I flew from Kansas City to Chicago, rented a car and drove to a resort called Pheasant Run. Tietge gave me a shot in my AC joint, and I flew back to Kansas City and then came back to Detroit with the team so that nobody would notice. I pitched a real good playoff game and we won, 1-0, to win the pennant.

"But when I pitched the third game of the World Series exactly one week later, my shoulder was bothering me again. If the World Series had gone to a sixth game, I was going to get another cortisone shot the night before and then pitch Game Six. So I was real glad it only went five games. I could hardly brush my teeth. We'd already known by September that I'd be having an operation on my AC joint after the season."

By August, in his determination to find relief and avoid ruining his arm through cortisone dependence, Wilcox fell upon what he hoped was a miracle cure. He was involved in harness racing, and a friend at the track suggested that he try a substance called DMSO, dimethyl sulfoxide, a wood byproduct that the trainers used on horses to ease pain and reduce swelling.

The Food and Drug Administration frowned upon it because there was no evidence that it was safe or effective. Wilcox created his own brew by cutting the DMSO with oil and applying it as a topical ointment after he pitched. Unfortunately, his teammates were quickly onto him. DMSO created an ungodly stink and also created cotton mouth and bad breath that seemed like it could peel the tiles off the clubhouse wall.

"I just figured," Wilcox shrugs, "why not try this? But it didn't really do anything but give me bad breath. I tried everything else. Did I tell you about the thing called electro-therapy with magnets?" No, and no thanks.

Wilcox had surgery after the season. He wanted to use Dr. Tietge but the Tigers insisted on a surgeon from Atlanta. "I was the first pitcher that James Andrews operated on," Wilcox says, none too fondly. "He wasn't famous when he operated on me. They brought him to New York to see me in September when we went there at the end of the year. He rotated my arm three times and said, 'It's your rotator cuff.'

I told him it wasn't, but they did arthro (arthroscopic surgery) on the cuff anyway and cleaned it up. But in December I couldn't use the shoulder at all. I knew I needed a second opinion, so I flew myself to the Mayo clinic and they told me that Andrews shouldn't have operated because there was nothing wrong with the rotator cuff, and they put me on a new rehab program. In early '85 it started acting up. I got another cortisone shot, and soon after I just said, 'Forget it.' Then they sent me back to Andrews and he operated on my AC joint."

Coming off his heroic '84 season, and in the final year of his contract, Wilcox could only pitch in eight games in '85. Before agreeing to sign him in '86, Lajoie asked Wilcox to go to the Dominican League to see if he could still pitch. Wilcox thought that he did well enough there to prove he had something left, but Lajoie passed on him. He signed with Seattle and went 0-8. It was the end of the line.

"My shoulder was dead, no strength at all. Two operations had taken a toll; '84 was basically my last year. I pitched my whole life for '84. That's what you dream of when you're eight years old, pitching in your back yard. You'd pitch against Roger Maris, Mickey Mantle and Willie Mays. And you're always pitching against 'em in the World Series."

Wilcox had his World Series and won his only start, 5-2, in Game Three. He had sacrificed what remained of his right shoulder in order to get that start. No doubt, he would have given his entire right arm, if that had been deemed necessary.

On Becoming a Michigander

By Dan Petry

I came up to the majors in '79, and I would go back home to California after the season. But one of my fondest memories and one of the major reasons why Michigan is my home happened after the '80 season, and before spring training in '81. I had just turned 22 and the Tigers asked me to go on the out-state promotional tour in January. I hadn't spent too much time in Michigan, so it sounded OK.

You'd hop on that bus and go around to the various cities and talk to fans and media. There was always a dinner at Win Schuler's in Marshall. Down in the basement was a room they had for us, and they had this huge stone fireplace, and this big fire is raging and the snow is piled up outside.

We'd sit down and they'd have this wonderful meal for us and Mr. Campbell and Mr. Fetzer, [Hall-of-Famer and executive consultant] Rick Ferrell and [director of radio and television] Doc Fenkell and a lot of Campbell's buddies would get together at their own table. Well, this time they said, "C'mere, sit down with us." I was like,"Wow, uh oh, I'm not with the guys anymore," and they asked me to have dinner with them.

I didn't say a whole lot. We sat around and I listened to them tell their war stories and this and that. There you are in this basement, with the rip-roaring fire, and the old guys are smoking cigars and the dark wood and this traditional setting and I go, "Wow," it was like nothing I'd ever experienced before. There's nothing like that in California—hell, we never start fires in California or the state burns down.

I was just in awe at the whole scene. Needless to say, I was very close with Mr. Campbell—in the way I felt about him, for those kinds of reasons. Like a dad or whatever. I never went up to his office to talk to him. I tried to stay away from him and those people, the executive types, as much as possible, but I just felt a closeness to him because of that dinner.

I know he took a little heat, but he just believed that the product sold itself. He didn't want any bells and whistles taking away from the product on the field. Today, things have changed. In recent years they've been promoting everything from the coaching staff to Ernie Harwell to the new stadium, but they're not talking about the product on the field, and that's what Jim Campbell never wanted to get away from.

Why Lance Had to Leave

By Lance Parrish

I'll always hold Jim Campbell responsible for me leaving Detroit, because he held that collusion deal to the hilt. [In the mid-'80s baseball owners were found guilty by an independent arbitrator of conspiracy to put a cap on free-agent salaries and were fined over $200 million.] When it came down to business he was very old-school, a very hard-line guy, but he was extremely nice to my wife and kids.

In spring training once, we were at that Holiday Inn (in Lakeland) and he was a few doors down, and he walked by our room one day and we had the blinds open, and he peeked in there and my son David, who was about three, was on the floor doing sit-ups and pushups and Campbell got the biggest kick out of that. He was a good guy, but there was another side to him that was just...my God.

In late '81, he called me into his office and threw a document in front of me. He told me that Tram had just signed the same one. I looked at it and was blown away. It was a seven-year contract for $2.8 million. I was making less than a hundred thousand and I couldn't even imagine that much money.

He could tell that I was shaken, but I told him, "Thank you, I'd like to talk it over with my wife and my agent." But that got him upset, and he thundered at me about what a great offer this was and that I should be thankful and just accept it. I wouldn't, but as it turns out, my agent eventually got the same deal but for one year less, six years. Turns out, it was the last deal I signed with the Tigers.

I became a free agent after '86, and there's not a doubt that the collusion thing was in full swing. We were this close (he puts his fingers an inch apart), to reaching an extension in spring training before '86. It was a three-year deal and it was ready to be signed.

But nothing got done. Even though I talked with Lajoie [whose job it was to sign players], I knew where it was coming from. And right before the last details were filled in, they pulled it back and said we're not going to negotiate with you 'til after the season's over. Naturally, I had to hurt my back and missed half of the '86 season. I'd still had a good first half and made the All-Star Game. I still had 20 homers and like 60 RBIs before the All-Star Game.

After the season, there was nobody out there who would bid on me, and Campbell could sign me for whatever he wanted to sign me for. I took extreme exception to that. Then they told me they were gonna offer me the same thing I'd made the season before [$850,000].

I said, "Wait a minute, you're not going to give me a one-dollar raise? I played half the season and had better stats than more than half the catchers in baseball, and you're not going to give me a one-dollar raise?" And they said, "No. Same thing as last year." I got so frustrated I said, "That's it. If anybody offers me anything, I'm leaving, because I don't feel that I deserve to be treated like this."

That's the most frustrating time of my career. I really wanted to stay in Detroit. I didn't want to go. I kept on saying, "Don't let me go into the free-agent market. I want to stay." I went to Philly for a million. Then at the last second the Tigers offered me 1.2 million. But that was past the deadline, and I couldn't have started the season 'til May and I said, "Forget it. You waited too long. You played your hand."

Gary Carter was making over 2 million a year and I was making 850 coming off the last year of a six-year contract. So, Campbell got me pretty good. I was ecstatic to sign it before 1982, but as baseball progressed, the salaries went up. I had the same numbers Carter had and he's making 2 million and I'm making 850. I thought that when this contract is over they'd take care of me because I'm still producing and then they threw that at me.

They did offer me arbitration, but I thought if I went to arbitration, they'd hold this injury against me. So I said pay me for one year what I'm worth, and they wouldn't do it. So I said, "That's it," and I couldn't believe it.

The Phillies were the only team that talked to me. [General Manager] Bill Giles flew in under the radar, came to my home in LA and told us, "Our hands are tied. But I will sign you because I think we're a catcher away from having a World Series team." Mike Schmidt, (Glenn) Wilson, Von Hayes, guys I knew over there were pushing me, "You got to sign, you gotta sign." Giles went out on a limb because he broke the ranks there with the collusion policy.

With Campbell, I maintained that I did everything he asked me to do, conducted myself the way he wanted, and I produced on the field. And when it got to where he was supposed to take care of me as the game dictates, he wouldn't. Salary negotiations are just comparative things anyway. So when it got to where I had played six years on the same deal and I was drastically underpaid according to the market, he didn't step up to the plate.

So long, Detroit. I hated to leave a city and a team that I had committed my career to. But I had principles.

The Ring

By Bill Scherrer

It happened in 1985. In mid-May we were getting ready to fly out to the West Coast to play the Angels. Before we went on the road, our trainer, Pio DiSalvo, was looking at my World Series ring. Anybody who knows me knows I'm not a big jewelry guy—doesn't make any difference to me. George Bush, who was the vice president then, had given us the rings in a ceremony over at Tiger Stadium on opening day...Women know about rings and furs, but I look at it, it couldda been anything. But we're wearing 'em around as proud as can be.

Then we're ready to go on the road trip, and Pio was looking at my ring and said, "It looks a little tarnished." He goes, "Let me get some polish on it." He tries to polish it up and says, "I can't get that stuff off." I just thought he was dumb about jewelry like we were. It also left a greenish residue on my finger. So I'm wearing it, going about my business and we go to California. There was that bar in Anaheim right near the stadium, I can't remember the name, but Jack and Gibby were there; Brooky, I'm sure Bergie—a bunch of us. Milt was definitely there.

One of the girls (in the bar) says to Milt, "Why don't you have your World Series ring on?" Milt points to me and says, "He does." So I came over and as I'm showing it to her, he's looking at my ring and saying, "You know, that ring looks a lot different than mine."

He picked it up and said it felt like it weighed a lot less and said to me, "Billy, you oughtta take this thing and get it appraised 'cause I don't think it's the same." The girl is doing the same thing, comparing mine to the one that Morris has, and I start getting defensive, like, "What are you talking about?" Like I actually know what I'm talking about. She looks at mine, and then Jack's, and yes, you can see a difference. Anyway, Jack and those guys felt worse than I did about it.

We flew to Seattle and Vern [Plagenhoef, a *Grand Rapids Press* beat writer] was there, and he and Milt and I were at the Red Robin and we told Vern about the rings, and Vern goes, "Oh my God" like he'd got the greatest story in the world. He says, "Listen, I'll pay for the appraisal." Milt went with us too. Milt loves that kinda shit anyway and we walk to some jeweler in Seattle.

The guy puts his magnifying glass on it and he says, "Is this a high school ring?" He's not looking at the insignia or the writing, he's just looking at the ring. I say, "No, this is a World Series ring," and the guy shrugs. I ask for the appraisal and he says, "Anywhere from $80 to $250." So now Vern's got it runnin'. He's calling this player and that player; calling Lajoie, calling Campbell, trying to get to the bottom of it.

While this is going on, everybody on the team was running to the jewelers to see if they got a bootleg or the real thing. The real ones were worth about three grand. After all this had happened, Lajoie came on the road and I sat down with him and said, "Bill, I don't really care. All I want to know is straight up, did I get a second-rate ring versus everybody else? I just wanna know." And that's when I found out for sure.

Somebody on the story called my sister and she said, "You could've given him a ring from a Cracker Jacks box and he wouldn't have cared if you told him the truth. But once you lie to my brother, he's your worst enemy."

Vern got the full story: There were three different rings. Frontline players got the good ones. Scouts and people like that got second quality, and guys like myself who were voted a one-third Series share got the third-class rings. Some guys, like [Roger] Mason and [Randy] O'Neal who didn't play in the Series, got watches. The whole thing was terrible.

But there was the other side—for being there just over a month—to have my teammates vote me a one-third share was very generous. They could have given me a fifth share and I would have been happy. And I will say this: when I scouted for the Reds in '90, everybody got a ring, and a real ring, even if the player had only played a day. And the Reds' wives got gifts too.

When it all came out, the guys said to management on my behalf, "If he wants to pay the balance, why don't you let him get a real ring?" That never went anywhere and a lot of us were disgruntled. And when we got our miniature World Series trophies, we had to pay $500 or so for 'em. The players thought that was ludicrous also. I don't know if it was Campbell running Monaghan's books and wanted to look like a star for saving him money, but Monaghan was a decent guy and I could tell from spring training that year that he didn't really know what was going on.

As it turns out, I very seldom wore it and I gave it to my dad and he wears it proudly like he's the Pope and it's worth millions. When you look at things in a practical sense, the ring's got a lifetime guarantee and if it turns to green again, they gotta turn it back to silver. I'm not kidding.

I have to send it to Balfour (the ring maker) and they clean it up and send it back. Whenever it gets tarnished, and it's happened a few times, I say "let me make a call" and they fix it for nothing because it's got a lifetime guarantee. Its comical, really. People have offered to buy it, but it's not for sale—it's too good a story.

One more thing—and it's why I have so much respect for everybody who I played with on that team. My ex-brother-in-law saw Jack Morris at a beach in Clearwater (Florida), and asked Jack about his Series ring. Jack said, "Once that happened (the three grades of rings), I didn't wear it any more." That's an example of how we bonded together—when one of us got screwed, all of us got screwed.

When somebody asks me about that team, I tell 'em, "I may have only been there a month and half, but I feel like I played all 170 games with the '84 Tigers."

The Meaning of '84

By Chet Lemon

That year, '84, and again in '87, when we won the division, were the two greatest years in Detroit for us, because we rallied against the odds and made special things happen. But '84, the "Bless You Boys" season and the way the city came together around us—the way everybody felt—it was like a glow that people had. I've gotten fan mail where people say they would wake up every morning and say a prayer because they were so happy for us and wanted us to keep going strong.

I had babies named after me, dogs named after me, because of what we accomplished that year and the way we were doing it. When I look back, those were moments that you can never take away from any of those players or their families—that's what life is all about—experiencing things together and the memories they make.

I talk to my youngest son, Marcus, he's 14, and he wasn't around (in '84) so he asks, "Dad, how was it?" And when he sees the Angels win a championship [in 2002], he can identify with what dad experienced, like "that's great—you guys were like that, right?"

He thinks his dad was the greatest player who ever lived. Whenever I go back to Detroit, people are so warm and kind and Marcus says, "Dang, Dad, you were pretty big." I say, "No, Dad was just one of many—he had the same oneness of mind and the same goal as the others and we went out and achieved our goal." And that's a rare feat—you want to remember that whenever you can do that together as a group —that's what makes it special.

It was a period of time that made people happy. It gave us a reason to go to the ballpark every day, to be excited about the way people piled into the ballpark, always anticipating a home run, or a great play or something that would give 'em a reason to walk away and say, "That's an amazing baseball team."

The Hope

The Tigers of the 21st century have floundered badly. From 1980 to 1988, they won more games than any team in the American League. Since 1988, the Tigers have lost more games than anyone else in baseball, including four seasons of 100 losses or more. From 1994 to 2003, they never finished over .500, and in six of those ten years, incurred 90 or more losses.

Bill Lajoie, Jim Campbell and Sparky Anderson all departed at different times, and in various shrouds of negativity. Lajoie left voluntarily after '91 for reasons difficult to ascertain. He claimed that inflated salaries had poisoned his love for the job of general manager. But it was also well known that his relationships with Campbell and Sparky had deteriorated along with the struggle to sustain the club's drafting success and on-field performance. At some point in the '80s, Lajoie, burdened by his general manager duties at the major-league level, abandoned his personal involvement in scouting and player procurement. The list of blown draft picks in the '80s and '90s is remarkable, providing the main reason why the team began its stunning free-fall through the standings.

To his credit, Lajoie never pointed the finger at the root cause of his Tigers discontent: From the late '70s on, the Tigers became a bare-bones, cash-strapped franchise. Shortly after buying the club in '84, Monaghan gutted a suspected $20-million-plus from the team's financial reserves to fund his struggling pizza business. He had entered the scene as John Fetzer's pet, a surrogate son, a deeply religious, seemingly innocent type who turned out to be a wolf in sheep's clothing.

But the Tigers had stopped investing in their product four or five years earlier when John Fetzer was preparing the club for sale. They were even cutting back on monies for draftees, the lifeblood of the team's future.

So here we are. You, me and Tigers fans everywhere. We collectively understand the complex set of circumstances—some lucky and some brilliantly conceived—that enabled 1984 to come to pass in all its glory and triumph. And, as well, we understand much about the myriad miscalculations and fractured relationships, as well as the unavoidable bad breaks, that produced the ensuing dark years.

I have always believed that, above everything else, Detroit is a baseball town. There is an innate love of the Tigers that was cultivated over the generations since the turn of the 20th century and still burns within individual minds and the collective psyche of Michigan. For now, this love and attachment, this lifelong baseball investment, is held at arm's length, symbolically tucked away in fans' intellectual safe-deposit boxes.

But the love is still there, available for withdrawal and renewal whenever the Tigers emerge from their long winter of hibernation.

Maybe fans will again find a reason to arrive in record numbers at the ballpark.

Maybe the heroes of 1984 directing the Tigers on the field in 2003 and beyond will be able to lead the franchise back into the sunlight. And when they do stand at the helm of a Tigers team that reflects the image of the greatness they achieved, Tigers fans will joyously cavort aside the green grass of Comerica Park, where a new group of baseball gods will become the latest of the great Tigers.